Paupers' Paris

Miles Turner is an impoverished American, living in Oregon. He spent his fourteenth birthday in Paris and never recovered from the experience. Over the years he has spent vacations there whenever possible, living cheaply, exploring the city, and researching this book. He has made numerous Parisian friends and contacts, whom he has persuaded to divulge up-to-the-minute hints, and some well-kept secrets, for the penniless traveller.

Miles Turner

Paupers' Paris

Pan Original
Pan Books London and Sydney

First published 1982 by Pan Books Ltd,
Cavaye Place, London SW10 9PG
Revised 1983 and 1984
This new edition published 1986
9 8 7
© Miles Turner 1982, 1983, 1984, 1986
ISBN 0 330 29159 9
Phototypeset by Input Typesetting Ltd, London
Printed in Great Britain by
Richard Clay (The Chaucer Press) Ltd,
Bungay, Suffolk

Contents

PARIS

Introduction

This book is for paupers – or if not paupers, cheapskates – who would love to spend some time in Paris, but would prefer not to spend much money. It sets out to prove that, while Paris has justly earned its reputation as one of the world's more outrageously expensive places, there are hundreds of ways to avoid the city's grasping hands and still share in its pleasures.

If we have a single motto, it's 'Sleep cheap and eat well'. It turns out that you can sleep *and* eat for next to nothing, and do both rather well if you set your mind to it. There are cheap routes to Paris; there is limitless cheap transportation all over the city; there are hundreds of low-budget hotels that are clean and friendly and charming; there are incredible meals to be had in the humblest restaurants; there are more – free – spectacles, sights and attractions per square block than anywhere else we can think of. We've tried to fill this book with specifics – a mere scratching of the surface – of all these subjects, and with some pointers on how to use the information.

To make maximum use of our information, you'll need at least some of the following:

A sense of adventure. If tripe is half the price of steak on a menu, and you've never had tripe before but have a queasy idea of what it is, still you're *driven* to order tripe.

A low entertainment threshold. That quality which makes a person a cheap date. In Paris it means that the clientele of the nearest brasserie are as interesting and amusing and exciting to you as the entire cast of Covent Garden.

Unqualified adoration for the city. Everyone loves Paris in theory. To relish that slightly Gorgonzola aroma in the lower depths of the Métro is a measure of true love.

A sense of self-mockery. If you can't enjoy the spectacle of yourself as a total imbecile when it comes to haggling (or saying 'good morning', for that matter) then you should go to Denmark where they speak English.

A tourist's loathing of other tourists. The best thing that can happen to you is when a Parisian asks *you* for directions.

More taste than money. While you can't actually bring back a Cézanne or two, or the contents of Lanvin's windows, at least you will have paid them a visit.

A good deal of low cunning. The ability to wash (and dry) your entire wardrobe in a hotel sink without leaving a trail of evidence for the chambermaid.

We suggest that you take with you at least a few words of French – even if they're all in a pocket phrasebook. Parisians are rather proud of their language, and on their own turf would rather converse in French than try their English out on you. If you need help, or just crave human contact, remember that the French help those who help themselves. The ice begins to break when you make the effort to communicate, but it's up to you.

It's this lack of linguistic hospitality – and also some misunderstandings about customs and manners – that has given the French a reputation for rudeness among travellers. *La politesse* is central to all transactions in France. The French are formal: they'll preface every question with 'Pardon, Monsieur . . .' or 'S'il vous plaît, Madame . . .' They'll consider *you* rude if you don't do the same.

Remember also that Parisians who habitually deal with tourists, with apparently ill-mannered Americans, Germans and English, who may in fact be less callous than tongue-tied, develop their own callousness for dealing with foreigners. If you stay off the beaten track (and with the help of this book you can) you'll avoid these unfortunates and come into contact with a friendly, garrulous, buoyant race of Parisians you've never met or heard of before.

You will note that certain *arrondissements* – the 5e, 7e, 8e, parts of the 19e and 20e – have been given fairly lengthy descriptions in the Footwork section, while others better-known apparently have been slighted. This is highly personal, the ones that are in are there just because they are places we have enjoyed which may have been missed out in other publications. The 6e, especially around St-Germain-des-Prés, has been written about everywhere; visited by everyone; as a consequence, the waiters are rude, the hotels overpriced, the meals in the main to be avoided. You'll go there anyway, and probably find your own pleasures without help from us. But it would be a pity to miss, for example, the less-known areas such as the Batignolles (p. 00), the hidden and charming parts of the haughty 7e *arrondissement*, and the pleasant rather domestic bits of the forbiddingly elegant 8e.

Paupers' Paris is the result of the labour and support of all my friends and relatives: most importantly, my mother, Martha Lomask, who researched and rewrote entire sections of the book; my father, Milton, who slogged around the galleries of the Right Bank and found out all about music in Paris; Rory Cellan-Jones and his student friends, who had the pleasant task of trying out restaurants all over Paris; Rachel Neaman and Antonia Cunningham for doing shops and restaurants; Guy Morris who visited hotels and turned up some new ones; Robin Duff, a resident pauper in Paris, who contributed enthusiasm, information, and diligence in tracking down hotels and restaurants, and inside information on the flea markets; Madalynne Reuter, of New York, who gave up a good part of her Paris holiday to recheck the shops mentioned in previous editions, and turned up some good new ones; Leonard Yoon, who helped me plot the book over countless bottles of wine; Charlie White, who closed his eyes to my long absences from his office; Edith Burtschell for her particular help in the revised editions; and many others, including Serge Dunis, Tanya Lévi, P. K. Mensa, Janey Mathéyrins and her son Jean-Luc and daughter Sabine, Sheila More, M. and Mme de Roberti, Giselle and Jean de Marigny, Adam Sedgwick, John Stewart, Antoine Messara, Michèle Veugeois of the Office de Tourisme in Paris, Martine Williams and Pauline Hallam of the French Government Tourist Office in London, Mme Dorothy Lecointe, Sylvie Pecolliet, Mme Paule Pinelli, Claire Durand, for all their advice and information.

Readers should note that prices in this book were correct in August 1985. Inflation in Paris has slowed to about 4%, partly because of the government freeze on many essentials, but has continued to have its effect even now. In August 1985, prices for bread, milk etc. were allowed to rise slightly, transport in Paris went up between 8 and 10%, hotels were preparing to raise their prices in 1986 – everyone still screaming about how they are squeezed for profit – but Paris continues to offer, at very good value, hundreds of good hotels, charming restaurants, and its own distinctive attractions for those who know how to look.

M.T.

Allons-y (Preliminaries)

Who?

Before anything else you must decide – who's going? Just you, your nearest and dearest, your bridge club? A few pros and cons:

Travelling alone is the best way to see and do exactly what you want. If you get lost or bungle seriously in a restaurant, feel like sleeping till noon, or decide to spend the rest of your life in Paris, the decisions (and the responsibility) are all yours. If you make mistakes, nobody else gets blamed. You don't have to adjust to anyone else's diet, or standards of hygiene, or attention span. If you can handle being on your own, it's the best way to go.

But if your gregariousness and your French aren't up to it, you can die of loneliness. You'll have to survive on a few encounters a day – in cafés, restaurants and shops. You'll always be treated well, if you make the effort to make yourself understood, but it's unlikely that anyone will adopt you.

Travelling in company guarantees that you'll have someone with whom to share the experience, and a helping hand if things get dicey. The drawback is that your tastes will differ. *You* will want to spend eight hours in one room of the Louvre; *she* will choose to spend the day playing pinball machines in a café behind the Bastille.

Our solution for days when your energy and interests don't coincide is to split up: plan to meet for lunch, and plan to meet again for dinner. (Agree in advance on the restaurants. No last-minute searches on an empty stomach.) If one person doesn't show up within fifteen minutes, the other forges ahead with the meal. We've found this to be a good way to avoid getting bored with each other. Travelling in company can have an odd, isolating effect. You can get on each other's nerves. And it's bad for your French.

Small groups can be worked the same way: you can pack the kids off to the Bois, send Granny to the flea market, and you're on your own. The one thing you must not do is travel in packs. Even a benign dictatorship can end up in communal misery.

When to go?

Of course it's best to go when the spirit moves you. When you can't stand the grind a minute more. When your boss *lets* you go. But if it's not purely a matter of impulse, desperation, budget, or tight scheduling, there are a few matters about timing to consider.

High season, low season, normal season

Naturally, this affects airline fares: get a good travel agent, or do a real study yourself of what the flying people are up to at any given moment. Equally important: there are certain times of the year when it is all but impossible to find a room in central Paris or anywhere near it at short notice. The Office de Tourisme in Paris has this advice:

Most heavily booked periods:
2–6 February
2–10 March
1–2, 4–7 April
5–10 June
4–10, 17–26 September
18–22 October
17–22 November

Do not arrive on any of these dates without a firm booking.

Second most difficult:
All of June, much of September, most of October. Wisest to book in advance if you can.

Normal periods:
Most of March, April, May and November, other than the heavily booked dates above.

Low season:
Surprisingly, July, August, December and early January are times
when you can almost always find a room somewhere, even on short
notice. However, it may be a good precaution to have a firm booking
for the first few days if arriving in July or August. For real Paris-
lovers, December and the first week in January (when the wonderful
sales are on) – when Paris is at its silvery best, the light shining
through the bare trees and the life of the city vibrating all around
– can be the choicest time to be there.

We once found ourselves, through ridiculously bad timing, in
Paris in the first week of March during two major trade fairs and
at the opening time of an important art show. We managed to get
a room in a very good low-priced hotel, in a great neighbourhood
we'd never stayed in before, which immediately became our second
home. This was done by exerting ourselves somewhat, visiting a
number of hotels until we found one that would have us for one
night, which stretched to six. We wouldn't care to do this if arriving
at midnight after a long flight, tired, drunk or travelling with small
children or an elderly companion.

Climate

The weather can influence your plans, and will certainly influence
your wardrobe. To give you a rough idea – the mean temperature
in February is 36.5°F (3°C), in July 65.5°F (18°C). East and north-
west winds keep Paris cool and fairly dry in winter and spring;
there can be stretches in December and January when bitter winds
come shrieking across North Europe from, apparently, Siberia, and
you'll be glad of woollies and a warm coat. Prevailing south-west
winds bring the heaviest rains in summer and autumn, so pack a
folding umbrella and a light waterproof coat then.

What to take

Your wardrobe naturally depends on what you have, and how much
you are willing to lug around. 'Travelling light' is a phrase that has
an adventurous ring to it – people who drag along only one steamer
trunk rather than three, probably consider themselves light travel-

lers – it's a relative term, but a worthwhile goal. We figure you can live comfortably, and indefinitely, on about fourteen kilos of luggage; more if you are strong of arm or not averse to porters; less if you're a wimp, anti-porter, or plan to switch digs every few days by Métro, not taxi. In either case, here are a few suggestions:

1 Dress in layers – for all climates and most seasons. Everything easily washable or dry-cleanable. Everything easily folded, or preferably rolled, which cuts down on creasing. Think twice about heavy items. If your overcoat is going to be a millstone, don't take it. In all but the dead of winter, rely on piling one sweater on top of another under that light waterproof coat.

2 Take nothing you haven't worn before, and nothing that you don't love. Take nothing you can't walk or climb in.

3 Take a couple of pairs of durable, comfortable, well-broken-in shoes; for women, they should be of different heel heights. Armies may travel on their stomachs – *you* travel on your feet.

4 *Indispensables*
A cotton kimono
A pair of rubber flip-flops (thongs, zoris, or whatever these Taiwanese sandals are called)
For cold weather, a really warm, soft scarf – lambswool for preference. And two identical pairs of gloves, because you're going to lose one glove the day you arrive
A telescopic umbrella – one that fits easily into the suitcase
A good plush hand-towel – not too small – which will help pad breakables and will supplement the sometimes meagre ones common to Paris hotels
Soap in a plastic box
Blow dryers, heated rollers, electric razors (see Electricity, p.200)
A plastic carrier bag for unwashed clothes. A few plastic bags and twist-ties. A featherweight bag that folds into your luggage, and can double as an overnight case or to carry home all the extras you will buy
Nail scissors and, even more important, toenail clippers – real agony-savers
Glasses or contacts if you wear them: take an extra pair and/or a recent prescription
Drugs: an adequate supply, and a refillable prescription.
Indispensable for picnics, hotel and otherwise: a cup and an immersion heater if you *must* have tea (see Electricity, p.200). A saucer-sized plate, a small sharp knife, a fork, a spoon. Be as ingenious as you want about this

Clip-on reading light (220 volts) if you can't live without it and
don't trust hotel lighting
Three or four lightweight plastic hangers for drip-drying. A few
clip-type clothes pegs. A little detergent in a plastic squeeze bottle
(see Hotels, p.62)
A corkscrew
And, not to belabour the obvious, don't forget your toothbrush.

All of this, excluding what you wear on your back, should fit into
a fairly small suitcase that could be carry-on luggage, bypassing
that awful wait at airport or hoverlanding. Take along a thin,
strong, nylon soft-sac for *en route* essentials such as book, flask,
camera, tissues, maps, whatever.

Money questions

How much to take. (For denominations, mechanics and equivalents,
see Money, p.210.)
   Some advance decisions are going to be necessary here. You'll
have to decide after considerable thought what's important to *you*,
not to us or your next-door neighbour. Budget for your extrava-
gance, and save somewhere else. Do you feel best in a room big
enough to spread out wet coats, luggage, bottles, flowers, newspapers? That's what you should budget for. Can't live without *petit
déjeuner* served in your room, or your own shower, a private loo, a
lift? A hotel within arm's length of the Louvre, or a quieter, cheaper,
possibly more spacious place ten minutes away on the Métro?
Budget for it. Save on museum entrance fees by going on Sundays
(free or half-price), or have a week of picnic lunches instead of
eating in restaurants, and spend your money how you will.

Transport to and from Paris

Maximum: will buy you airfare,
London-Paris and back, open-   £142
dated ticket and ultimate convenience

Minimum: provides the cheapest
bus/boat/hovercraft service, and
a modicum of discomfort.   £43
See pp.20–26 for details

Hotel per night

Maximum: a nice, bourgeois hotel in a 'good', close-in district, all facilities including shower and loo. 225F

Minimum: cheap, clean, away from it all, no frills. See pp.56–90 for details. 75F

Food per day

Maximum: breakfast in bed; a lunch that will take up half the afternoon, and dinner half the night. 160F

Minimum: coffee at the *zinc* of the local café, a picnic lunch indoors or out, a modest but satisfying dinner.
See pp.91–131 for details. 75F

Getting around

Maximum: includes a few taxis for quick getaways to station or airport 150F
(20F per day)

Minimum: unlimited Métro/bus/ RER travel for seven days. See pp.36–55 for details 39F

The sights

Maximum: full-price museum admissions; a movie; innumerable cups of coffee, seated. 120F

Minimum: everything gratis, or very, very cheap.
See pp.132–68 for details. 25F

The shops

Maximum: a matter of taste and
income.   ?F

Minimum: don't buy *anything*.
See pp.169–92 for details   0F

Necessities

Maximum: enough to get your
laundry done, your hair cut,
your baby sat, your post sent,   250F
and your pockets full of change.

Minimum: an afternoon in the
launderette and one postcard.   30F
See pp.193–226 for details.

Emergencies

Maximum and minimum depend
entirely on you. If you're
accident-prone, provide extra
money for crises. If you have an
invisible plastic shield, or a lot of
sensible insurance, take less. But
always keep some money in
reserve.
See pp.227–37 for details.

How to carry money

Cash

You'll need some within five minutes of your arrival in Paris: enough
to get your *Billet de Tourisme* or *Carte Orange*; enough to get a bite

to eat and transport you to your hotel; a few more francs for a
check-room for your luggage; possibly a phone call, or to pay the
Hôtesses de Paris for locating a room for you. Even better: arm ·
yourself before you leave with enough francs in cash to carry you
for a day or two. Change pounds or dollars before you leave home,
at a bank or *bureau de change* where you know you'll get a good rate.

Traveller's cheques

Your own bank may offer them as a free service (but avoid the
lesser known brands which can be difficult to cash in some Paris
banks or bureaux). Size of denominations depends on how often
you want to sign your name, and how careless you get when you've
cashed a big one.

Personal Cheques

Fortified with a Eurocheque cashing card from your bank (or your
Visa card in case it's Barclays), you can get up to £100 a day –
Barclays let you cash one cheque in that amount and charge 7F50;
other banks insist on two £50 cheques and two fees. Some English
banks issue special Eurocheque books and cards; others let you use
your standard cheques.

Visa, Access, Mastercard, Diners Club and such

Only in a pinch. The exchange rate at which you are billed is
calculated by the issuing company on the day they bill you, not the
day you used the card, so you can't know in advance how much
you are spending. And it's an easy way to run up bills that can
curl your hair when you get home. If you're travelling for a long
period, remember that after an initial grace period you start paying
interest on the unpaid amount at a horrendous 24 per cent per
annum. Be advised, too, that many hotels, most of the smaller
shops, and almost all the restaurants you frequent *do not* accept
credit cards.

Booking hotels in advance

If you know more or less what you want, and where you want to be, and how much you want to pay (see 'Au lit', pp.56–62), it's a good idea to reserve in advance. It's not in the least difficult if you have a little time to work it out. It can save you energy and anxiety at the moment of your lowest ebb – your arrival in the chaos and confusion of the Paris airport, terminal, or railway station.

Once you've picked a hotel, write a letter to the management. In French. Use, if you like, the form letter – a service of the Office de Tourisme – reproduced below. Specify the dates of arrival and departure (if you can), number of people, and your requirements – with or without a loo or *salle de bain*, single or double room, and so on.

Form letter to hotels (freely adapted from that used by the Paris Office de Tourisme):

Le Directeur
Hotel_____
Address_____

Monsieur le Directeur,

Je vous serais obligé de me communiquer vos conditions
(I would be grateful if you would let me know your terms)
et tarifs pour un séjour de_____ nuits, commençant le _____
(and prices for a stay of _____ nights, beginning _____)
à _____ heures, et se terminant le _____ à _____ heures.*
(at _____ o'clock, and ending _____ at _____ o'clock.)

Nous souhaiterions réserver _____ (chambres à un lit)
(We would like to reserve) _____ *(single rooms)*
(chambres à grand lit) (chambres à deux lits) (avec WC/bain/douche).
(double rooms) (twin-bedded rooms) (with WC/bath/shower).

Avec mes remerciements,

*Use the 24-hour clock.

Use an International Reply Coupon

Whether you're reserving a room or just asking for information from any French source (other than a government tourist agency). The hotel, shop, or agency, or whatever, can exchange the coupon for return postage. Many of these operations are running on a tight margin, and are not about to send free information to rich tourists. The courtesy will be appreciated. A self-addressed airmail envelope is another form of good manners, and can help ensure that you do get a reply.

IRCs cost 35p in Britain and are available at post offices.

Postscript to preliminaries

Life-saving tips from the most experienced travelling paupers we know:

1 Never travel without a good supply of soft toilet paper (not just for obvious purposes, but for blowing noses, mopping brows, even as napkins for picnics)
2 Never travel with more luggage than you yourself can carry in comfort, without porter or taxi
3 For dire emergencies never travel without a little bit of cognac in a flask

En route (Getting there)

Your choice of routes to Paris will depend on your finances and need for comfort; how much you want to spend *en route*, how long you want to stay, what time of year (or time of day) gives you the best deal.

London to Paris and back

Myriad possibilities, listed from the cheapest to the dearest.

Euroways

Coach/Boat/Coach: If you can face the prospect of a coach ride to a Channel port at night, disembarking and crossing by boat, getting back into the coach and rolling into Paris with the dawn, this is for you. Euroways is a good service, buses equipped with reclining seats and reasonably good ventilation (not air conditioning). They offer night trips the year round, day trips 1 April to 30 September. Prices vary with the season, so check before booking. The prices below refer to the summer season. Spring (up to 31 May) fares are less.

Cost: One way £20.50.

Departures: Nightly from Victoria Coach Station, Bay 18, 7:30 p.m. Daily (during season) 8:30 a.m.

Arrival: Coach station, place Stalingrad, Paris 19e (*Métro* Stalingrad), 7:15 a.m. Paris time (night trip), and 7:00 p.m. (day trip).

London office: 52 Grosvenor Gardens, SW1; telephone 01–730 8235, or through travel agents.

Paris office: VIA Tourisme, 8 place Stalingrad, Paris 19e. Telephone 4 201 70 80.

Hoverspeed

Coach/Hovercraft/Coach: This bus service is faster than the above but more expensive. It is now called City Sprint, and the buses are clean and comfortable, but if you are a non-smoker get there early to choose a seat. In the high season (22 July–5 Sept) there are four departures a day from either end, dropping down to two a day in March and April. None between 1 November and 1 March. The first bus leaves London at 8:00 a.m. to 8:45 a.m., depending on the season, and the last at 10:30 to midnight. It's a useful way to go if you plan to return from Paris by some other route, or are going on to other European stops, as tickets are sold singly and it's pretty cheap, almost £10 less than the faster Train/Hovercraft/Train deal.

Adult, one way	£21.50
Student*	£20.50
Ages 4–15	£16.50

No Senior Citizen fares on this route now.

Coaches leave from Victoria Coach Station, Buckingham Palace Road, London SW1
Paris Office: 135 rue Lafayette, 10th *arrondissement*

Tickets and information from travel agents, or telephone London 554 7061

Train/Hovercraft/Train: Three to five flights a day, depending on the season. It's clean, inexpensive and surprisingly fast – can be as little as 5½ hours from Charing Cross in London to the Gare du Nord, depending on weather conditions. There's time at the hovercraft terminals, (Dover, Calais) to collect some duty-free stuff

*Under 18, or under 26 if in full-time educational or vocational training

and have a snack. Cost depends on whether you buy a 5-day excursion ticket, or an open return good for up to two months.

Trains on both ends are usually fast and comfortable, the French ones especially so, with airplane-type seats and drop-down trays for having sandwiches and drinks from the rolling carts in the aisles. In between trains, you get a fast, bumpy trip in reasonably comfortable hovercraft seats. It's noisy, and there's a lot of vertical motion. People who order drinks usually get their comeuppance.

	2nd class single	2nd class return	5-day excursion
Adult	£35.50	£71.00	£45.00
Child 4–11 inclusive	£17.75	£35.00	£22.50
Child 12–15 inclusive	£24.50	£49.00	£30.50
Senior Citizen*	£21.00	£42.00	£45.00

Children under 4 TRAVEL FREE

Hovercraft tickets available from British Rail centres and travel agents. But beware! Some travel agents, including the best known, slapped a £5 surcharge on *any* fare, in 1984/5, which included continental rail travel. Other agents won't handle Senior Citizen rail tickets. If this happens to you, make your displeasure known on the spot and go to a more amenable agent.

Sealink

Train/Boat/Train: The traditional approach. Slower than Hoverspeed, but at least you can jog around the decks.

	Single	Open return	Night fare single	5-day excursion**
Adult	£27.00	£54.00	£18.00	£35.00
Ages 4–15	reduced rates: check BR for exact fares			
Senior Citizen†		£35.00		£35.00

*You must have a Rail-Europ Senior Card now – these special fares are no longer available to those who hold only the purple Senior Citizen British Rail (UK) card
The Rail-Europ Senior Card costs £7, from British Rail ticket offices and post offices
**Check BR for specific restrictions on travel dates
†With purple Senior Citizens' Railcard

Inter Rail – a good deal for under-26s

If you are under 26 years old, a £125 Inter Rail card gives you a month's unlimited travel in 19 countries of Europe, plus Morocco, plus half-price ticket concessions in Great Britain and Ireland, plus half-price on Sealink shipping services. From travel agents or British Rail.

Cheap flights

The best deals from London to Paris and vice versa come through a funny loophole in the rules set up by the great international fare-setting cartel. Something called the 'fifth freedom' of the skies allows long-haul airlines which fly primarily to the Middle and Far East, but make stops on the Continent, to give lower fares for these short hops. Paris-bound paupers discovered in 1985 that they could hop back and forth for as little as £65, instead of the £78 price charged by the big airlines – with an open return ticket good for up to two months. It is also possible to buy a one-way ticket, for about £45, allowing travellers to come back any way they choose, when they like. In 1985, the big travel agents decided to join the bucket shops in offering these bargains, so check their prices. Both the return and one-way fares worked out better than the iron-bound 'Super-Pex' tickets from major airlines, which require you to make a firm, non-cancellable booking at the time you book your outward flight. You can thus save enough for a good dinner for two in Paris.

Gulf Airways: Heathrow to Charles de Gaulle, £65–£69 return, about £45 one way. Flights at 7:00 p.m., Monday, Tuesday, Thursday, Friday and Sunday. However, the return flight from Paris is an excruciating 7:00 a.m. Agents for Gulf include Thomas Cook, High Street Kensington, London W.8.; Jupiter Travel, 91 Regent Street, London W.1 (01–734 1812); Travel Arcade, Suite 305, Triumph House, 189 Regent Street, London W.1. (01–734 5873); Bhanji Travel, 127 Praed Street, London W.2. (01–402 8794).

Thomas Cook, London, also offered flights at £58 return, by Pakistan Airways, one flight a week each way: Heathrow Saturday at 1:00 p.m. to Orly; from Orly Wednesday 2:40 p.m.

One way from Paris: You can buy tickets for 365–400F, depending on the day and the season, for Pakistan Airways flights Orly/ Heathrow, from Paris-International Travel, 43 blvd Haussman, 9e, and USIT Voyages, 4 rue de Vaugirard, 6e. Seats are limited, and go fast in the summer.

Not-so-cheap flights

British Airways and Air France offer many more flights at reason-able prices, but their conditions are rigid: return tickets only, and you must book your return when you make your purchase – non-cancellable, so make sure you have insurance to cover you in case of severe illness or any other emergency condition.

Air France, British Caledonian and British Airways – Heathrow to Charles de Gaulle/Roissy.

Cost: £78 high season, £74 off season.

Available through travel agents.

Package tours

These come in all shapes and sizes, and, naturally, all prices. They range from the antiseptic (everything through a coach window, with English commentary) to the spartan (transportation, bed and breakfast, no frills).

The advantage of a no-frills package is that it takes the guesswork out of the basic amenities, and leaves you free to explore the city on your own. The means of transportation (air, hover, coach, and the rest) and the types of accommodation (1-star to 4-star) are varied, and you'll want to sort through the possibilities carefully.

The drawbacks: package tours are inevitably more expensive than flying solo, and the more all-inclusive ones tend to isolate you from the French. They can also be fraught with fine print; irritating little conditions and restrictions. And with expensive enticements: exaggerated supplemental fees for an in-room shower or bath; the 'Just Married Special', which includes a Special Romantic Dinner, a guided tour of Montmartre, with a Drink in a Typical Montmartre Café and a Métro ticket to the place de Clichy. All very fine, but at a price.

If you're a beginner in Paris, and you'd really rather not do it *all* on your own, here are some possibilities. You may well be able to find a better deal, or a tour that fits your own tastes and timetable to a T – a travel agent can help – and if so, go for it.

Some London agencies that offer budget deals:

Travel Young
28 Bloomsbury Way
London WC1A 2SL
Tel: 404 5287

Good Times Holidays Ltd†
134 Clerkenwell Road
London EC1
Tel: 278 9569

French Travel Service*
Francis House
Francis Street
London SW1P 1DE
Tel: 828 8131

Paris Travel Service†
54 Ebury Street
London SW1
Tel: 730 0654

Time Off Ltd†
2A Chester Close
Chester Street
London SW1
Tel: 235 8070

A typical fee schedule from an excellent agency (Time Off in Paris) includes four transportation routes (airfare, Gatwick–de Gaulle or Heathrow–de Gaulle; train/boat/train or train/hovercraft/train); five levels of accommodation (from 1-star to 4-star luxury hotels); choice of bed-and-breakfast or half-board. There are supplemental fees for single room occupancy, private bathroom and optional excursions; and there are charges for altering or cancelling your schedule. Some of the route options permit travel on certain days of the week only, but overall the package is flexible, allowing you to write your own menu, as it were, and taking care of some of the basics.

*No relation to French government.
†Available through Cook's and other agents.

Costs based on double occupancy, bed-and-breakfast, in £:

	train-boat-train	*train-hovercraft-train*	*air: Gatwick-de Gaulle*	*air: Heathrow-de Gaulle*
2 nights				
1 star*	£66	£67	£106	£117
2 star**	£80	£81	£120	£131
3 nights				
1 star*	£75	£76	£115	£126
2 star**	£96	£97	£136	£147
4 nights				
1 star*	£83	£92	£131	£134
2 star**	£112	£121	£160	£163
5 nights				
1 star*	£92	£93	£132	£142
2 star**	£112	£121	£160	£163
5 nights				
1 star*	£92	£93	£132	£143
2 star**	£127	£128	£168	£179
6 nights				
1 star*	£101	£102	£141	£152
2 star**	£143	£144	£183	£194
7 nights				
1 star*	£109	£118	£157	£160
2 star**	£159	£168	£227	£259

* without bath
** with private bath

Rooms with twin beds are £1 a night extra.

Excursions: Historical Paris £10
Modern Paris £10
Artistic Paris £18
Versailles £13
Chartres £18

Entrée/sortie
(Arrivals and departures)

Passports, visas, customs

You ought to have a valid passport to enter France (although strictly speaking it isn't necessary for EEC residents). In Britain, standard passports are good for ten years, and cost from £15 up to £30. Get forms from your local post office. Two photographs needed. Return the application, with fee and photos, countersigned by someone impressive who knows you – vicar, solicitor, doctor or JP – either to the passport office or to the nearest main post office in your city. Expect to wait about ten days for the passport in winter, or up to a month in heavy periods. Don't leave it till the last minute.

A British Visitors Passport is good for one year only. The fee is £7.50. Apply for forms at the post office. Two photos. No counter-signature needed. Valid only for Europe. This seems an expensive way to travel, but the waiting time for issue is less than for the standard one.

Length of stay

Up to three months, a resident of the EEC countries needs no visa. For longer stays, apply at the Préfecture de Police nearest to where you are living. Take along your passport and a good reason why you want to remain in Paris. They will issue a *Permis de Séjour*. Keep this with your passport and produce it when necessary (in time of trouble or when leaving France). If you are going to study in France, take to the Préfecture some kind of proof of enrolment in a school or college.

On leaving Britain, you must for some reason show your passport to an immigration official. On entering France (airport, or at boat or hovercraft landing) a French official looks at it but probably won't bother to stamp it. Likewise on the return. As a foreigner entering either country, you could be asked the reason for your stay (business, tourism, family matters), how long you'll be around. With the advent of the EEC, this has become – in France, at least – the merest formality.

Customs/Douanes

Again, these days, it's mostly a matter of waving you on. If they're looking for you they'll stop you, or they may hold you up briefly by pure chance, rifle your luggage, and leave you to repack. Contraband is illegal drugs, firearms (except hunting guns with permits), explosives, pornography. A respectful demeanour and a blank face will probably keep you from getting hung up in Customs at either end. Do not attempt to charm or chat up a customs officer anywhere. They are not susceptible to charm.

Duty-free allowances

For those arriving from EEC countries (including Britain) – 300 cigarettes, 75 cigars or 400 grams of pipe tobacco, 3 litres of wine (would you seriously consider taking wine into France?), 1½ litres of spirits, two (used) cameras, ten rolls of film.

There are duty-free shops on the departure side of airports, ship- and hoverports. However, if you're travelling late at night these shops may be closed. Payment is in cash at boat and hoverports, cash or credit cards at airports.

Arriving

First impressions can make or break your trip. If you step off the train or plane confused and disoriented, you can expect to stay that way for days. It helps to know what to expect: instead of floundering around in the chaos of the Gare du Nord you can begin immediately to develop a Paris expertise which will see you through your visit.

The airports are smoothly organized, well signposted and furnished with *bureaux de change*, information services and so forth. But like airports everywhere, Charles de Gaulle/Roissy and Orly are sterile, unamusing places, pervaded by a kind of travel *angst*, and you'll want to be on your way at once.

At both airports, you can arm yourself with the invaluable *Billet de Tourisme*, good for 2, 4 or 7 days as it suits you (more about that on pp.40–1). At Charles de Gaulle/Roissy, get it from the SNCF (French Railways) office. A 2–day pass costs 51F; for 4 days it's 77F, for 7 days 128F. At Orly, get it from the SNCF office in the arrival lounge.

At Charles de Gaulle, you can buy a 10-ticket *carnet* from the automatic distributor and from some of the shops in the airport; these tickets can be used on the city and suburban buses (but not on the Roissy/Rail bus link (see below)), and on the Métro. At Orly, inquire from the Paris Information service as to whether or not you can buy a *carnet* in the airport.

To reach central Paris from either airport, you have several choices.

Charles de Gaulle/Roissy (where Air France, British Airways, British Caledonian and Gulf Air land you)

Roissy/Rail: An excellent, cheap and fast service by bus and rail takes you to the Gare du Nord in the centre of Paris in 25 minutes. It leaves every 15 minutes, from 6:30 a.m. to 11:00 p.m. You board the free bus at the airport, it takes you to the SNCF station where you buy your ticket: 24F to Gare du Nord or 28F50 if you are changing then to the ordinary Métro to your destination. Note: during heavy tourist periods, in hot weather, on weekends, avoid the Gare du Nord if you have to take a taxi to your hotel; the queue can number from 200 to 400 people. Go on to Châtelet, which, since it is not a main-line railway station, rarely has queues for taxis.

Bus: Regular service buses, 350 to Gare du Nord and the Gare de l'Est and 351 to place de la Nation. If you have the *Billet de Tourisme*, there's nothing to pay: show the pass to the driver. Do *not* put the little ticket into the automatic stamping machine as this will invalidate it. Without the *billet*, the cost is six tickets from your *carnet*.

It's an interesting ride in, but not very fast and can be trying if you have more than a minimal amount of hand luggage.

Air France bus: Goes to Porte Maillot in the 17e *arrondissement*. (For an explanation of the *arrondissement* system see pp.37–8, and the map on pp.238–9.) Faster than the service buses, and takes your luggage off your hands – 27F. About every half hour.

Orly

Orly/Rail: Fast service to nine stations on the Left Bank, every 15 minutes from 5:30 a.m. to 9:00 p.m. then every 30 minutes until 11:00 p.m. 15F.

Express Bus: New in 1983, a high-speed, low-fare bus direct from Orly to Denfert-Rochereau Métro station in the 14e *arrondissement*. It is a smartly designed double-size articulated bus, plenty of luggage space, and does the trip in about 30 minutes. Every 15 minutes from 6:00 a.m. to 11:30 p.m. 13F50.

Air France bus: To the Gare des Invalides, Left Bank, 7e *arrondissement*. About every half hour, and your luggage is taken care of –25F.

Railway stations

Boat and hovercraft are linked to the Gare du Nord by fast train – about 2½ hours from Calais or Boulogne, and included in the cost of your ticket.

Railway stations are large, chaotic, and always crowded, even early in the morning. It takes five minutes and three wrong answers to find anything but there are centrally located information booths, usually with English-speaking personnel, who can provide authoritative answers.

If you're burdened with luggage, look for the free, energy-saving luggage carts. Avoid porters: the fixed charge per bag is 7F50.

If you haven't provided yourself with some francs in cash before arrival, seek out the *bureau de change* and pick up some survival money. Not much: you'll probably get a better rate of exchange at one of the large commercial banks in Paris itself.

Help

If you haven't already reserved a room, and need help . . .
If you need a simple but comprehensible map of Paris, the Métro,
buses . . .
If you need to know how to use the telephone, figure out the
transportation system . . .
Or if you are merely tired and totally disoriented . . .

Look for the Hôtesses de Paris: These run a service provided by
the Office de Tourisme de Paris, they speak all useful languages and
they know almost everything. For the first-time traveller arriving in
Paris without a place to lay the head, for someone arriving after
dark, the Hôtesses can be invaluable. They have a list of hotels in
each price range where they know there are vacancies at that
moment. They will not call a specific hotel of your choice (they
figure that if you know that much, you can fend for yourself), but
they *will* find you a room no matter how many phone calls it takes.
The charge is 12F for a one-star hotel, 17F for a two-star, 30F for
a three-star, and it's worth it.

It has been our experience that they will not necessarily find the
cheapest room in the best-value hotel. Usually, there is a sign
displayed showing the minimum price for a single room as single,
150F; for a double 250F. This may be broadly true, but in practice
you can do better for yourself (see 'Au lit', pp.56–90).

Still, it doesn't do to get too independent at this point, if you
don't speak much French, can't face the telephone system, and
haven't quite the nerve to tackle the Métro with your luggage at
heel. Let the Hôtesses book you a room for your first night, and
strike out on your own the next day.

If the Hôtesses de Paris at the railway station where you arrive
look slightly weary and sceptical, especially at the end of a long hot
day, don't be too surprised. Considering the number of idiot travellers who fall into their offices at all hours, often armed with nothing
more than touching faith and a copy of an out-of-date or fanciful
guidebook, expecting to find a double room near Pigalle for 40F,
their slightly disillusioned air may be justified. And they will indeed
make umpteen phone calls, until they place you in a room.

Gare d'Austerlitz (arrival hall)	Mon–Sat 9 a.m.–8 p.m.
	(10 p.m. in summer*)
Gare de l'Est (departure hall)	Mon–Sat 8 a.m.–1 p.m.
	5 p.m.–8 p.m. (10 p.m. in summer*)

Gare de Lyon (arrival hall)	Mon–Sat 8 a.m.–1 p.m.
	5 p.m.–8 p.m. (10 p.m. in summer*)
Gare du Nord (mainline hall)	Mon–Sat 8 a.m.–8 p.m.
	(10 p.m. in summer*)
Main tourist office (Bureau de Tourisme de Paris)	Mon–Sat 9 a.m.–8 p.m.
	(10 p.m. in summer*)
127 Champs-Élysées, 8e	Sundays and holidays 9 a.m.–6 p.m.
	(8 p.m. in summer*)

Métro: George-V.

Tel: 4 720 88 98 for announcements in English of almost everything you need to know, 24 hours a day.

The tourist offices are a mine of information and a great source for free maps and other handouts. Most useful of these are several varieties of Métro and bus folders; individual pamphlets on certain sight-seeing bus routes; a comprehensive list of hotels and restaurants listed by *arrondissement* (see map pp. 238–9), alphabetically, and classified by price and amenities. In addition, the main tourist office in the Champs-Élysées has posters displaying current cultural events; they give information about other parts of France; and there is a travel bureau in the basement run by SNCF. Across the street is a *bureau de change* open seven days a week (see Money, p. 210).

If you're just a little knocked out, but don't need the immediate assistance of the Hôtesses for hotel booking or map help, take time to get your breath. We strongly advise you to spend the next half hour getting acclimatized to Paris (what could be more pleasant?) before jumping on a bus or Métro.

First: find somewhere to leave your luggage. In all the stations and at the air terminal there is a left-luggage place, the *consigne*. Cart your bags there in your trolley, and check them in. *Cost*: 8F50 per bag. If you are travelling light, a storage locker (2F for a small one, up to 7F for a big one) will do nicely, if you can find one that's empty when you need it.

Then: get a bite to eat, a glass of wine, or a cup of coffee. A brasserie is perfect, but don't head for one in the terminal (too hectic), or directly opposite (double the cost, as they know how to

*Summer indicates Easter to 1 November.

soak the tourist). Walk one street away, in any direction, find a
bar-tabac or a brasserie. Here you can sit down, catch your breath,
relax for a bit before you go on. Try out your first five words of
French. Begin to figure out how the money system really works.
Don't be shy about laying the coins on the table, getting used to
the colour and feel. Plan the route to your hotel, with the aid of the
Plan de Paris (see p.36).

For a little basic brasserie vocabulary, see under 'La nourriture',
pp.91–94. Smile. And finish with 'Merci, au revoir, monsieur (or
mademoiselle)', which will surprise them so much they'll smile
back.

If you haven't already booked a hotel, and have (as you should
have) absolute confidence in this book, consult the chapter 'Au lit',
pp.56–90, for information, and pp.221–2 to find out how to use the
phone.

Getting to your hotel

If you are really weighed down, take a taxi. If necessary, write
down the address and show it to the driver. There are taxi ranks
outside all the stations and terminals. See the information on p.223
for tipping.

If you are ready to brave the Métro or the bus, see pp.38–42, in
'Getting around'. At railway stations, airports, and major Métro
stations you can pick up a *Billet de Tourisme* or *Carte Orange* (see
pp.40–2 for how to do it), and start using it to travel for almost
nothing right away. The process for *Carte Orange*, including getting
a picture taken in a photomatic booth, takes about five minutes;
for *Billet de Tourisme*, a fast thirty seconds.

Leaving Paris

By the time you're ready to wrench yourself away from Paris, you
should be able to do this part walking on your hands. But just in
case:

In railway stations: departure times, train numbers, destinations
and track numbers (*voies*) are marked in huge letters, on an immense

blue board in mid-station. Trains leave very strictly on time, and with almost no warning whistles or horns. If anyone is coming to see you off they will need a platform ticket, although as there are few officials actually at the gate this can sometimes be dispensed with.

Airport buses: Air France takes you to Charles de Gaulle from Porte Maillot; allow about 1¼ hours for the journey. Buses leave about every twenty minutes to half an hour – check on the spot for time of departure to catch your plane. Fare: 28F. (Unless you are actually staying near this terminus, the Roissy-Rail service from Gare du Nord is faster and easier.)

Trains: *Roissy/Rail*: Gare du Nord to Charles de Gaulle. Tickets from automatic dispensers in the hall leading to the train, marked Roissy/Rail, or from a ticket window – but be wary of this last, as the booking clerk also issues the *Carte Orange* and *Jaune*, student passes, etc., and you can get blocked for ever while he does the paperwork. If you are well organized and don't lose things easily, get your *return* ticket to Charles de Gaulle when you arrive from the airport and are not pressed for time, and put it with your airline ticket. Trains every 15 minutes from 5:30 a.m. to 11:30 p.m., 24F.

Service buses to airports: DON'T, unless you're a masochist with plenty of time to waste, take the bus to Charles de Gaulle, even if you have the *Billet de Tourisme* and the ride is free – the nervous strain is just too much. However, the new fast direct service to Orly, from Denfert-Rochereau in the 14e *arrondissement*, is great – about 30 minutes' travelling time to Orly-Ouest, 35 minutes to Orly-Sud. Every 15 minutes, 6:00 a.m. to 11:30 p.m., 13F50.

Buses and Métros to railway termini: Consult your maps. If you're on a direct route, with no changes, there should be no problems. But if you must change anywhere on the Métro, forget it: negotiating stairs and intersections with luggage is out of the question. Take a taxi. In hot weather, and in rush hours, Paris buses are intolerably hot; the windows are made to keep out draughts, not to let in fresh air. Doors are closed when the bus is in motion – and sweaty human bodies can be really unpleasant.

If you read French and plan to use buses often and for a long period, invest in *Le Guide de Paris-Bus*, from bookshops and some news kiosks. Great detail, well organized, which bus takes you where, precisely where each bus stop is located, how to get to main points of interest. You can quickly learn which combination of buses will serve you best and save a lot of walking.

Remember, most Paris streets are one-way, so a bus going east may run along one main street and its westbound route will be on another street, possibly a quarter of a mile away.

Aux alentours
(Getting around)

You'll probably spend much of your time in Paris getting from place to place, or just wandering around with eyes open. Nowhere in the world will you have such beauty to absorb as you go, but getting muddled can take the shine off anything, even Paris. Make the most of your wandering by arming yourself with a really first-class 'atlas' of Paris.

The best we know is a thick little book called *Plan de Paris*, published by Éditions A. Leconte and available in bookshops and *papeteries*. The hardcover edition is dark red, and costs 55F, which seems like a lot, but it's packed cover to cover with everything you need to know. There are cheaper, paperback editions of the *Plan*, but with hard use they tend to lose the cover, the maps drop out, and you end up frustrated. Other atlas-type books exist, some with larger and more legible maps, but none we have found includes so much and such accurate information.

The *Plan* of M. Leconte lists all streets, alleys, *quais* and squares alphabetically, with their beginning and ending points, *arrondissements*, nearest Métro stops, and a keyed map reference which takes you to the individual, coloured *arrondissement* map.

Each *arrondissement*, from 1 to 20, has its own pages. Métro lines and stops are printed in red. The maps themselves are laid out with alpha-numerical grids. Make sure your copy is crisp and clear. Some plans (not, to be sure, the estimable M. Leconte's) are smallish and blurry, and therefore useless no matter how cheap. A good copy is child's play to use, and a treasure to keep long after your visit to Paris. Don't lend it to anyone.

The suburbs (*banlieues*) are also mapped in this book with the same format of street listings, map reference, etc., but probably won't be of much interest to you at this point.

A highly useful section lists addresses and map references for anything you want to know, and quite a lot you might never need: embassies, theatres, hospitals, schools, churches, monuments, police stations, city halls, race tracks, museums, post offices, state ministries, stadiums, tennis courts, swimming pools, shops, radio and TV stations, principal cinemas, cabarets, concert halls.

All the Paris bus routes are listed in numerical order, and what is even more important, shown in bar-chart form, each with its starting and ending point and the principal stops in between. For that alone, the Paris Office de Tourisme should give M. Leconte a gold medal, as it is the only thing lacking in their own otherwise excellent bus folder.

If you are in Paris for more than a day or two, and intend to move more than a quarter mile from your hotel in any direction, the *Plan* is indispensable.

Less detailed but very useful maps of Paris, with pictured locations of principal tourist attractions – museums, monuments, and so forth – are available free from the Bureau de Tourisme. And the big department stores (Printemps, Galeries Lafayette, among others) have prepared very much the same sort of thing, showing of course where *they* are located.

The streets of Paris

The *arrondissement* system

In the mid-nineteenth century, Paris was thoroughly overhauled by Napoleon III's urban planner, Baron Haussmann. Slums were cleared (fortunately, he didn't get around to the Marais), sewers and aqueducts installed where the Romans had left off, and a web of wide thoroughfares, the Grands Boulevards, was laid. The city was thereupon divided into twenty *arrondissements* (there had previously been twelve, based on the old traditional *quartiers*, some dating back two thousand years). Numbers 1 to 7 cover the three historic parts of Paris: the *cité* (official and religious, located on the central islands), the *ville* (the Right Bank, commercial and industrial), and the *université* (Left Bank, commercial and scholastic). To a great extent these medieval distinctions hold true today.

The *arrondissements* spiral clockwise from the centre of Paris (1er, part of the Ile de la Cité and the area around the Louvre). The

numbers which you will see on street signs and in newspapers and
magazines (and in this book) are expressed thus: 1er, which means
Premier; 2e, which stands for *Deuxième*, and so forth. Each *arrondissement* has quite distinct identifying features or landmarks which can
serve to give you your bearings. The Eleventh (you might as well
get used to seeing it written as 11e) is roughly the area which
stretches outwards from the Bastille; the 8e is Gare St Lazare and
the Madeleine; the 7e is the Invalides and the Tour Eiffel. Street
signs in Paris are large, legible, and almost always include the
arrondissement number (thus: avenue de l'Opéra, 1er).

With map, *arrondissement*, landmarks, street signs and clearly
written house or shop numbers, you shouldn't ever get *totally* lost,
but it can happen, and for some reason even people with a good
sense of direction find it hard to work out which way is north in
Paris.

When you do feel really lost, the simplest thing to do is seek out
the nearest Métro station: ask anyone, with the simple formula,
'Pardon, monsieur (or madame) – le Métro?'

Le Métro

It's impossible to lose your way in the Métro. You can't walk ten
paces without a clear explicit sign informing you of your destination.
How to use all this information:

1 In the *Plan de Paris*, look up the name of the street you want to
go to, and you will find the nearest Métro stop.
2 Find the station on the Métro map in the front of the *Plan*, or in
one of the small free maps dealt out by the municipal transport
system at every chance. Or look on the big map outside the entrance
to the nearest Métro station, or near the ticket office, or on the
platform from which the trains run.
3 Trace your route. Each Métro line is known by its beginning
and ending points. Between any two stations in the system, you
will be coming from and going towards one of the terminals of the
line. For example, to go from Gare St-Lazare to Pigalle, you would
take a train in the direction of Porte de la Chapelle. From St-Lazare
to Sèvres-Babylone, your direction is Mairie d'Issy. On Métro
maps, each line is numbered and colour coded. The terminals are
marked in good big capital letters on the map, at the outskirts of
the city.

4 If you need to change trains to get to the stop you want, it's equally easy. Paris Métro lines are linked together in a remarkable system of *correspondances* (intersections) of two, three, sometimes five or six lines. You may have to walk underground for what seems like miles before you find your train, and it's hard on the feet. But keep calm, and you will never be lost. The signs simply don't allow that to happen.

The Métro runs every day, but with reduced services on Sundays, holidays, and after about 8 p.m. when intervals between trains become longer. Most trains begin running at 5:30 a.m., and stop at 1:15 a.m.

L'autobus

Trickier, and takes longer to get you from A to B, but infinitely more fun than the Métro. Like the train system, each bus is marked large and clear with its point of origin and destination. The buses are designated primarily by number. On the sides of the bus, the major stops are displayed so that when it moves past you, you can read the route in a flash. An overall bus map, available at Métro stations, bus termini, and the Office de Tourisme at 127 Champs-Élysées, gives a fairly clear, colour-coded overview of the routes. But it's intricate, and you could miss your bus while you're trying to work it out. Best of all is the chart-form bus information in the *Plan de Paris*.

Bus stops are recognizable by yellow kerbside shelters, with a red disc on a standard above them. This displays the number(s) of the bus or buses that stop here. Inside the shelter is a clear chart of the bus route, all its stops, and even a helpful marker that shows exactly where you are on the route.

Inside the bus – just in case you've missed the other information – there are two or three route maps, either overhead or on the sides above the windows at eye level for those standing. This makes it easy to keep track of where you are, what the next stop will be, and even if the worst comes to the worst and you are really mixed up, which direction you are going in. The bus stops have their names clearly and legibly displayed so you know where you are at all times.

Times: In general, buses leave their starting points at 7:00 a.m., and run to about 8:30 or 9:00 p.m. Others have a night service (these all begin at the place du Châtelet, avenue Victoria, 3e). Sundays and holidays: buses 20, 21, 26, 27, 31, 38, 43, 44, 46, 52, 62, 80, 91, 92, 95, 96, and the Petite Ceinture bus which runs around the outskirts of Paris.

All Paris buses run on the request-stop system. If you are at a stop marked for only one bus, the driver will stop (if he sees you) but it may be safer to wave your arm or an umbrella. If more than one bus serves your stop, you *must* signal the one you want.

The same system applies when you want to get off. No automatic stops. You must push a small, well-concealed button on one of the upright stanchions near entrance and exit doors. This activates a sign in the front of the bus: *Arrêt demandé*. This system lets Paris buses move fairly fast, considering the narrow, often crowded streets in which they run.

Métro and bus tickets

With few exceptions for distance and for the RER (see below) tickets are interchangeable from Métro to bus. You can buy them singly (extravagantly), or in *carnets* of ten (more economical) from bus drivers and at Métro stations. Prices given are as of November 1985, and should hold for at least a year.

Single tickets, 2nd class	4F40
1st class (Métro only)	6F50
Carnet of ten, 2nd class	26F50
1st class (Métro only)	40F

Billet de Tourisme (valid from whatever date you choose)	
2-day	51F
4-day	77F
7-day	128F

Rather dear, unless you are going to spend a lot of time travelling. The *Billet* gives you unlimited travel (first class on the Métro) on all Paris and suburban buses, the Métro, RER, and the Sacré-Coeur funicular. You can't use it to reach central Paris on the RER from Charles de Gaulle, nor on the new express Orlybus – however, if you're game to take the slower public buses to or from airports, the *Billet* is good. Available from main Métro stations, rail stations, and from Barclays Bank, 1 Cockspur St, London W1. For *our* francs, a better bet is:

Carte Orange (good for one *calendar* month)	
2nd class	139F
Carte Jaune (good for one *calendar* week)	
2nd class	39F
C: New: *'Formule'* 24-hour pass	19F

Unlimited travel within the two inner zones of Paris (all that counts for the tourist, anyway), on Métro or bus. Some RER lines and surburban buses.

Take a passport-size picture with you, or have one snapped in a machine in the rail station. The *Carte Orange* itself is free and good for a year. Each month you buy a *coupon mensuel* which is slipped into a pocket in the front of the plastic holder of the *Carte*, and used as any Métro or bus ticket. The coupon goes on sale about a week before each month begins, and it's smart to buy it then as the crush the last day of a month, or the first of the next, is unbelievable.

On the bus

You will need one or two ordinary tickets depending on how many zones you will pass through. Tell the driver where you are going and he will tell you how many you need. Ordinary tickets are 'composted' by pushing into a ticket-punch machine. But DON'T do this with your *Carte Orange* or *Billet de Tourisme* ticket – it perforates the ticket and makes it unusable again. Flash the entire *Carte* or *Billet* at the driver. If you composte the ticket there are no refunds for your idiocy.

Now that you know how to get around – where to?

You might just want to set off at random – head in any direction on foot; hop on the first bus that comes along; take the Métro to the end of the line and try to find your way back as a pedestrian – no matter what, something will come of it.

Or perhaps you could use some pointers on the *quartiers* before you set out – a few landmarks – some guaranteed bus routes. Possibly some areas to avoid, as well.

Major monuments (the Tour Eiffel, the Arc de Triomphe, the Louvre, and such) you should be able to find with one hand tied behind your back. If you're really in doubt, ask a tourist. What follows is a sampler: general reflections on a few *quartiers* (central and out of the way) and some routes you might like to try, on foot and otherwise. It's anything but exhaustive. You'll discover far more than we have space for on your own.

Paris by bus

Commercial sightseeing buses in Paris cost an arm and a leg, as the saying goes. Why pay 80F for a trip when the glorious RATP (the municipal transport system) offers you an incomparable set of bus trips for practically nothing? If you are armed, as you should be, with the indispensable *Billet de Tourisme* (see page 40), or the possibly even more useful *Carte Orange* (page 41) your sightseeing is on the house, so to speak. The RATP has laid out, in a well-designed folder called 'Billet de Tourisme', available at all major Métro stations, a list of seventeen 'sightseeing' bus routes that can show you the most beautiful, historic, curious, and provocative parts of Paris. These seventeen could take up your entire time in the city, of course, so we've narrowed down the choices to a magic seven – some of which will show you parts of Paris most tourists haven't even heard about.

If you have time for only one leisurely, luxurious bus ride, choose No. 24.

Bus 24

From Gare St-Lazare, it takes you round the place de la Madeleine (luxurious shops) into the place de la Concorde, then sweeps along the quai des Tuileries beside the Seine, past the Louvre. As you go, you have a most enticing view of the silvery buildings lining the opposite side of the river (the Rive Gauche). Glancing to your left, you can see the exquisite church St-Germain-l'Auxerrois, where all the kings of France worshipped privately. At the pont des Arts, look across the river at the Hôtel des Monnaies (the Mint) and the Institut de France which houses the 'Immortals' of the Académie Française. Crossing the river on the pont Neuf to the Ile de la Cité, the bus passes the Palais de Justice before continuing over the Petit Pont to the Left Bank. From the boulevard St-Germain, the route follows the quai St-Bernard, skirting the edge of the four-centuries-old Jardin des Plantes. If you stay on the bus all the way to its destination at Alfort, you will catch sight of the monumental new Palais Omnisport built on the site of the razed wine warehouses along the quai de Bercy – passing a real working-class area on the way. On the return journey, the bus goes along the left bank of the Seine, with a good look at Notre-Dame; then past the Mint and along the quai Voltaire (where Ingres, Delacroix, and Wagner lived at various times), before recrossing the river by the pont Royal and returning to St-Lazare by way of the place de la Concorde and the magnificent rue Royale. Monday to Saturday, 7:00 a.m. to 8:30 p.m.

Bus 29

Also from Gare St-Lazare, the 29 takes you around the Opéra, down the rue du 4 Septembre, passing the Bourse, the stock market headquarters, the place des Victoires with its statue of Louis XIV on horseback. You suddenly come to the great ultra-modern dazzler, Beaubourg (Centre Georges Pompidou), towering over the small crooked streets of the Marais, almost the oldest part of Paris. The bus goes past the elegant place des Vosges, built for the king in 1612, then into the wide boulevard leading to the place de la Bastille. The Bastille prison itself is gone, but the immense circle is very impressive. If you like, get off here and catch the No. 87 bus for another fabulous sightseeing trip to the Champ-de-Mars (for the Tour Eiffel and Napoleon's tomb), or stay with the No. 29 and go on, past the Cimetière de Picpus where many of the victims of *la guillotine* lie buried. Monday to Saturday, 7:00 a.m. to 8:30 p.m.

Bus 32

It begins at the Gare de l'Est, but you may want to catch it at one of its more interesting stopping places, such as place de la Trinité, going in the direction of Porte de Passy. The route takes you through the 'Quartier d'Europe', so-called because almost every street is named after a capital city: Amsterdam, Budapest, London, Stockholm. Past the Gare St-Lazare, you are in the faded elegance of the boulevard Haussmann, named after the man who reshaped the city in the 1860s. Along the rue de la Boëtie, look for the wildly expensive and beautiful boutiques and galleries. Then up the Champs-Élysées, and to the Trocadéro, the palace built for the Paris World's Fair in 1937 and now the home of three museums. You may want to stop off here and see the Museum of Mankind – fascinating. The bus goes on to the smart, but not entrancing, Passy neighbourhood with its mansions and streets overhung with huge old trees. On the return trip, the route is slightly different, and you'll pass along the avenue Matignon and through Faubourg St-Honoré, wall-to-wall with the great couture houses. The bus will give you an overview, but this is really pedestrian territory. File it for future window-shopping. No. 32 runs Monday to Saturday, first bus from Gare de l'Est at 7:00 a.m., last one at 8:30 p.m.

Bus 52

Begins at the Opéra, takes you around the lovely shopping area of the boulevard des Capucines, past the Musée Cognacq-Jay (again, file for future reference), and through the place de la Madeleine with its magnetic food shops: Fauchon, Hédiard and Michel Guérard. Around the place de la Concorde (a circus of killer traffic has taken the place of the guillotine that stood here for years), and a wonderful view up the vista of the Champs-Élysées. The big avenue de Friedland takes you to the Étoile/place Charles de Gaulle, where there is always a silent crowd at the Eternal Flame that burns over the tomb of France's Unknown Soldier. Beyond that, you are in the streets of the 16e *arrondissement*, a smart, conservative residential area. The avenue Mozart on the return journey is charming; the local café is called The Magic Flute. This is a pleasant place to step off the bus and have coffee, and walk round a neighbourhood that is real Paris, far off the tourist beat. The bus continues to the place de la Porte d'Auteuil and finishes at the pont de St-Cloud, a pretty sterile area, so you might want to end your trip at the place de la Porte d'Auteuil and either walk west into the Bois de Boulogne, or head back into central Paris on the Métro. No 52 runs seven days a week, including holidays, first bus at 7:00 a.m. weekdays and 8:00 a.m. Sundays, last bus about 10:15 p.m.

Bus 63

Begins at the Gare de Lyon, takes you along the quai St-Bérnard, and almost at once you are in the Quartier Latin, the home of Paris students from the time of the monks in the Middle Ages to the motorbikes and demonstrations of the 1960s. It traverses the rue des Écoles, crosses the boulevard St-Michel, and passes the church of St-Sulpice before threading its way through the stately streets of the 7e. The 63 touches the fringe of the boulevard St-Germain, then takes you along the quai d'Orsay (political and diplomatic Paris). If you stay with it to the end of the route at Porte de la Muette, you see 'untourist' Paris – but it's more interesting to get off at the Trocadéro stop for an unparalleled view of the city from high on the hill. Take the bus back in the direction of the Gare de Lyon, and this time step off at St-Germain-des-Prés: yes, it's a cliché, but not to be missed because of its bookshops, its galleries, its cafés. There are still those who swear that a costly coffee at the Deux Magots is worth the price, just to see and be seen by *le tout Paris*. And it costs nothing to browse in the side streets, to see Picasso drawings or primitive paintings. Bus 63 runs seven days a week, from 7:00 a.m. to midnight (leaving times from the Gare de Lyon).

Bus 72

Runs from the pont de St-Cloud to the Hôtel-de-Ville, and back again, and on the way gives you sight of both modern and historic Paris. In between you will see some of the glitter and splendour, and some of the less savoury and picturesque parts too. To get the most from this 'tour', catch the bus at the Hôtel-de-Ville end: from here you have a view of the pont Neuf (begun in 1578, so only relatively new), the great sweep of the Louvre, the Cours de la Reine and the Horses of Marly rearing over Paris on their pedestals. It passes the Jeu de Paume; get off here if you want to visit the most famous collection of Impressionist paintings in the world, or stay on the bus which goes on along the Seine, along the boulevards named after the City of New York and after President Kennedy. The bus runs along the avenue de Versailles, most interesting for its buildings such as No. 142 by the architect Hector Guimard, in art nouveau style. Beyond this point, the ride isn't particularly exciting, except as all Paris's 'real' neighbourhoods are; you may want to get off in the avenue de Versailles, wander a bit and absorb its feeling, then return by No. 22 to the Opéra. Mondays to Saturdays, first bus from pont de St-Cloud at 7:00 a.m., last one at 8:50 p.m. On Sundays, there is a partial service, from pont de St-Cloud to Concorde only.

Bus 83

Begins at place d'Italie, in the 13e *arrondissement*, a seldom-visited but quite interesting part of Paris (some very good hotels and restaurants there, see pp.82 and 123 for more about them). Running down the avenue des Gobelins, it traverses the boulevard du Port-Royal. On Saturdays, there's a street market worth stopping for in this street, near the rue St-Jacques. Here it skirts the 5e *arrondissement*, the Latin Quarter. The rue d'Assas on this route is absolutely littered with good little bistros and cafés. The bus passes the Jardin du Luxembourg, where you might want to stop to inhale some fresh air and watch the Paris kids at play; then it runs along the river by the quai d'Orsay, past Invalides. Along the way, you glimpse the Tour Eiffel, and the dome of the Invalides with Napoleon's tomb. The bus crosses on to the right bank into fashionable haute-couture Paris, around the Rond-Point des Champs-Élysées and the Métro station of St-Philippe-du-Roule. The bus goes as far as Levallois, but you have really had the most interesting part of its route by now, unless you want to see working-class Paris as it really lives. If you prefer, finish your trip at the Rond-Point, and sit for a while on a bench in the pretty little park while all Paris goes by, or walk up the Champs-Élysées towards the Étoile. This is a wonderful bus ride to take late in the afternoon (but be prepared for crowds during rush hour), as you may be lucky enough to see the lights along the Seine and the Champs-Élysées coming on as dusk approaches. Mondays to Saturdays, first bus from place d'Italie at 7:00 a.m., last one at 8:30 p.m.

Montmartrobus a minibus service for the inhabitants of the steep streets that snake around the Hill of the Martyrs, new, enchanting, hardly publicized, and as yet sussed out by only a handful of tourists. For one ticket, or free with *Carte Orange* or *Billet de Tourisme*, you get a breathless, bumpy, roller coaster ride from Pigalle to the end of the line at Métro Jules Joffrin. On the way you are treated to the Moulin de la Galette, the place des Tertres, the lovely place des Abbesses, the pure-Utrillo rue Tholoze, the centuries-old Montmartre vineyards, and more views up and down each winding street than you can take in. If the scenery goes by too fast, you can hop off, take pictures or merely wander and gasp, and catch the next bus in fifteen minutes or so. The return trip takes a slightly different route, if anything even more *pittoresque et historique*. The drivers are nerveless and daunted by nothing: not even a beer camion stuck in a hairpin turn will blow their cool. The marvellous thing about Montmartre is that the moment you're out of the sleaze of Pigalle, the landscape reverts to quotidian serenity: an area in which real people live and work as they have for centuries. If you jump off the bus at the northern end (Mairie du XVIII) you can pick up a snack lunch in one of the unbelievable places in the rue Poteau, and sit in the exquisite Square de Clignancourt among flowers, trees, and children. If you have any luck at all you'll get there when the band is playing in the toy-town bandstand. The Montmartrobus runs from 7:30 a.m. at Pigalle to 7:30 p.m., last trip back from Mairie du XVIII at 8:17 p.m.

In addition to these free or almost free bus routes through Paris, the RATP has some extraordinary tours of its own from the place de la Madeleine (8e) to – among other places – the châteaux of Chambord, Chenonceaux, Poitiers, to Bayeux for the Tapestry, to Colombey-les-Deux-Églises to see de Gaulle's house, to Beaune for the wine country, to Cabourg for Proustiana, to Mont-St-Michel, to Domrémy for the route of Jeanne d'Arc – and even a day trip to Luxembourg if that's a thrill for you.

Information

Services Touristiques de la RATP, place de la Madeleine, near the flower market. Pick up the yellow folder called 'Excursions (plus de 100 circuits)' from major Métro stations and all railway stations. Prices are low, compared to commercial bus tours, but you will need at least a minimal command of French to make sure you understand their instructions about leaving times and boarding places. They also have guided tour buses to Versailles, Malmaison, Paris by night, and so on, but only in French.

Footwork

The Batignolles

Just north of the Gare St-Lazare (8e), in the web of streets named after European capitals, begins a pleasantly varied, fairly gentle cluster of neighbourhoods. Heading north up the rue de Rome, you begin to run into music stores: luthiers, guitar makers, violin shops, sellers of sheet music. This is the *quartier* of the Paris Conservatoire. The bar-tabacs, cafés and restaurants cater to music students; the prices are accordingly low and the whole neighbourhood is a find for the pauper astray in Paris. And it leads you, very quickly, into an oasis of calm. Take a left on the boulevard des Batignolles, past the Théâtre Hébertot, and you are in the beginning of the rue de Lévis – a street market, jammed on Saturday mornings, which most tourists miss because they've never heard of it. This leads to an airy little square, and you are in the rue Legendre, heading towards Montmartre. In three blocks, you've arrived at the Église Ste-Marie. Behind it is the square des Batignolles – placid, delightful, a good place to sit for a while. It's a small park rather than a 'square', and contains a series of artificial duckponds, a carousel, and raked gravel paths. If you're still energetic, continue eastward and gradually uphill into Montmartre. The Batignolles is a backwater of calm in Paris – quiet, unimposing houses, a petit-bourgeois population. At one edge is the place de Clichy, the epitome of sleaze; at the other, the tracks that lead back to the Gare St-Lazare. In between, absolute peace.

The rue Mouffetard and the Fifth

Since medieval days, the precincts of the 5e *arrondissement* have been the student quarter of Paris. The rue Mouffetard itself has somewhat more diverse origins. It began as a Roman road from Lyons, developed into a rich residential area in the twelfth to fourteenth centuries, then fell into the hands of skinners, tanners and dyers (the Gobelins factory nearby is the only remnant of this period). The resulting stench gave the street its name: *mouffette* is French for skunk.

The Mouffetard today consists of a street market at its southern end, and a string of small shops and restaurants running north: *boulangeries, triperies, boucheries chevalines* (for horsemeat), *fromageries*. The restaurants run mostly to Greek, Arab, and Vietnamese/ Chinese food. Everything here is startlingly good value: it's impossible to pinpoint a restaurant that offers a better meal than its neighbour, for about 42–55F, usually with reasonably drinkable wine and service thrown in.

At its north end, the rue Mouffetard becomes the rue Descartes. At No. 39, the poet Verlaine lived and died – it has always been a *quartier* for the artist, the writer, the poet, the student, the poor scholar, and although it has been thoroughly discovered by generations of tourists, the Mouffetard and its neighbouring streets remain triumphantly what they are.

The surrounding streets include the rue Geoffroy-St-Hilaire with the only fully-fledged mosque in Paris; the Arènes de Lutèce (remains of a Roman arena), the place Monge (outdoor market), the Panthéon, and the Bibliothèque Ste-Geneviève, probably the first use of structural steel supports and lots of glass, worth having a look at. The 5e is loaded with schools, technical colleges, branches of the sprawling University of Paris, and at odd times of the day bands of students flood the streets. It's wonderful walking country. The most you'll spend, perhaps, will be the price of a good, cheap lunch or a sandwich eaten sitting on a college wall, or, extravagantly, a coffee, sitting at a café table resting your feet and watching the world of student Paris wander by.

Rue St-Dominique and the Seventh

The 7e is rich but sterile. You'll see that the hotels and restaurants we have picked in this area are rather few and far between. Lots of trees, wide streets, and most of the *arrondissement* seems to be made up of the mouldering Tour Eiffel and its gravelly park, and the Invalides – haunted grandeur, with Napoleon's tomb as the major *frisson*. In general, we find the neighbourhood parched and almost devoid of interest, certainly very low on anything that counts for strolling, listening, enjoying the free delights of Paris.

But turn the corner off the boring boulevard de la Tour Maubourg into the rue St-Dominique, and it's like opening the top of a magic trunk. Bustle, laughter, shops, sales, ebullient cross-bred dogs instead of blanketed Yorkshire terriers, girls in tight skirts and men in faded jeans, a most typical and joyous neighbourhood restaurant or two (see p.113), even a few hotels that are worthy of note (p.71). The little side streets that dangle from St-Dominique are equally delightful, and it's almost impossible to believe that a hundred yards away are the flat-faced, dull apartment buildings and pompous antique shops. Spend a day in that street: you'll spend almost no money unless you decide to splurge on a down-filled ski jacket for a big 110F, or a slightly used Christian Dior scarf from a street barrow.

Another startling street that redeems the whole 7e from its sterility is the little rue Cler, a pedestrian precinct that is like a microcosm of a French provincial town set down whole in one of the richer areas of Paris. The shopping is entrancing, and there is an hotel (see p.71) which has a faithful year-after-year clientele, French, English, American, Japanese. Perhaps there are other rue Clers and rue St-Dominiques which we haven't found; if so, we apologize to the 7e and some day will perhaps take time to discover its 'villages'.

The astonishing Eighth

One of the least homogeneous *arrondissements* of Paris that we've encountered is the 8e, which ranges from the quiet music-student life beyond Gare St-Lazare, to the bustling commercial area around Au Printemps department store, the boulevard Haussmann, and the rue Caumartin; and takes in the supreme elegance of the rue Royale and the place de la Madeleine. Imagine a neighbourhood that encompasses both a public bath-house where a hot shower costs 5F, and the super-luxury atmosphere of Fauchon, the most expensive food shop in the world! Hermès, with its silk scarves and perfectly made saddlery-stitched handbags – £400 is nothing here – is in the rue Boissy d'Anglas. So is Lanvin, which seems to exhale Arpège from its windows.

The Jeu de Paume on the edge of the place de la Concorde is the jewel of this area, undoubtedly. If you think of having a meal within a thousand yards of its doors, be prepared to blow the week's budget – Maxim's is a few steps away. Yet in the same street that houses the creations of the couturiers is a pleasant little café which feeds the mannequins and the *vendeuses* (not the customers, of course) for about 35F a lunch. The Hôtel Crillon is only a few feet away from the American Embassy, and it costs nothing to smell the expensive hyacinths in its window boxes, or to sit for a few minutes in the downy chairs in the lobby (looking as though you are waiting for a rich friend). Yet in the immediate neighbourhood, just off the place de la Madeleine, are *four* good budget-priced hotels. One is such remarkable value that it is only sheer generosity that makes us put it in this book, instead of keeping the name for a few favoured friends.

The bit of the 8e that surrounds the Gare St-Lazare is too little known to those who merely take trains or buses from the station.

Real people live here, work here, send their children to school, look for jobs, buy flowers and pastry, newspapers, electric toasters, shoes, get their hair done and their cars repaired. Walk along the rue Rocher, or the rue de Vienne, have a very good meal at a price that would not even buy you a pub lunch in London, go into a sheet music shop in the rue de Rome and you might find a flat, a cello, a baby-sitter, a ride to Marseilles, a tandem bicycle or a chance to play chamber music. Walk ten minutes towards the river, and (if it pleases you) go in and try on a Dior mink jacket, or decide whether you really like the new Hermès scent or not.

The 8e is not as beautiful or as historic as the Marais, not as bubbling as the student quarter, the 5e, not as snobbish as St-Germain-des-Prés, not as pretentious as Passy and the 16e – it's dead at night except for the rich sweeping out of Maxim's – but for daytime walking its mix of characteristics makes it very special indeed.

The other Paris

Jewish, Tunisian, Algerian. If you have a fancy for seeing what foreign parts of Paris are like, take the Métro to Pyrénées or Belle-ville, in the 19e/20e, on a Saturday night after sundown, or from about 9 o'clock on Sunday morning. Walk the length of rue Belle-ville, and here you will find that the old traditional Jewish working-class quarter is gradually meeting and mingling with the new wave of Arab Paris, without political thought or collision. Belleville dies at sundown on Friday, comes alive again on Saturday nights and Sundays. Whatever the weather, all Belleville is out on the street, talking, eating, embracing, arguing, smoking, shopping. Here you gradually begin to realize that almost every face you see is male. Arab women, if they have been brought to Paris, keep steadfastly to their houses and families. The Arab man in Paris lives to work, and works very often in the low-end job no one else wants to do. On weekends, they are all out drinking coffee in crowded cafés and socializing on street corners. The women, if any, are buying fruit, vegetables, dripping-sweet pastries, fresh-killed chickens.

Here in the rue Belleville and the rue Ramponeau, you have the feeling of being surrounded by a world infinitely more exotic than anywhere else in Paris. Half a dozen varieties of Arabic, plus Yiddish or a strange French that is heavily injected with words from both languages, are all around you.

It is true that the civilization of North Africa has affected Parisian life in all its aspects. Hardly a quarter of Paris (except perhaps the stuffy 7e and the formal 15e and 16e *arrondissements*) is without its restaurant serving couscous, mloukhia, merguez, bric à l'oeuf, sugary Oriental pastries. But none is like Belleville.

In the last few years, the racial mix of Belleville has been further enriched by a new wave of Chinese residents, restaurants, shops, and mini-supermarkets. The Belleville area, historically, is the preserve of not very well-to-do Jews, many who survived concentration camps, many strictly orthodox. Then came the influx of Arabs, and with them many North African Jews; from Algeria, Tunisia, Libya, Morocco, Yemen. It is intensely alive, with a cosmopolitan mixture of cinemas, posters, news-stands, food stalls – and if you want to get your hair cut on a Sunday, make for Belleville.

If you are there on a Sunday morning, and of an adventurous turn of mind, go into one of the numerous places that sell take-away food. A 'sandwich tunisien' is a North African/French sandwich: a crusty loaf split open and crammed with tuna, black olives, tomatoes, lettuce, hot green peppers, capers, bathed in an orange sauce that could start a fire. Drink only beer or mineral water, not wine. Finish with ruinously sweet Arab pastries and you will have made a very adequate meal and it will have cost you about 18F all told.

Tourists are not exactly fawned upon in Belleville, any more than in Brixton, but nor is the casual stranger sent packing. We suggest you keep a low profile: flashy clothes and expensive cameras will do nothing for your image; at best you'll feel uncomfortable and out of place. But if you can manage not to look or behave like a gawker, there's no reason to avoid the area.

If you decide that you do want to see this *quartier*, so rich in life and colour, don't wait, as its crumbling buildings are coming down fast before the push of modernization. Already the bulldozers have done for the worst slums, and modern proletariat housing is going up. The boutiques will be the next to move in. One wonders where the Arab men – lounging, smoking, spitting, kissing – will go when the last 'hotel' is levelled.

Street scenes

Much of the beauty of Paris, ranging from the small and exquisite to surprising grotesques, is alive and thrilling to the eye and the –

possibly furtive – touch of the fingers. Not just the endless turning vistas of streets, trees, mansions and monuments, but the decoration in the form of carvings, capitals and statues which reveal themselves often in unnoticed places, and always free.

Paris churches are part of this 'living museum', and although there is never an admission charge, it's a civilized gesture to leave a few francs in the unobtrusive offering boxes near the doors.

In the oldest surviving church of Paris, St-Julien-le-Pauvre (in the street that bears his name), look for a marvellous group of flying harpies among its twelfth-century stone capitals. Otherwise it's a dull little place crowded with columns, which comes to life only when its occupants, a Greek Catholic sect called the Melchites, sing on Sunday mornings.

The oldest bell in Paris is in the tower of the Church of St-Merri, 78 rue St-Martin, 4e – it was cast in 1331. The bell-tower porch of the church of St-Germain-des-Prés was begun in 1040, and two of the windows in the church itself date from the middle of the eleventh century; while just outside in the little garden is an astonishing head of a woman by Picasso.

The last period of Gothic architecture, known as the Flamboyant, blazed out as though in reaction to the stark horror of the fifteenth century (plague, civil war and occupation by the English were all visited on Paris in a space of about thirty years). Perhaps the most fascinating survival is in the vaulted interior of the church of St-Séverin, at 1 rue des Prêtres-St-Séverin, 5e: an extraordinary spiralling central column seems to move and vibrate as it flings upwards and outwards a series of interlocked ribs.

This might be an appropriate place to mention that Paris churches *are* churches, and are primarily for worshippers. It would be wisest and nicest not to talk loudly, walk heavily, or jostle the chairs and benches: and as for the groups of tourists who chatter and flash their way around Notre-Dame, we would cheerfully see them suspended by their cameras from the mouths of gargoyles.

It is almost impossible to write dispassionately about the Sainte-Chapelle, the most queenly example of Gothic architecture of Paris, built to hold relics of the Passion and consecrated in 1248. It is no longer a church, but an historical monument, and in changing identities it has been very nearly vandalized. Its lower chapel now sells guidebooks and cassettes, its frescoed walls are scratched with graffiti, and one of the unforgettable sights of recent years was a tourist who had taken off her shoes and was peacefully eating a sandwich under the great Rose Window.

For uncompromising medieval grimness, have a look at the tower of Jean the Fearless, built about 1374, and tacked on to the Hôtel de Bourgogne, at 20 rue Étienne-Marcel, 2e. At the other extreme is the Hôtel de Sens, aristocratic and elegant, standing at the corner of the rue de l'Hôtel-de-Ville and rue Figuier, 4e. Its conical tower and superb doorway are among the gems of the Marais. All through this district are scattered beautiful examples of noble buildings of the sixteenth and seventeenth centuries, which survived wars, plagues, riots and revolutions but nearly went down in the heedless twentieth century. Mercifully, they have been saved, restored, cleaned. See the Hôtel de Lamoignon at 24 rue des Francs-Bourgeois, 3e, dating from 1580, and another beauty, the doorway with pepperpot turrets of the Hôtel de Clisson, even earlier, and now tucked into the National Archives at 58 rue des Archives, 3e.

Centuries later, Paris produced a most tremendous variety of 'pompous' architecture – a riot of academic taste, from about 1850 to 1900, so bad as to be utterly endearing. A classic is the Hôtel de Ville (4e). Don't miss the main staircase, whose decorations mix up cowboys, Indians, and French merchants who seem to be wearing sola topis in Ceylon or Equatorial Africa.

The Universal Exposition of 1900 produced art nouveau and 'Le Style 1900', which has been loved, hated, collected and argued about ever since its birth. Many of Hector Guimard's sinuous, serpent-green Métro entrances still survive, and are now especially prized since the Museum of Modern Art in New York bought a discarded one and re-erected it in its garden.

At 10 rue Pavée, 4e, there's a synagogue designed by Guimard in 1913. A less famous architect, Jules Lavirotte, did a block of flats at 19 avenue Rapp, 7e, that has *everything*: peacocks, butterflies, enamel, entwined flowers, and – peering out of the maze of design – a bust of Ophelia with streaming hair that turns into tendrils of vines. At 33 rue du Champ-de-Mars, not far away, art nouveau lilies crawl all over the front.

At the corner of the rue Victor Massé and rue Frochot (9e), where whores patrol the street from about 4 o'clock in the afternoon, there's a most delightful piece of art deco stained glass set into the walls. And don't fail to see a perfect Paris townscape: the avenue Frochot, a locked private road with sedate houses, small front gardens, and an academy of painting, a prim little island in the midst of beginning-to-be-squalid Pigalle.

A series of Utrillo paintings unrolls when you walk into the rue Germain-Pilon (18e), just off the place de Clichy. At No. 13 is a

delightful courtyard and house, and nearby is the Grand Boulan-
gerie Viennoise with beautiful painted glass art deco panels
bordering its doors. Oddly enough, many Paris bakeries of the early
1900s have these little works of art.

At the top of the street you emerge into the rue des Abbesses –
another Utrillo – and nearby is the tranquil place des Abbesses,
with a famous and perfectly preserved Guimard Métro entrance.

Paris abounds in statues and carvings on its buildings, balus-
trades and pedestals – it's impossible to describe or even to list the
main ones, and anyway they've been photographed and written
about almost to the point of boredom. Our personal picks: the
brackets that support the flying buttresses of the church of St-
Germain-l'Auxerrois, in the place du Louvre (1er), a delightful
nightmare of hippopotamuses, monkeys, madmen, and a rat busily
destroying the globe of the world; the heart-stopping 'St Francis in
Ecstasy' of the sixteenth-century master Germain Pilon, in the
church of St Jean–St François, at 6-bis, rue Charlot, 3e; the rearing
Horses of Marly at the bottom of the Champs-Élysées; and the
Seated Lion, of the 19th-century sculptor Barye, on the quay side
of the Tuileries.

Scheduling

Prime time for Paris-watching varies for various events.

Early morning (really early) from about 7:00 a.m. is the time to
see what Parisians are really made of. For the most part, they
actively enjoy work. Sidewalks are sluiced and swept, shopfronts
washed down (with soap and polishing cloths), market stalls are
arranged like jewellery shops. The cafés are full of banter.

From noon on, life becomes more leisurely. Lunch may be drawn
out over a couple of hours; by 4:00 p.m. the population strolls
rather than bustles. At dusk, the fountains and monuments are
illuminated: at least once, try to be standing in the place de la
Concorde, ideally inhaling the scent of money from the Hôtel
Crillon, at the magical moment when the lights in the square, along
the river, and all up the Champs-Élysées, go on.

Au lit (Sleeping cheap)

The hotels that follow have been personally and recently vetted by our experienced Paris people. We emphasize *recently*, because it has been our experience that hotels can change, renovate, redecorate, re-price, even disappear, with extraordinary speed in Paris. Because of the uncertainties of the French economy in 1985/86 – despite our diligence – we're certain that many hotel prices will shoot up after this book has gone to press. So be warned, and try not to be affronted.

Many of our choices are those officially classed as 1-star in the *Guide des Hôtels* produced by the Office de Tourisme in Paris. They collect their information from three professional bodies (the Syndicat Général de l'Industrie Hôtelière, the Chambre Syndicale des Hôteliers, Caffetiers, Restaurateurs de Paris, and the Syndicat Nationale des Chaines d'Hôtels et de Restaurants). With all that expertise, you aren't taking much of a chance. This professionalism means that hotels have been inspected for adherence to certain standards, their prices have been registered, their amenities and number of rooms verified.

On the whole, the *Guide des Hôtels* is accurate, but between the time the data comes in and publication date, many things – including prices – can alter, especially if the hotel has upgraded its services or accommodation.

Every hotel we have included here is clean, well run, and well above what we would consider minimum standard of comfort. A certain number we have found are actually classed as 2-star, but with prices that bring them within our budget. Most of them are, as you would expect, walk-ups, but a surprising number even of 1-star hotels have lifts, which makes life easier with luggage, for older people, and for those with small children. About 98 per cent of them have a telephone in each room, and a switchboard service night and day. In most cases, someone on the hotel staff speaks

English, and where no English is spoken we have noted the fact. You will then have to get by with smiles, goodwill, and a little French remembered from school.

The price of every room in any hotel vetted by the tourist office must be displayed at the registration desk and again in the room. Many hotels, in the last year or two, have taken to displaying their range of prices, coordinated with the accommodation offered, on a printed notice on an outside door or window, so you know even before entering what you are getting into.

These days, few hotels include *petit déjeuner* (the Continental breakfast of croissants, bread, jam, coffee, tea or chocolate) in their prices. If it *is* included, and you don't want to eat it or pay for it without eating it, say so politely but firmly *when you register*, and ask how much the room *alone* costs. Breakfast in a hotel can range from a fairly moderate 10F to a shocking 16–20F. Even at its cheapest it will be double the price of coffee and croissants taken standing at the zinc counter of the nearest bar-tabac or brasserie – and there you have the fun of tuning in on the conversation of Parisians going to work.

The 1-star classification of hotels is rather a loose mesh, taking in anything from a radiantly clean, newly painted hotel ten minutes from Beaubourg – efficient but not the friendliest in the world – to a strange little hostelry where the hot water runs out early, the towels are child-size, the proprietor never visible – but where you can have charcuterie lunches in your room, hang dripping laundry from the radiators, without anyone taking the least bit of notice. A sweet, rather shabby, warmly friendly place right off the glossiest part of the rue St-Honoré is 1-star, and so is a much statelier, frighteningly clean, chillingly unfriendly hotel in the newly fashionable Marais.

A very few of the hotels we have found have no stars at all, although they are comfortable and spotless – many of them hope to be in the next guide, but the inspectors haven't got around to them yet.

On the whole, we have found that even in this time of inflation you can get a single room with a *cabinet de toilette* (that is, basin, bidet, and constant supply of really hot water) in a pleasant hotel for as little as 75F. A double room with a big bed is even more of a bargain, as it costs as little as 115F even in a very remarkable hotel about a hundred yards from the Madeleine, in the luxurious 8e. If you want a shower, expect to pay from 90F for a single, and up to 160F for a double room with large bed. Twin beds, and a bath instead of a shower, can push prices up towards 190–200F, but in terms of other capital city prices, they are still cheap. Usually, the price of a room with shower or bath and WC is the same for one or two persons; cheaper rooms, with running water or *cabinet de toilette* alone, may charge less for a single occupant. Some rooms have a big bed, plus a narrow single, meant for a family but perfectly okay for three travelling paupers.

Rooms that have no lavatory are always within ten feet or so of such a facility, and every hotel we have listed is careful to keep these loos clean, sweet-smelling and tidy. Every hotel but one has a shower or a tub on almost every floor, for which you can expect to pay about 10–15F for each use. You'd be surprised at how clean you can keep without a daily bath, in a room with that luxurious and versatile necessity, the bidet.

On the whole, expect to pay the highest rates for location: near the Opéra, around the Louvre, almost anywhere in the 1er, 6e, 7e, 8e, or 16e. St-Germain-des-Prés, which was for decades the refuge of the poor traveller, is now one of the costliest areas of Paris. A few old faithful hotels in the much loved Latin Quarter (5e) try to keep their prices down, but they seem to be closing for good or else renovating and upgrading. The Grand Hôtel des Balcons, near the universities, was home from home for generations of American, English and German students. It has finally tottered under the weight of breadcrumbs, empty wine bottles and dripping laundry, and has been renovated to emerge blazing with three stars.

If you are willing to spend an extra ten minutes on the Métro, away from the tourist heart of Paris (with your *Billet de Tourisme* or *Carte Orange*), you can save up to 25F per day for hotel rooms. Some of the hotels we have found are in what may seem unlikely neighbourhoods often brushed off by travel writers as 'uninteresting, working class, too far from the action' – beyond the Bastille, around the place de la République, up near the place d'Italie, in quiet Passy, and so forth. Actually, every one of these *quartiers* has an indigenous life of its own, well worth getting to know. Far more truly Parisian than the more obvious areas known as 'historique et pittoresque', where they've seen tourists floating around for generations, and where they sometimes couldn't care less if they never see *you* again. In more out of the way places, you have only to take breakfast two days running at the counter of a bar-tabac, and on the third day it will be 'Bonjour, Monsieur – comme d'habitude?' – the usual? The news-stand lady will be ready to hand you *Le Figaro* without being asked.

Some hotels which have been mentioned repeatedly in guide books begin to lean back and take it easy. One of our researchers spent a night recently in a well-known, well recommended 1-star place in the Quartier d'Europe, the quiet and pleasant area beyond the Gare St-Lazare. There, the shower head had fallen off the wall, the windows didn't quite close, and the blankets were like Kleenex. Since the clients didn't actually storm out, the management didn't see much reason to make improvements. However, it *is* in this book because its convenience, its location, the general niceness of the management – and its still low prices – make it good value still.

In contrast, one of our Paris-wise friends recommended a hotel in a quiet courtyard in the 18th arrondissement (Montmartre, but far from the brassy connotations of that word), with pretty coloured glass windows in the attractive rooms – where you could sleep for 52F; and a double with shower and WC is only 146F50 (about £12 at the time of writing).

Most hotels listed here have shaver points with 220-volt current, so you can use your electric razor, blow dryer, mini-boiler for a cup of tea, and so on. For Americans used to 110 volts, all appliances must be dual voltage, or carry a converter (see Electricity, p.200). Almost every hotel has reading lights above or near the bed, which is a must for those who can't close their eyes without a book in hand, or if you want to have a lie-in with the newspaper.

If you use the telephone from your hotel, expect it to cost more than a phone box would, but you do have the convenience of having someone else deal with getting the number for you. If the concierge has done anything extra for you – getting a taxi, theatre tickets, or whatnot – it's polite to leave about 10F in an envelope at the end of your stay. If the *femme de ménage*, who cleans the rooms and brings fresh linen daily, does anything like washing or ironing for you (not something our readers will want, probably), leave her some money when you go. How much depends on what you feel the service saved you.

If you can dust off your school French and smile a lot, you will find that in almost every case the atmosphere in these hotels will be astonishingly warm, personal and friendly. A few phrases of hotel French are on pp.60–1, and more general conversation about *la politesse*, which oils the wheels of Paris, on page 218.

Eating and laundry in your room

Many Paris hotels have had their hospitality really abused by travellers brought to France by budget airfares and charters, in the last fifteen or twenty years. So they are, many of them, now posting polite notices in their lobbies or in their rooms: Please, no eating and no washing. We can well understand this, having seen such places as the Grand Hôtel des Balcons as it was before renovation in late 1979 – an absolute mess. We can only advise that if you *do* want to picnic, for breakfast or lunch (and it's a great temptation, with the most succulent pâtés and jewel-like patisserie sold almost under your nose), do it with neatness and discretion. Tidy up after yourself. Don't carry an obvious, warmly smelling roast chicken in a plastic bag right past the desk. Put down newspapers on the floor, pick up your crumbs, don't stain the table with wine-glasses, don't get grease stains and lipstick on the towels. We have picnicked with impunity, and perfect neatness, in hotels in Paris from the elegant Montalembert to our current favourite small hotel a few streets from the place de la Concorde without anyone ever saying boo.

When it comes to laundry, it's obvious that it isn't the washing, it's the *dripping* that drives Paris hoteliers up the wall. Hangers with wet shirts, draped over radiators, can make a soggy mess of a carpet. In one hotel, since completely renovated, students draped wet tights, bras, jeans and jerseys on the curtain rails until even the walls ran with damp.

If you must wash your smalls in a hotel basin or bidet, and why not, have the courtesy to blot them reasonably dry in a towel, and hang them over the basin or a tiled floor so that no drips will damage the carpet or curtains. And be discreet enough to whip them into the cupboard before the chambermaid comes to clean. She's not a management spy, but part of her job is to let the front desk know what condition the hotel is in every day.

Indispensable for staying in inexpensive hotels: a few extra light-weight plastic-coated hangers, four clip-type clothes pegs which can serve to hang up socks or tights, or to pull together curtains over an open window. An oversized safety pin comes in handy, too, for all sorts of things.

Hotel French

The notice-board dealing with prices of rooms is often couched in an esoteric shorthand, but once you've cracked the code it's quite easy.

Chambre avec e.c. – room with hot and cold running water, basin, no bidet

Chambre avec cabinet de toilette – room with basin and bidet in their own compartment

Chambre avec douche – room with basin, bidet and shower

Chambre avec bain – basin, bidet and tub (often with a hand shower)

Chambre avec douche/bain et WC – basin, bidet, shower or tub, and lavatory

Petit déjeuner – Continental breakfast (see p.57)

En sus means 'extra charge', e.g. *petit déjeuner en sus, 10F*.

Baths, showers

As noted, if you are staying in a room without these amenities, you can command one by ringing down to the office. The charge will appear on your bill at the end of your stay. Really skinflint travelling couples can manage to work in two showers for the price of one if they are quick and wily, but don't say you read it here.

Part of a poor traveller's experience in Paris can be the public baths. Don't shudder and turn the page. They are clean, supervised by the city, offering showers with plenty of really hot water in private cubicles, and catering to the nearly 700,000 Parisians who have no baths in their homes. They are open four days a week, and a fairly fastidious friend agreed to try one recently. Great value, is the report, clean as can be. For 5F you get a shower stall and a dressing cubicle with mirror, tiled floor, hooks and shelf, endless hot water for twenty minutes which is plenty of time to get really clean and to wash your hair. Everything is mopped up between clients. It's a good alternative to spending 12F for a shower in your hotel. See pp.194–5 for addresses and more information.

Finding a hotel on your own

If all the hotels listed here are full, wander around the neighbourhood you like best, after stashing your luggage at the station. Even have a look at hotels that have no stars at all. They are often clean, respectable, cheap, run by a couple who may not speak much English but want you to be satisfied. If you are staying more than three days, you could try asking if they have a weekly or monthly rate. They save on laundry, you save on hotel costs.

Note: the hotel day begins and ends at noon, sharp, and if you overstay you will be charged for an extra day. Most of the hotels in this book are very good about letting travellers leave a small amount of luggage, coats, and so on (at their own risk, of course) in lobby or office until time for the train or plane. Some, however, have been so thoroughly imposed upon by those who dump rucksacks, skis, carrier bags and raincoats for days on end, that they are no longer so willing. Others may have little space and really don't want their lobbies cluttered up with the increasingly hideous magenta and bright orange nylon luggage that travelling paupers lug around – don't be offended if they politely refuse to keep them for you. Take the stuff to the nearest *consigne* at a railway station, making careful note of their opening and closing times.

Never book without looking

Go hotel shopping in the middle of the day, or not later than teatime, not at night or when you're dropping with fatigue. If they won't let you look, say a polite 'merci' and be on your way.

For some cheap alternatives to hotels

See Other options, p.88.

Note: As this book went to press, we were advised that some hotel prices may rise by as much as 20 per cent in 1986.

Recommended Hotels

1er arrondissement

Hôtel Lion d'Or   1-star

5 rue de la Sourdière, 1er
Tel: 4 260 79 04
Métro: Tuileries

Room with *cabinet de toilette*	1 or 2 persons	63F
with shower or bath, no WC	1 or 2 persons	115
Petit déjeuner		13
Use of shower		13

NB The little Lion is due for renovation soon, so the low prices must go up. It is in a street with good restaurants, in the rue St-Honoré; the rue du Mont-Thabor, very close by. Few of the rooms have bathrooms, but the showers and loos are very clean. Choose it for its proximity to the Louvre, the Palais Royal, the Seine. And it's run by people who speak English. No credit cards. *Patron*: M. Bekhouche.

Hôtel de la Place du Louvre   1-star

rue des Prêtres St-Germain-l'Auxerrois, 1er
Tel: 4 233 78 68
Métro: Louvre

Room	with *eau courante*	1 or 2 persons	77F
	with cabinet de toilette		77
	with shower or bath, no WC	1 person	99F50
		2 persons	99F50 to 150
Petit déjeuner			15
Use of shower			15

About three minutes from the main entrance of the Louvre, almost on top of the most exquisite church in Paris (St-Germain-l'Auxerrois itself), and just alongside the great Samaritaine department store – this small (only 25 rooms), charming family hotel has a devoted clientele. 'Les professeurs d'Oxford, du Cambridge et du Dublin' found it out years ago, and so did a good number of knowledgeable French, so book three weeks to a month in advance. The rooms are old fashioned, clean, comfortable, and the street is blissfully quiet at night. One of the best lunchtime places we know, Brasserie l'Auxerrois, is almost next door, and a new restaurant is opening just beneath the hotel. Rather basic English spoken. No credit cards. *Patron*: M. Viallet.

Lux Hotel 2-star

12 rue du Roule, 1er
Tel: 4 233 00 71
Métro: Louvre

Room with shower and WC	1 person	146–153F
	2 persons	165
with bath and WC	1 or 2 persons	172
Petit déjeuner		14F50

This 2-star hotel is tremendous value, with good wallpaper, carpets, towels and plumbing, and a lift. The staircase, says our hotel-wise Paris friend, is grand and wide and makes climbing almost a pleasure. The owner is polite, not over-friendly, and efficient, which means a lot. The location is fantastic: a peaceful street very close to the Louvre, minutes from the river, a short walk to the Samaritaine store – not only a good shopping place but with one of the better 'Selfs' (see p.128) for quick, inexpensive lunching. English spoken.

3e arrondissement

Hôtel Chancelier Boucherat 1-star

110 rue de Turenne, 3e
Tel: 4 272 86 83
Métro: Filles-du-Calvaire

Room with *eau courante*	1 person	78F50
with *cabinet de toilette*	1 person	106
	2 persons	122
with shower or bath, no WC	1 person	171
	2 persons	187
with bath or shower and WC	2 persons	233F50
Petit déjeuner included		
Use of shower		15

On the edge of the delightful Marais, this hotel on a quiet street is one of our best discoveries. Don't be misled by the frayed stair carpets: the rooms are freshly painted and papered, the bathrooms immaculate, the managers speak perfect English and know and love their neighbourhood. Book about three weeks in advance at high seasons, as it has its 'regulars' who stay here every year. No credit cards. *Patron*: M. Philippe Talavera.

4e arrondissement

Grand Hôtel Jeanne d'Arc   1-star

3 rue Jarente, 4e
Tel: 4 887 62 11
Métro: St-Paul

Room with *eau courante*	1 person	63F
	2 persons	83F50
with *cabinet de toilette*	1 person	111F30
	2 persons	143F50
with shower, bath and WC	1 or 2 persons	155
	4 persons	201F50
Petit déjeuner		15
Use of shower		15

Very clean and very pretty – this is on a very quiet street leading towards the rue de Turenne. The rooms are well arranged, and those who have stayed here praise it highly. But you will need to book several weeks in advance at all times except the really low seasons. This is partly because the hotel is in the Marais which is now everybody's 'must', and partly because it has been discovered by quite a lot of astute young Americans. Write in French, using the form on page 18, and enclosing an International Reply Coupon. A *little* English spoken. No credit cards, but Eurocheques accepted. *Patron*: M. Aymard.

Grand Hôtel Malher   1-star

5 rue Malher, 4e
Tel: 4 272 60 92
Métro: St-Paul

Room with *eau courante*	1 or 2 persons	58F
with *cabinet de toilette*	1 or 2 persons	70
with shower, no WC		101
with bath or shower and WC	1 or 2 persons	150
Petit déjeuner		13F50
Use of shower		10

Just across the street from the Hôtel Sévigné, this is rather a mystery hotel. Spotless, good carpeting and wallpaper, marble-floored lobby, perfect location in the Marais, great restaurants all around. English is spoken by the *patronne*, Mme Fossiez (if you can ever find her). So why isn't it packed out? The floors and walls are thin, but fortunately the clientele is mostly middle-aged, quiet, sedate, with no radios or unseemly jumping about. A very good place if you don't mind the cool atmosphere. Reading lights by all beds. No credit cards.

Hôtel Castex   no stars

5 rue Castex, 4e
Tel: 4 272 31 52
Métro: Bastille or Sully-Morland

Room with *eau courante*	1 person	74F
	2 persons	80
with *cabinet de toilette*	1 or 2 persons	80
with bath or shower	1 or 2 persons	107
Petit déjeuner		13
Use of shower		10

(No rooms with private WC, but the facilities in the halls are clean and tidy.)

This little family hotel is being redone and smartened up, and has applied for classification as a 1-star establishment. Therefore its prices have escalated sharply over a period of about 18 months. However, it's still a very good buy, and the location is superb – surrounded as it is by restaurants of remarkable quality at almost unbelievable prices. The rooms in the Castex are shining clean, the furniture old-fashioned, the management pleasant and helpful. But skip breakfast: it's a staggering 13F. The rue Castex isn't one of the really picturesque streets of the Marais, but only two minutes away, across the rue St-Antoine, is the place des Vosges, and the haunting beauty of the Hôtel de Sully, the Hôtel Lamoignon, and the Carnavalet Museum.

Hôtel des Célestins   2-star

rue Charles-V, 4e
Tel: 4 887 87 04
Métro: Bastille or Sully-Morland

Room with shower and WC	1 person	170F
	2 persons	190
with bath and WC	1 person	210
	2 persons	260
Petit déjeuner		22

This is a hotel that has risen like a phoenix from the premises of an unassuming little place. The young owners have beautifully modernized it, exposing 17th-century oak beams, equipping it with superb furniture, plumbing, every possible comfort including a little jewel-box lobby and push-button electronic opening for the front door. Every room has a complete bathroom and WC. It's possible for a couple to stay luxuriously in one of the less expensive rooms for no more than the cost of a double room in a much more ordinary hotel. The grander rooms are huge, with bathrooms the size of some Paris hotel rooms, but they are above our budget level. This will be the small, smart, 'snob' hotel discovery of the next few years. Reading lights, and extra outlets in rooms. No credit cards. *Patron*: M. Jacquemine.

Hôtel de Nice   1-star

42 bis, rue de Rivoli, 4e
Tel: 4 278 55 29
Métro: Hôtel-de-Ville or St-Paul

Room with *eau courante*	1 person	86F
with *cabinet de toilette*	1 or 2 persons	95
with shower or bath, no WC	1 or 2 persons	146
with shower and WC	1 or 2 persons	173
	2 persons	250
Petit déjeuner included		
Use of shower		15

This is a treasure, as it is sparkling clean, well painted and wall-papered, and run by a group of eager, helpful young people who have recently taken it over. However, traffic on the rue de Rivoli is continuous, night and early morning, and you are advised to take earplugs. The situation is superb, only minutes from Beaubourg and on the edge of the Marais. Very popular, so book at least two weeks in advance for peak periods; at low season it is sometimes possible to walk in and get a room. *Patron*: M. Roger Davy.

Hôtel Sévigné   2-star

2 rue Malher, 4e
Tel: 4 272 76 17
Métro: St-Paul

Room with shower and WC	1 person	182F
	2 persons	192
with twin beds		226
with bath and WC	1 or 2 persons	238

Petit déjeuner included

Formerly known as the Grand Hôtel du Sud et du Pole du Nord – madness to change such a sonorous name! The easy-going atmosphere is gone, but it's still well-run, and extremely clean and tidy. The lobby now has a shiny, mirror-faceted column in it, which is pretty weird, and they will no longer accept groups of three to sleep in a two-bed room. The rates have necessarily risen as the name has become more literary. It's completely and expensively reno-vated, with a smart new breakfast room on the ground floor, a lift (which starts half a flight above the lobby) like a padded cell, and every room now has a bath or shower, or a complete bathroom.

They say English is spoken, but the day we were there, the manager said *he* didn't. Drawback: hard by the rue de Rivoli, hence noisy. No credit cards but Eurocheques accepted. *Patron*: M. Claude Rantier.

Hôtel Speria   1-star

1 rue de la Bastille, 4e
Tel: 4 272 04 01
Métro: Bastille

Room with *eau courante*	1 person	89F
	2 persons	121
with shower	1 or 2 persons	149
with bath and WC	1 or 2 persons	212
Petit déjeuner included		
Use of shower		10

Nothing in this hotel is new, the paint needs attention, the furniture is past its prime. But those who like it are devoted to it: the beds are comfortable, the management pleasant, English is spoken, and, rare in a 1-star hotel, there's a lift (although this starts on the first, not the ground, floor). The rue de la Bastille is noisy in the daytime but quietens down after about 6:30 p.m. The hotel is clean, and the prices – especially for a place on the fringe of the Marais – are still remarkably low. It's close to the lively and typically Parisian life of the area around the Bastille, which most tourists know only as a horrendously large Métro stop. Actually, there are many good small restaurants within five minutes' walk, and across the place de la Bastille into the 11e are some delightful food-shopping places, good for that inevitable picnicking. Visa cards accepted.

5e arrondissement

Grand Hôtel d'Harcourt   2-stars, NN

3 boulevard St-Michel, 5e
Tel: 4 326 52 35
Métro: St-Michel

Room with *cabinet de toilette*	1 person	77F50
	2 persons	115F50
with shower or bath, no WC	1 person	115F50
	2 persons	147F50
with shower and WC	1 or 2 persons	129
with bath and WC	1 or 2 persons	178F50–220
Petit déjeuner		15
Use of shower		20

A new find, highly recommended by a well-travelled American acquaintance: a recently redone two-star hotel *with a lift* in an area where prices are usually over the top. It faces the St-Michel fountain, and is a short walk from Notre-Dame, the Cluny Museum, Luxembourg Gardens, and the liveliness of the St-Michel and St-Germain streets. Rooms are freshly painted and papered, there's a spacious breakfast room, and even in summer rooms are sometimes available on very short notice. The street can be noisy, early and late into the night, so take earplugs. No credit cards. The *patron*, M. Abed, speaks good English.

6e arrondissement

Hôtel Sèvres-Azur   2-star, NN

22 rue Abbé-Grégoire, 6e
Tel: 4 548 84 07
Métro: St-Placide

Room with *eau courante*		85F
with *cabinet de toilette*	1 or 2 persons	129
with shower, no WC	1 or 2 persons	180
with shower or bath and WC	1 or 2 persons	238
Petit déjeuner		17
Use of shower		17
Voltage: 220		

A world away from some of the student-type hotels listed above. Newly painted, papered and carpeted (the NN rating means *Nouvelles Normes* which means that the hotel has been recently renovated), with a tiny lift, this hotel is exceptionally pretty. Even the one bottom-price room is big enough to be comfortable. The top prices are fairly high, but considering the standard of quality, and in comparison to many other Left Bank hotels, it's very much worth the money. English spoken. Visa cards accepted. *Patron*: M. Roger Jolin.

7e arrondissement

Hôtel du Champ de Mars   2-star

7 rue du Champ-de-Mars, 7e
Tel: 4 551 52 30
Métro: École-Militaire

Room with shower and WC	1 or 2 persons	240F
with bath and WC	1 or 2 persons	255–280
Petit déjeuner		18

A 2-star hotel with more spacious rooms than some others in the neighbourhood. While not very cheap, it does offer good value for two people travelling together, not so economical for a solo voyager. It's clean, comfortable, and with a friendly atmosphere, highly recommended by people who stay there year after year. However, breakfast in one of the nearby *tabacs* or bars is a far better idea than paying 18F here. The street by day is a microcosm of 'neighbourhood' Paris, with children, dogs, sparkling shops. At night it is very quiet. A little English is spoken, but smiles and goodwill on both sides fill the gaps. *Patron*: M. Guillochon.

Grand Hôtel Leveque   1-star

29 rue Cler, 7e
Tel: 4 705 49 15
Métro: École-Militaire

Room with *eau courante*	1 or 2 persons	85–107F50
with shower	1 person	135
	2 persons	175
with shower or bath and WC	1 or 2 persons	205
Petit déjeuner included		
Use of shower		10

Most of the 7e *arrondissment* is so correct, so sterile, that it's a happy shock when you turn a corner and stumble into anything as vital and sparky as the rue Cler. It's a pedestrian street bubbling with shops and stalls and life all day, and at night as quiet as a country lane. The Hôtel Leveque has smallish, cosy, nice rooms. M. Pierre, the *patron*, is fluent in English. He says, with great charm, 'No eating, no laundry in the rooms', and he means it, he runs a tight ship. He's so kind and helpful that even a scrounger at heart can't take advantage of him. Rates are remarkably low, and people seem to stay for ever. No credit cards.

Hôtel Malar   1-star

29 rue Malar, 7e
Tel: 4 551 38 46
Métro: Latour-Maubourg

Room with shower	1 person	92F
	2 persons	104
with shower or bath and WC	1 or 2 persons	150–200
Petit déjeuner		15

This isn't exactly an undiscovered hotel, as people keep rushing up to us and divulging its existence. But it is very good value still, well-kept, friendly and with a feeling of warmth and welcome. It's not very far from the very amusing rue St-Dominique, one of the streets that makes the 7e worth living in. Prices (except for the rather expensive breakfast) are still low enough to come as a surprise in this rather pricey neighbourhood. All rooms have shower or bath, many have WCs, and at 92F a room for one with a shower is a great bargain. No credit cards. *Patronne*: Mme Sudraut.

Hôtel Prince   2-star

66 avenue Bosquet, 7e
Tel: 4 705 40 90
Métro: École-Militaire

Room with shower and WC	128–180F
with bath and WC facing courtyard	190
facing street	217
Petit déjeuner	13F80

A spectacular bargain – only 29 rooms, each with bath or shower and its own WC, on a broad boulevard which is typically haut-bourgeois Parisian. The neighbourhood has a life of its own which makes it considerably more interesting than most of the rest of the bland, rich 7e. The Prince has a lift, and facilities for those in wheelchairs. It gets very booked up in summer and autumn, with many businessmen and their families staying there, so write or phone several weeks in advance. English is spoken, and Visa and Amex (American Express) cards accepted.

Hôtel du Résidence du Champ de Mars   2-star

19 rue du Champ-de-Mars, 7e
Tel: 4 705 25 45
Métro: École-Militaire

Room with *eau courante*	1 or 2 persons	41F20–71F
with *cabinet de toilette*	1 or 2 persons	111
with shower	1 or 2 persons	129–173
with shower or bath and WC	1 or 2 persons	179–230
Petit déjeuner		16F50

A two-star hotel with a lift, just off the smart, tree-lined avenue Bosquet – at prices that are no more than some one-star establishments. The rooms are adequately furnished, not very large, but well arranged for comfort. One room with *cabinet de toilette* is a rock-bottom 55F, but your chances of getting it are about nil except on a rainy day in February. The street is one of the few lively 'shopping' ones in the staid 7e. For a picnic lunch, explore the delights of Marc Tattevin at No. 15, whose prepared foods are seductive; and 'Fromage in Più' nearby makes cheese-lovers faint with pleasure. Amex accepted and Eurocheques in French francs only. *Patron*: M. Carvel.

Le Royal Phare   2-star

40 avenue de la Motte-Picquet, 7e
Tel: 4 705 57 30
Métro: La Motte-Picquet

Room with shower and WC	1 person	128F
	2 persons	147–180
with bath and WC	1 or 2 persons	190
Petit déjeuner		13F80

M. Le Rouzic, the *patron*, speaks little English but understands it well and is extremely helpful. He is gradually redoing the hotel with new carpets, wallpaper, curtains, bedspreads, and it all shows his considerable personal involvement. A happy atmosphere and very good value. Close to excellent shopping (a good Prisunic and Francprix), and close to the charm of the rue Cler for shopping, strolling, gazing. The avenue de la Motte-Picquet traffic begins early, about 7:00 a.m., if that matters to you, but it's quiet at night. Reading lights; and a lift. Amex and Visa cards accepted.

8e arrondissement

Hôtel de Marigny   2-star

11 rue de l'Arcade, 8e
Tel: 4 266 42 71
Métro: St-Lazare

Room with cabinet de toilette	116F
with shower or bath and WC 1 or 2 persons	221–230
Petit déjeuner, delivered to your room	16F50

A truly remarkable bargain, if you can manage to get one of the less expensive rooms in this charming 2-star establishment, with a lift, about a hundred yards from the Madeleine and five minutes' walk from the Gare St-Lazare and the place de la Concorde. It is sparkling clean and run by bright young people who speak excellent English. The Marigny actually provides pillows in addition to the usual Paris hotel bolster, and is one of the few that provide an individual piece of soap for the traveller. Prettily furnished, too. But watch out for the self-service lift as the doors can give you a rap on the elbow if not firmly controlled. Reading lights. No credit cards. *Patron*: M. Mangars.

9e arrondissement

Hôtel Confort   2-star, NN

5 rue de Trévise, 9e
Tel: 4 246 12 06
Métro: Rue Montmartre

Room with *cabinet de toilette*	1 person	90F
with shower or bath	1 person	130
	2 persons	160
with shower or bath and WC	1 or 2 persons	195
Petit déjeuner		14
Use of shower		10

This is a pleasant hotel with not much to distinguish it from hundreds of others, except that it is 2-star with the NN classification, which means they have done a lot of painting and sprucing up. And it has a lift. In addition, it has facilities for people in wheelchairs, and you can bring your dog with you. It's cheap, considering all these amenities, and is run by agreeable and helpful people, who speak English. Reading lights. Eurocheques accepted. *Patronne*: Mme Francis.

Hôtel de Lille   no stars

2 rue Montholon, 9e
Tel: 4 770 38 76
Métro: Cadet

Room with *eau courante*	1 person	63F
with *cabinet de toilette*	1 or 2 persons	82
with shower or bath	1 or 2 persons	105
with shower or bath and WC	1 or 2 persons	135
Petit déjeuner		14
Use of shower		13

A few years ago our Paris hotel scout remarked that the Lille could do with a few licks of paint and some new tiles – it has now been smartened up and is very clean and tidy. Although it is now more expensive than in past years, it is to be recommended. Some English is spoken. They no longer take Visa cards. *Patron*: M. Amir.

Hôtel Mattlé   2-star

8 rue du Boule-Rouge, 9e
Tel: 4 770 23 10
Métro: Rue Montmartre

Room with bath or shower and WC 1 or 2 persons	185–270F
Petit déjeuner	15

NB All rooms in this medium-sized, well-run 2-star hotel – with a lift – have fully-equipped bathrooms. At these prices it's remarkable value. As you can imagine, it gets very booked up at peak times so write at least ten days to two weeks in advance. Visa cards accepted. *Patron*: M. Cohana.

Hôtel Montyon   2-star

15 rue de Montyon, 9e
Tel: 4 770 92 70
Métro: Rue Montmartre

Room with *cabinet de toilette*	1 person	81–91F
	2 persons	122F50–135
with shower or bath	1 person	103
	2 persons	171
with shower or bath and WC	2 persons	226F50–268
Petit déjeuner		15F50
Use of shower		Free

This attractive hotel isn't cheap, but it has a lift, a pleasant small reception-breakfast room with a TV, and a bar in the lobby which sounds rather awful but in fact is quite a good idea if you feel like having a quiet drink before dinner. Reading lights. No credit cards, but Eurocheques accepted. *Patronne*: Mme Annick Plusquellec.

10e arrondissement

Hôtel Centre Est   1-star

4 rue Sibour, 10e
Tel: 4 607 20 74
Métro: Gare de l'Est

Room with *cabinet de toilette*	1 or 2 persons	94–108F50
with shower	1 or 2 persons	121–135F50
with shower or bath and WC	1 or 2 persons	164
Petit déjeuner included		
Use of shower		10F50

In this rather unpromising neighbourhood – notable mostly for its
bargain shoe and handbag shops – a little gem hotel has turned up.
It was found when one of our researchers fell into its doorway out
of a cloudburst. Five minutes from the railway station, which is a
centre of bus and Métro lines that will take you anywhere, the
Centre Est has a lift, facilities for wheelchairs, even accepts dogs.
The rooms are big, the bathrooms spotless, the *patron* speaks
English, it has reading lights. Altogether a 1-star place with 2-star
facilities, at prices lower than one would expect. The French know
this hotel, so it's wise to book two weeks in advance if you can, or
leave your luggage at the station and come in person. No credit
cards. *Patron*: M. Glas.

Hôtel Jarry   2-star

4 rue Jarry, 10e
Tel: 4 770 70 38
Métro: Château d'Eau

Room with *cabinet de toilette*	1 or 2 persons	77F
with shower	1 or 2 persons	103
with shower or bath and WC		136–155
Petit déjeuner		13
Use of shower		16

In the not very interesting 10e *arrondissement*, this hotel is a pleasant
surprise: as we write, it is in the process of being done up in

considerable taste, and the concierge speaks good English. Conveniently located for the Gare de l'Est, and there are some goodish restaurants and brasseries in the neighbourhood. (But the prices of breakfast and use of a shower are far too high!) No credit cards accepted, but Eurocheques in French francs. *Patron*: M. Mahfouf.

Hôtel du Jura   1-star

6 rue Jarry, 10e
Tel: 4 770 06 66
Métro: Château d'Eau

Room with *cabinet de toilette* 1 person		85F
	2 persons	115
with shower	1 or 2 persons	170
Petit déjeuner included		
Use of shower		10

A more modest place, but comfortable and neat, and a remarkable bargain with well-arranged rooms and breakfast included. And while the 10e isn't one of the 'historic' areas of Paris, it has its own neighbourhood character, and some very good shopping. Those who run the hotel are kind, helpful, and willing to speak English of a sort and to help you with your French. *Patron*: M. Soc.

Hôtel de la Nouvelle France   1-star, NN

23 rue des Messageries, 10e
Tel: 4 824 70 74
Métro: Poissonnière

Room with *eau courante*	1 or 2 persons	60–93F
with *cabinet de toilette* 1 or 2 persons		103
with shower and double or twin beds		150–170
with shower or bath and WC, double or twin beds		
		160–180
Petit déjeuner		16
Use of shower		10

A complete delight: a 1-star hotel with the significant letters NN (*Nouvelles Normes*), which means that it is recently renovated and may soon be raised a step to 2 stars. Go *now*. Glossy paint, pretty wallpaper, smartly tiled baths, and a young manager fluent in English. Book a month in advance – and for summer, two months isn't too much. On the Métro, two stops to Gare du Nord. No credit cards. *Patronne*: Mme Pierrette Closier.

Hôtel de Verdun

5 rue Saint-Laurent, 10e
Tel: 4 607 70 93
Métro: Gare de l'Est

Room with *eau courante*	1 person	72F
with *cabinet de toilette*	1 person	82
	2 persons	102
with shower or bath	1 or 2 persons	107
with shower or bath and WC		165
Petit déjeuner		14
Use of shower		15

Unpretentious is the word for the comfortable Verdun – the rooms make no pretence at decoration, but they are spacious. Ask for a room at the back, facing on a quiet courtyard, as the short rue St-Laurent leads from one busy thoroughfare to another and can be noisy. No credit cards. *Patron*: M. Jacques Marsaud.

11e arrondissement

Hôtel Notre-Dame   2-star

51 rue de Malte, 11e
Tel: 4 700 78 76
Métro: République

Room with *cabinet de toilette*	1 or 2 persons	103F50
with shower		138
with bath or shower and WC	1 or 2 persons	198-218
Petit déjeuner		17F50
Use of shower		11

(These last prices are a fairly steep jump, and bring the Notre-Dame into the price bracket of some 2-star hotels we know in more fashionable neighbourhoods.)

The rue de Malte seems to be rich in good small hotels, and it's close to an amazing selection of family restaurants and good shopping. This hotel is beautifully run, with a lift, newly painted, immaculately clean. Book a month in advance in high seasons, as the canny English have already nosed out the Notre-Dame.

Hôtel Plessis   1-star

25 rue du Grand-Prieuré, 11e
Tel: 4 700 13 38
Métro: Oberkampf or République

Room with *cabinet de toilette*	1 or 2 persons	90F
with two beds		135
with shower	1 or 2 persons	127
with shower and WC	1 or 2 persons	160
with bath and WC		175
Petit déjeuner		15F 70

A 1-star hotel, yes, but with a lift. Very well run by an enterprising couple, M. and Mme Montrazat, who speak English and know a great deal about this quite interesting neighbourhood. They say that prices may have to go up in 1986, but even so, this hotel will probably remain quite remarkable value. The TV in the lobby is fun to watch, especially for sports and (incomprehensible) game shows. No credit cards.

Hôtel Rethia   1-star

---

3 rue Général-Blaise, 11e
Tel: 4 700 47 18
Métro: St-Ambroise

Room with *eau courante*	1 or 2 persons	65–75F
with shower or bath	1 or 2 persons	125
with shower or bath and WC	1 or 2 persons	147
Petit déjeuner included		
Use of shower		10

In the past three years, rooms have been redecorated but prices have climbed hardly at all. Although it is in a rather out-of-the-way neighbourhood, this would be our choice for a long inexpensive stay: for writing; for exploring Paris; for discovering a quiet and peaceful bourgeois *quartier* where one soon puts down roots. A pretty square opposite is bubbling with children after school. No credit cards, but Eurocheques accepted. *Patron*: M. Aguer.

12e arrondissement

Hôtel de Marseille

---

21 rue d'Austerlitz, 12e
Tel: 4 343 54 22
Métro: Gare de Lyon

Room with *eau courante*	1 or 2 persons	87F
with *cabinet de toilette*	1 or 2 persons	87
with bath, no WC	1 or 2 persons	135
Petit déjeuner		15
Use of shower		12

In a short street lined with hotels, only about 200 metres from the Gare de Lyon, this is a good new discovery. The rooms are clean and tidy, and although not much English is spoken there is an air of welcome and good will. No rooms have private loos but the communal ones are well-kept. Two of our best recent restaurant finds (Le Bercy and Le Vaucluse) are literally around the corner. *Patron*: M. Soumar. No credit cards.

Modern's Hôtel

11 rue d'Austerlitz, 12e
Tel: 4 343 41 17
Métro: Gare de Lyon or Gare d'Austerlitz

Room with *eau courante*	1 or 2 persons	56F
with *cabinet de toilette*	1 or 2 persons	66F30
with bath and WC	1 or 2 persons	138
Petit déjeuner		12F50
Use of shower		12

The decor is patchy but adequate, according to our fairly critical hotel spy, who also comments that 'the reception is very laid-back', which seems to mean that they pay little attention to you. At these prices, would you expect more? Oddly enough, there's a telephone in every room. No credit cards, but Eurocheques in francs accepted. *Patron*: M. Joseph Kouby.

13e arrondissement

Pacific Hôtel   1-star

8 rue Philippe-de-Champagne, 13e
Tel: 4 331 17 06
Métro: Place d'Italie

Room with *eau courante*	1 person	63F50
with *cabinet de toilette*	1 or 2 persons	100
with shower or bath	1 or 2 persons	124
with shower or bath and WC		138
Petit déjeuner		14

A fairly large hotel, with a lift, unusual in a 1-star establishment. It's rather old-fashioned and agreeable in every way. Some English is spoken. Prices are remarkably low considering the standard of comfort, and in fact went up less than 10% in two years. The rooms are comfortable, the baths small but with very good tiles and plumbing, and *shower curtains* – not a usual thing in moderate-priced Paris hotels. It's a few minutes from the place d'Italie (good shopping and a big branch of Au Printemps), and just off the avenue des Gobelins which is rich in small good restaurants. No credit cards. *Patronne*: Mme de Roode.

Hôtel Rubens   1-star

35 rue du Banquier, 13e
Tel: 4 331 73 30
Métro: Campo-Formio

Room with *eau courante*	1 or 2 persons	64F
with *cabinet de toilette*	2 persons	80
with shower or bath	1 or 2 persons	115
with shower and WC	1 or 2 persons	115-135-150
Petit déjeuner		14
Use of shower		12

A lovely hotel in an interesting 'bourgeois' neighbourhood, high up, good transport (the No. 83 bus from place d'Italie is one of the great ones). This is another 1-star hotel with a lift. The street is very quiet with no through traffic. The hotel has been freshly painted and the rooms are delightful, the baths unusually large. It is close to a variety of good restaurants (Lebanese, Vietnamese, Italian), and is just off the avenue des Gobelins which has a great *traiteur* (takeaway for hot and cold delicacies). Reading lights. No credit cards. *Patron*: M. Quintino Caputo.

14e arrondissement

Hôtel des Bains   1-star

33 rue Delambre, 14e
Tel: 4 320 85 27
Métro: Edgar-Quinet

Room with *cabinet de toilette*	1 or 2 persons	79F50
with shower and WC	up to 4 persons	154-180
Petit déjeuner		12F50
Use of shower		10

Walking distance from the Tour de Montparnasse, a towering purgatory if there ever was one, and near the immense and formidable Gare Montparnasse with its spiderweb network of Métro lines. The rue Delambre is a happy hunting ground for bargain clothes and food. And the Hôtel des Bains would be a pleasant place from which to explore the less touristic parts of Montparnasse itself. It's very inexpensive, hardly raising its prices from year to year. Facilities are nothing extraordinary, but like many 'ordinary' Paris family hotels, it is comfortable, well run, and English of a sort is spoken. Recently some rooms with shower and WC have been added, and the communal WCs are all perfectly clean. Eurocheques in francs accepted. *Patron*: M. André Regis.

16e arrondissement

Hôtel du Ranelagh   1-star

56 rue de l'Assomption, 16e
Tel: 4 288 31 63
Métro: Ranelagh

Room with *eau courante*	1 person	54–60F
	2 persons	75–80
with *cabinet de toilette*	1 or 2 persons	69–72
with shower or bath·	1 or 2 persons	103–120
with shower or bath and WC	1 person	150
	2 persons	165
Petit déjeuner		15
Use of shower		12

Pleasant, undistinguished hotel which has barely raised its lowest prices for two or three years – though the better rooms have gone up a good deal. The rooms are exceedingly comfortable and clean. The Ranelagh is very near the delightful avenue Mozart, with good cafés and shops – much quieter than the more obviously touristy parts of Paris. Little English, no credit cards. *Patronne*: Mme. Chevé

Hôtel Stella 1-star

---

133 avenue Victor Hugo, 16e
Tel: 4 553 55 94
Métro: Victor Hugo

Room with *cabinet de toilette*	1 person	87F
	2 persons	112
with shower or bath	1 person	122
	2 persons	157
with shower or bath and WC	1 person	166
	2 persons	201
Petit déjeuner		15
Use of shower		15

Rooms are very pleasant with handsome modern cane beds, good bedspreads, and beautiful little gilded bamboo chairs (like ballroom chairs); the bathrooms with WC are small but comfortable and the showers have shower curtains. The bath-towels are large enough to be comfortable. In the summer it gets very booked up and one should reserve one month to six weeks ahead; off season, at times when Paris is not crowded with visitors for fairs or special events (see holidays, p.204), it is sometimes possible to get a room at a day's notice, but hardly ever possible to walk in and get one for that night. 'English is no problem,' said the man at the desk, in French – you decide for yourself when you go in. Considering its amenities, it's one of our best choices. Amex and Visa cards accepted. *Patron*: M. Abderamane.

Résidence Trocadéro   2-star

3 avenue Raymond-Poincaré, 16e
Tel: 4 727 32 96 and 4 553 89 67
Métro: Trocadéro

Room with *cabinet de toilette*	1 person	103F
	2 persons	124
with shower and WC	1 person	158
	2 persons	183
with bath and WC	1 person	170
	2 persons	196
Petit déjeuner		15F70
Use of shower		15

The 'Troc' has always been one of our more expensive hotels, but its prices have remained fairly stable over the past years, increasing at slightly less than the inflation rate. Its location is magnificent, about 100 feet from a glorious view over Paris, and very near the stately Avénue du Président-Wilson (see Museums, pp.140–153). Pleasant people run it, which makes up for the uninteresting decor of the rooms. While good little restaurants are not plentiful in this opulent corner of the city, a few stops on the Métro will take you to one of our many favourites. And one of the best street markets of Paris (Wednesday and Saturday) is just around the corner, for discreet picnicking. Amex and Diners' Club cards accepted, and English spoken. *Patrons*: M. and Mme Khek.

18e arrondissement

Hôtel André Gill

4 rue André Gill, 18e
Telephone: 4 262 48 48
Métro: Pigalle

Room with *eau courante*	1 person	52F
with *cabinet de toilette*	1 or 2 persons	110
with shower or bath	1 or 2 persons	130
with shower and WC	1 or 2 persons	146F50
with bath and WC	1 or 2 persons	165

Petit déjeuner	14F50
Use of shower	18

An oasis of peace and calm, on the Montmartrobus route and very close to Pigalle yet a world away in feeling, the André Gill is in a pretty courtyard with trees. The rooms are pleasant and some have attractive coloured glass windows. English is spoken, and they accept American Express, Visa and Diners' Club cards, but not Eurocheques. *Patron*: Benzina Tajeb.

Hôtel du Bouquet de Montmartre

1 rue Durantin 18e
Tel: 606 87 54
Métro: Abbesses

Room with *cabinet de toilette*	1 or 2 persons	97F70
with shower or bath	1 or 2 persons	144–161
with shower or bath and WC	1 or 2 persons	167–201
Petit déjeuner		15F50
Use of shower		12

The rue Durantin leads directly into the green and tranquil space of the place des Abbesses, where one of the rare canopied art deco Métro stations of Hector Guimard still survives. It's hard to believe that a quiet little hotel can be only three minutes' walk from Pigalle with all that it implies. Use this as a base to explore, on foot, or with the miraculous Montmartrobus (see p.46), the hidden streets of the Butte Montmartre (staying well away from the place du Tertre.) The rooms here will benefit from some redecoration, meant to be started in late 1985. English spoken. *Patron*: M. Gibergues.

Other options

Bed and Breakfast: B & B on the English plan is slowly catching on. 'Café Couette' is an organization which operates all over France and has recently started up in Paris. Write to, or visit, them at 8 rue d'Isly, 75008 Paris. An English-speaking representative is usually in their office which is at the back of a courtyard and hard to find, but persevere. Single rooms with bed and breakfast are about 90F, doubles from 120F.

Rooms to let: check the notice-boards at the American Church, 65 quai d'Orsay, 7e (*Métro:* Alma Marceau, Invalides) which is a mine of room and flat offers, usually for two weeks or a month in holiday seasons. Take a notebook; go early, provide yourself with a pocketful of one-franc pieces, and start phoning. (See p.221 for peaceful un-vandalized phone locations.) St Michael's Church of England, 5 rue d'Aguesseau, 8e (*Métro:* Madeleine) has a similar service, very helpful staff and delightfully friendly atmosphere.

Student Housing: students are well catered for in Paris. Take your International Student Identity Card, or if you don't have one, a current photograph and proof of your full-time student status with 30F, to CIEE, 49 rue Pierre-Charron, 8e (*Métro:* Alma-Marceau).

The Cité Universitaaire, in the quiet southern part of Paris, often has rooms to let during university holidays. Contact them at 18 boulevard Jourdan, 14e (*Métro* Cité-Universitaire), where you may find someone who speaks English.

Accueils des Jeunes de France: (AJF) at 16 rue Pont Louis-Philippe, 4e (*Métro:* Pont-Marie or Hôtel de Ville) is first class at finding accommodation for the young. They have a bureau at the Gare du Nord, and at 119 rue St-Marten, 4e (*Métro:* Rambuteau, Châtelet or Les Halles).

There are four beautiful and historic converted houses in the Marais, 4e, given over to housing students. Check at the Maubisson Hotel des Jeunes, 12 rue des Barrès, 4e. (*Métro:* Hotel de Ville, Pont-Marie.)

Youth hostels: the Ligues Françaises des Auberges de Jeunesse (LFAJ), 38 boulevard Raspail, 7e (*Métro:* Sèvres-Babylone), is *the* address to use if you have a YHA card, no matter what age you are. Paris hostels are not comfortable, not very well located, and certainly offer little privacy, but at their prices who can complain? Three-day stay is the limit, but that's probably all you would want.

Your own college or university may be able to add to this very brief listing of student-type places to stay. For longer stays, look for notices of short rentals of flats or studios, which may be posted in the entrance halls or around the restaurants and cafeterias in the various university buildings scattered around Paris. A friend of ours, on sabbatical from Cambridge, found himself a free room for a year in exchange for teaching the flat's owner some English. Check these:

CROUS, 39 avenue George Bernanos, 5e (*Métro*: Port-Royal)

Assas, 92 rue d'Assas, 6e (*Métro*: St-Placide)

Cité Universitaire, 19 boulevard Jourdan, 14e (*Métro*: Cité-Universitaire)

CIDJ, 101 quai Branly, 7e (*Métro*: Bir-Hakeim)

Renting a flat: in Paris, for a family or group planning to stay a long time, can work out cheaply: two agencies which handle furnished, well-equipped flats or studios, for a minimum of two months, are Paris Promo SARL, 18 rue du Cardinal-Lemoine, 5e, and Inter-Urbis, 1 rue Mollien, 8e. Both charge tenants a fee but are said to be efficient. Find out everything that can be a problem: lease, electricity, gas, service charge, inventories, and if possible take along a French-speaking person to deal with this.

Exchanging: perfect for paupers. A French person or family occupies whatever you have to offer, from a bed-sit to a house, and *you* go to their room/studio/flat. An experienced 'exchanger' has these tips to offer:

1 If you can, make your arrangements through an exchange agency which lays down certain well-established rules. Or check the Announcements column in *The Times*, London.

2 Be specific about what you are offering – number of bedrooms, baths, equipment, use of telephone, daily help, linen, washing machine, car, motorbike, exact dates when you plan to leave and return.

3 Be sure you understand what you are getting: same as above, but with such important extras as how many flights of stairs, lift, concierge, etc.

4 Pets and plants can be catered for in exchanges, but specify *that* early on; some exchangers may be allergic or not willing to tie themselves down.

Everyone we know who has done exchanges has been satisfied, and plans to do it again. Most have had happy surprises: one family thought it was getting a four-room house and found they had four *bedrooms*; another was invited to spend the weekend in a Normandy cottage during their Paris stay; a third has established a long family friendship which includes the free use of a Paris flat over Christmas week. *Not* so great: the exchanger who arrived late at night and found the cupboard bare, not so much as a teaspoon of instant coffee or a slice of bread for breakfast, in an intimidatingly clean kitchen!

Recommended: Worldwide Home Exchange Club, 139a Sloane St, London SW1. Also: Intervac, 6 Siddals Lane, Allestree, Derby DE3 2DY.

La nourriture *(Eating well)*

What to expect

For anyone coming from a country where a serving of vegetables in an Indian restaurant can now cost £1.50 or more, Paris has now become the bargain paradise of the world.

The great Paris restaurants, admittedly, can cost you a month's salary at one sitting, but that's not what this book is about. Everywhere in Paris there's an immense range of affordable and very good food. There's no equivalent whatever in English cuisine at any price that can compare with Paris food today. To eat well in England in 1986 comes far too high for the likes of travelling paupers.

Our basic requirement in setting out this list is what is called *le menu*, or sometimes *menu touristique*. It is price-fixed, posted in the window (even the great Lapérouse has a publicly displayed *menu*, but that's 225F). Some offer a three-course menu, with a quarter litre of wine, beer or mineral water and service (at 15 per cent) included in the overall price. Others will include service but not drink – but this is in every case modestly priced at about 3.50–4F the quarter-litre. A few now are including drink but not service, which is added on at 15 per cent. Some we have picked do not offer *le menu* but their à la carte choices seem so good, and add up to such modest totals, that they are included here.

Many Paris restaurants close on Sundays, and some are open only for lunch or only for dinner. Most close on public holidays, some close Christmas Eve and New Year's Eve. Many which open on Sunday are closed one other day during the week, and very many still, despite the tourist demand for food, do the traditional thing of closing for the entire month of August, when all Paris moves to the beach. But even that is not immutable!

Paris restaurants are changing their hours of opening, weekly and annual closing times with the speed of light to adjust to the changing patterns of tourism and variations in economic circumstances. Many that formerly closed in August are now taking off earlier or later in the year – some not at all, others disappearing for six weeks in slack times. The information herein was accurate in early August 1985, but don't be too disappointed if things have changed when you arrive.

We have grouped these restaurants by *arrondissements* (see p.37 to find out how these work), so that if you find your first choice is packed, another won't be far away. Almost all of them offer remarkably good food and a certain pleasantness of atmosphere. Many of these places hardly ever see a tourist, because they are good bourgeois eating-places patronized by serious eaters, and no one eats more seriously than the French. A few, not many, accept credit cards. In the main they are clean, simple, usually with a spotless paper tablecloth put down over a longer-lasting cotton one; paper napkins – but sometimes linen ones – endless baskets of fresh, good French bread, and undistinguished but palatable wine, beer, or mineral water.

A few are really bars, with sawdust on the floor, and a little knot of serious drinkers who stand a few feet from your table: these details we have noted in the specific information about each, and if you find this sort of thing disturbs you, don't go. There are plenty of more conventional restaurants to choose from. Sanitation (*le lavabo*) varies from spotless to mildly squalid. Not once in our experience has the bill been padded in any way. Coffee is never included in the fixed price menu, and ordering it in a restaurant can bump up the price by as much as 5F. You'll sleep better without it anyway.

Now for the good news: Almost every one of these restaurants will provide you with a three-course meal, wine and service included, for not more than 50F, which at today's rate of exchange (11F50 to the pound at date of going to press) is about £4.50. One or two can be as much as 75–85F, roughly £7–£8, but they have been chosen, despite the extravagant price, for something quite notable.

Follow the lead of many Parisians: if wine, beer or mineral water is not included in the price of the set meal, skip it. All restaurants and cafés must offer you a carafe of drinking water ('Une carafe d'eau, s'il vous plaît') *if you request it* – clean, safe, and just as agreeable as many of the bottled waters which can cost 3F50 to 7F. Not all Parisians drink wine at every meal, despite what you have heard all your life.

Have the occasional snack lunch or dinner in your room (or outdoors), which can save you 18 to 20F on a restaurant meal (see p.60, about hotel eating). Or go to one of the very good value 'Selfs' (p.128), where three courses with your choice of drink can be as little as 25 to 28F.

Café eating and snacks can tear the carefully calculated budget wide open. Avoid sitting at a café table (called *la terrasse*) for breakfast: take your coffee and croissants at the counter (*le zinc*) where it will be half the price.

Never order tea in Paris! It is always made with a teabag, the water isn't boiling, and it can cost a ludicrous 5F. Brandy is cheaper.

All tap water in Paris hotels and flats is safe to drink, but if you are worried about what a change of water can do to your digestive system, it's good to know that you can buy a huge (1½ litre) plastic bottle of Vittel, or private-label, *still* mineral water, at supermarkets for as little as 2F. *Eau gazeuse*, such as Perrier, obviously comes only in glass bottles, but even so, 1½ litres costs only about 4F, and the supermarket will give you 1F back when you return the bottle.

Restaurant manners

Restaurants – except for Les Selfs (pp.128–31) – are run by a *patron* or *patronne*, with waiters and waitresses. All very human, all very connected to their clients. We're not talking here about McDonalds or their like. Contrary to myth, those who work in restaurants are not to be addressed as 'Garçon!'. If you want fast, friendly service, and advice if you need it, it pays to be polite. As you enter the restaurant it doesn't hurt to say 'Bonjour', or 'Bonsoir, Monsieur'; as you leave, 'Au revoir, m'sieur/m'dame'. In between, you should fill out your sentences with 's'il vous plaît', and 'merci bien', and such. In very small family-run restaurants, it's usually polite to include the entire clientele as well as the management in your goodbyes: 'Au revoir, messieurs-dames'.

French restaurants – especially the ones you'll find listed here – don't give you a lot of elbow room, and curiously enough you find that you don't need it. You may find yourself just barely able to squeeze into your seat; or seated opposite a stranger instead of with a table to yourself; and seated very snugly at that. Yet, such is the general air of *politesse* and enjoyment that such tight spacing doesn't seem like encroachment on your personal living space.

You'll find it easy to adapt to; your neighbours are absorbed in their food, or each other, and there is no lack of privacy. A 'bonsoir' or 'bon appétit, Madame' will not be taken amiss if you happen to catch someone's eye. If no one wants to get into conversation, it will be obvious; if everybody does, this soon becomes known. In any event, there is no stuffiness or awkwardness about your proximity. Best of all, women who eat alone in restaurants need not worry about being put at the worst table, near a draughty door, or in a forgotten corner. They are never ignored, and are always treated with respect, and even a little encouragement.

Recommended restaurants

1er arrondissement

Au Vieil Écu

164 rue St-Honoré, 1er
Métro: Louvre

A pleasant place if you can stand piped music (mercifully soft) and really vulgar décor. A short menu at 44F *tout compris* with some unusual choices: flaky cheese pastry or soup or good smoked sausage, then faux filet, or turkey niçoise served with ratatouille, or fish; six kinds of cheese on a platter left for your choice, or fairly conventional desserts. Quick, amiable service, good food, good value, no wonder it is always crowded. Open 11:45 a.m. to 3:00 p.m., 7:00 p.m. to 12:30 a.m. Closed Sundays and holidays; no annual closing. Visa cards accepted.

L'Incroyable

26 rue de Richelieu, 1er
Métro: Palais-Royal

This is on everyone's discovery list, but success hasn't gone to its head: the perfection of French bourgeois cooking and ambience. Very crowded at lunchtime on weekdays; Saturday is a better bet. Choices: herring fillets with potato salad or pâté, etc., then steak tartare or a chicken dish with a green veg or salad, and cheese or fruit tartes (have the pear tarte if it's on offer) – all for 32F, wine and service included. L'Incroyable is not easy to find, on its narrow street near the entrancing Palais-Royal gardens, but persevere. Open 11:45 a.m. to 2:15 p.m., 6:30 to 8:30 p.m. Closed Monday and Saturday evenings, and all day Sunday. Annual closing 15 July to 1 August, and closed in the evenings for the first two weeks of August.

China Express

120 rue Rambuteau, 1er
Métro: Les Halles

A pretty and comfortable place, overlooking the exciting developments at Les Halles. They'll feed you good Chinese food from noon to 1:30 a.m., 365 days a year. Their menu at 39F, plus 15% service and drink, offers such starters as Chinese soup, then six choices of main course which is more than most Oriental restaurants provide – the chicken in black bean sauce was excellent – and among other desserts, Chinese nougat. Drink is not cheap, a quarter-litre of wine 9F and jasmine tea 8F, so you may want to leave it out. Visa, Amex, Access and Diners' Club cards accepted.

La Fauvette

46 rue St-Honoré, 1er
Métro: Louvres, Les Halles

When Les Halles packed up and left, it left behind a semi-wholesale area of butchers and charcutières and a few of the very characteristic small 'market' restaurants. Fortunately, most tourists attracted by the glassy elegance of the new Halles are too snobbish to go into this little hole in the wall. What they are missing is a great meal for about 48F: huge serving of herring and potato salad, for example, civet de lapin or steak or a bountiful omelette, served with frites or salad, and, among other dessert choices 'Floating Island'. The food is hearty, and so is the clientele, it's noisy and always crowded. Open noon to 2:30, 7:00 to 9:00 p.m., closed Saturday, Sunday, holidays and all of August.

La Fauvette St-Honoré

90 rue St-Honoré, 1er
Métro: Louvre, Les Halles

This is 'the other Fauvette', equally unprepossessing from the outside, but serving massive portions of really good food. You must go early (before 12) as the powerful men from the neighbouring butchers come swarming in about 12:30, and the best choices of food go early. Lunch is 39F *tout compris*, with a choice of salads or charcuterie to start with, then steak or pork chops or Toulouse sausages with delicious flageolets, and pastries or cheese; wine is full-bodied and good. Open noon to 2:30, closed Saturday, Sundays and holidays, and from the Saturday before the first of August, until the first Monday in September.

La Grande Marmite

Corner rue Pierre Lescot and rue de la Petite Truanderie, 1er
Métro: Les Halles

Many of the newish restaurants around Les Halles are rip-offs, but not the Marmite. It's a small, attractive room with an old-fashioned bar and old movie-star photos on the wall. The food is exceptional and there is almost too much of it. At lunch the menu is 37F50 plus service – drink is quite expensive. A meal not long ago was so lavish that our restaurant spy commented 'A boiled egg for supper is all I could manage after that. A huge salad of frizzy chicory with warm chèvre (goat cheese) was followed by a monumental choucroute with ham, sausage, potatoes and frankfurters, then very good ice cream. At night, the menu is 49F70 plus service and drink – adding up to about 75F (roughly £6.75). Open noon to 1:00 a.m.' Closed Sundays and holidays.

Monoprix

21 avenue de l'Opéra, 1er
Métro: Pyramides

The lunchtime bargain of Paris, one flight up in the largest of this chain of shops: big, smartly decorated with tiled walls and soft lights, and air-conditioned. One can have three courses – pâtés and salads to start, from 2F50 to 4F, a hot main dish such as choucroute garnie 23F, or others as low as 14F, and such luxury desserts as sachertorte for 9F50. A whole meal including wine could be as little as 32F (less than £3). Open 11:30 a.m. to 2:30 p.m. Closed Sundays. Go early, as queues from noon on are long.

Le Petit Ramoneur

74 rue St-Denis, 1er
Métro: Châtelet or Les Halles

Very near the Forum des Halles, and about five minutes from Beaubourg (where no one should eat) – this is a most delightful and popular place in an (almost) pedestrian shopping centre. It's jammed at lunchtime, while other inexpensive places are three-quarters empty. The menu is 41F20 *tout compris*, and they do a nice thing: a bottle of red wine is put on the table and you help yourself. Food is hearty, bourgeois, big helpings of everything. Nineteen first courses, including lentils vinaigrette and pâté de foie with green peppercorns; about ten choices of main dishes such as veal escalope, petit salé with haricots, omelettes; superb tarte maison and a lot of cheeses. Very drinkable wine. Open noon to 2:30 p.m., 7:00 to 10:00 p.m., closed Sundays and August. Go early at lunchtime – between 1:00 and 2:00 p.m. it is packed.

Pizza Pino

43 rue St-Denis, 1er
Métro: Les Halles

One of a big chain, newly opened and a great choice if you long for a pizza, outdoors, near Les Halles. A pleasant view of the lovely Fountain of the Innocents. Clean, bright décor, friendly waitresses, good service. À la carte, but not too dear: 11–13F for a first course of green salad or tomatoes palermitaine; 22F for an excellent pizza; 17–31F for various pastas; 11F for 3 scoops of super ice cream. Service 15% extra. Wine is rather costly at 9F50 for a quarter-litre, mineral water 6F. Open daily from 11:30 a.m. to 4:30 a.m. the next morning! No annual closing, open holidays.

Relais du Sud-Ouest

148 rue St-Honoré, 1er
Métro: Louvre or Palais-Royal

An astonishing place so close to the Louvre, and why it hasn't been
mobbed by tourists we can't think. Stone walls, posters, faux-bois
painted wall panels – two rooms, upstairs and down. The service
is brisk and efficient rather than charming, but the food is very
good and the portions dauntingly large. Menu 48F at lunch, *tout
compris*, 65F at night. Very large portions of crudités (six vegetables),
pâté servings big enough for two, and some recherché things like
artichoke hearts stuffed with vegetables. Entrées include steak au
poivre, osso bucco, and in summer cold roast chicken and salad.
Desserts are beautiful tartes and cakes or big wedges of cheeses
always in perfect condition. You drink red wine, rosé, beer, or
mineral water – no white wine offered. Very busy from 12:15 to
1:15 p.m. Open noon to 2:30 p.m., 7:00 to 11:00 p.m., closed
Sundays. Open most holidays, no annual closing.

Le Stado

150 rue St-Honoré, 1er
Métro: Louvre or Palais-Royal

If you can't get into the Sud-Ouest, the Stado is even more
attractive. The food is extremely good, and the service is warm and
charming. Stone walls, tile floors, huge pictures of the Tarbes rugby
team. Cooking is south-western France (Pyrénées), lunch menu is
48F which at dinner and on Sundays goes up to 65F. Both prices
include wine and service, and it's worth every franc. Starters are
the usual pâtés, crudités, salads (big servings). Recently one of us
had a big plate of boeuf bourguignon, and his companion can never
resist the wonderful tender faux-filet steak with tarragon butter and
mounds of hot crisp matchstick potatoes. Cheese, a fluffy chocolate
mousse, or a not-too-sweet prune and apricot tart are always on
the menu. 'Drink beer with this kind of food,' advises a greedy Paris
eater who regularly lunches there. Open noon to 2:30 p.m., 7:00 to
11:00, seven days a week. No annual closing, but closed on major
holidays, 14 July, Christmas, New Year's Day.

Le Ver Luisant

26 rue du Mont-Thabor, 1er
Métro: Tuileries

In this very elegant and expensive street, close to the Jeu de Paume and to the Meurice and other classy hotels, an astounding restaurant, very narrow, full of mirrors, and very crowded at 12:30 even on a Saturday. Go after 1:15. It's charming. For 41F50, *service compris*, wonderful salads, choice of veal escalope, steaks, platter of charcuterie, omelette, steak haché, or a couple of plats du jour, one of which is a very good ravioli. Tarte or fromage (both fine), or a sensational chocolate mousse. Wine 5F. It's hot in summer, but has a lively, local, well-dressed crowd. Open noon to 2:30 p.m., closed Sundays, holidays and August. You can eat quickly at the bar near the door.

2e arrondissment

Le Clos Chabanais

3 rue Chabanais, 2e
Métro: Pyramides, Bourse

The 'Clos' has changed greatly in the past two years, and is now run by a very flamboyant *patronne* in turban and caftan, who calls all those who eat there 'mes enfants', 'coucou', 'ma biche'. The menu at 52F *tout compris* is available only at lunch; evenings are à la carte. No matter when you eat there, you are ushered downstairs into a dim, cavernous, candle-lit room. The food is generously served, well cooked. You help yourself to imaginative hors d'oeuvres, then have steak or trout or a plat du jour which might be chicken and rice with ratatouille. The hot tarte aux pommes was delicious. Open 12:00 to 2:30 p.m., 7:00 to 10:00 p.m. closed Saturday evening and Sunday, and in summer, all weekend. No annual closing, and Madame hasn't decided whether to stay open on holidays or not.

Le Drouot

103 rue de Richelieu, 2e
Métro: Richelieu-Drouot

The same management as Chartier (p.117), it's large, too well known, but excellent value. A four-course meal with wine recently was 38F, plus 12% service – leek salad, boeuf bourguinon with steamed potatoes, and caramelised apple tart, with a quarter litre of slightly better than ordinary wine. A cheese or ham omelette was only 8F50! Open 11:30 a.m. to 2:30 p.m., 6:30 to 11:00 p.m., seven days a week. No annual closing, but closed on major holidays.

Signor Pronto

18 rue Favart, 2e
Métro: Richelieu-Drouot

'Pronto' here means fast – impersonally quick, and as one of our Paris restaurant scouts commented, 'Upmarket McDonald's à l'italienne'. But it's inexpensive, as pizzas and pastas range from 10F to 22F, with desserts from 8F to 10F, and wine by the glass for 5F, so a meal could cost you as little as 32F even with 15% service added. Open 11:00 a.m. to 11:00 p.m., closed on Sundays, but open on holidays, and no annual closing.

Tout au Beurre

5 rue Mandar, 2e
Métro: Sentier

We can't claim this as a discovery – but it remains one of the spectacular values of Paris and seems to change little, in friendliness, popularity and consistently good food, from year to year. The menu is 40F, including wine and service. First courses are mainly salads and pâtés – the salade niçoise very good indeed – then boeuf bourguignon, roast veal with ratatouille, cassoulet, and the ever-present roast chicken and steak with frites. The most delicious (and popular) dessert is the gâteau Chantilly, light flaky pastry with lavish cream filling. Tout au Beurre is always crowded, and you're not encouraged to linger – go early, about 6:30 p.m., or latish, about 9:00. Open noon to 3:00 p.m., 7:00 to 11:00 p.m., seven days a week. In June or July, the room can be too hot for pleasure, so make it a spring or autumn choice. Closed in August.

4e arrondissement

Au Rocher de Cancale

8 rue de la Tacherie, 4e
Métro: Hôtel-de-Ville

The wallpaper is the epitome of bad taste, the tables are crowded, but the food is delicious and the service as swift and smiling as ever. For about 37F *tout compris* you can have a huge piece of pâté en croûte, quenelles en brochet with a spicy sauce and cheese, and a wonderful crème de marrons. Or herring fillets in a wine sauce, followed by paupiettes de veau and a wonderful light tarte. The crowd has become less 'straight' in the past couple of years, but all attractive, well-dressed 'neighbourhood' types, and much livelier than when the clientele consisted of rather quiet people reading newspapers. Open noon to 2:30 p.m. and 7:30 to 10:00 p.m., closed Saturday nights, Sundays, and from the end of the first week in August to the beginning of the last week.

Le Bar Cristal

13 rue Beautrellis, 4e
Métro: St-Paul, Bastille or Sully-Morland

The only thing wrong with Le Cristal is that it closes Saturdays and Sundays; otherwise it would be an all-week favourite. A lively neighbourhood with many painters among its regulars – crowded, uproarious, but all with good manners. The menus are 40F to 55F, service included, but drink extra. In the summer of 1985 they had the happy idea of offering a bottle of their own 'Cristal' red wine, to take home, for the diners who plunged for the 55F menu! Open 12:00 to 2:15 p.m., 7:00 to 11:15 p.m., Mondays through Saturdays, but closed for Saturday lunch, and Sundays. Annual closing dates are fluid, the 1985 closing was from 10 August to 2 September, 1986 is anybody's guess.

La Calanque

2 rue de la Coutellerie, 4e
Métro: Hôtel de Ville, Châtelet

For 54F, service included – about £4.75 as we write – the Calanque serves an extraordinary seafood menu. This is worth noting because fish is expensive in Paris. They offer many starters, then bouillabaisse or grilled salmon or whatever fish is in season, and a choice of 14 desserts or cheese. Drink is not included, but a half-bottle of white wine isn't too costly at 16F. Open noon to 2:30 p.m., 7:00 to 9:00 p.m. Closed Saturdays, Sundays, holidays and August.

La Canaille

4 rue Crillon, 4e
Métro: Sully-Morland

One of our student scouts of years past wrote, 'Very cool – it is assuré par les jeunes assez sympa-décontracté!' Which was then current Paris argot. More recently, a resident Parisian pauper says, 'Brilliant restaurant! Top-class food at good prices.' Not very substantial portions, so don't go there if you are really starving or setting out for an afternoon of heavy sightseeing. For 36F (lunch) or 42F (nights), you could choose from tarama, tabbouleh – delicious Lebanese rice salad – or a terrine, then progress to curried pork, a good grilled steak with vegetables or salad, and finish with excellent tarte maison, cheese, or yoghurt. Service included, drink extra and inexpensive, quarter-litre of quite good red wine only 4F. The street itself is bleak, dead-feeling, but the restaurant attracts a fascinating selection of people. Open 11:45 a.m. to 2:00 p.m., 7:30 to 11:30 p.m. Closed Saturdays, Sundays, mid-July to mid-August, and all holidays.

Le Petit Gavroche

15 rue Ste-Croix de la Bretonnerie, 4e
Métro: Rambuteau, Hôtel-de-Ville

The Gavroche has always been great value for money, and its menu at lunch is still only 32F, plus 15% service and wine which is quite expensive. At night it climbs to 38F, still a bargain even when you add in drink and service. The menu is not elaborate, but it changes daily and everything is well cooked. 'Great ambience, lively, small, busy, in a street that leads you to Beaubourg,' reports one of our restaurant-wise Paris friends, 'a meal for two with coffee and drinks shouldn't run to more than about 100F.' A heart of palm salad was 10F, boeuf bourguignon with steamed potatoes 25F (one of five main courses offered), and tarte Alsacienne very good at 8F. Service is not included, but a sign says 'Tip as you feel', so leave about 15%. Wine is expensive. Open noon to 2:00 p.m., 7:00 to 11:00 p.m., closed Saturdays and Sundays, on holidays, and all of August.

Restaurant Victoria

4 rue de la Coutellerie, 4e
Métro: Hôtel de Ville, Châtelet

An agreeable Oriental couple run the Victoria, which is within walking distance of Beaubourg; take a stroll to the river. We've never had a bad meal there, and no tourists have wandered its way. Consider 16 choices of hors-d'oeuvres, a tender steak, a platter of cheeses to choose from, or a delicious lemon tart or various sorbets and ice creams. 39F including service, with wine at 4F50 a quarter-litre. Open noon to 2:30 p.m., 7:30 to 9:30 p.m., closed Saturday night, Sunday and holidays. No annual closing.

Le Temps de Cerises

31 rue de Cerisaie, 4e
Métro: Bastille or Sully-Morland

As the Marais changes and becomes fashionable and expensive, it's a joy to find this perfect little local restaurant which we have known for years, still there and unchanged. It's run by an energetic young couple, Gerard and Marie-Claire, and always wall-to-wall with young people busy eating, talking, laughing and gesticulating. The walls are papered with posters, old photographs, postcards and snapshots. The menu is short, offering pâté, oeuf mayo or crudités to start with, and a few very good family-type hot dishes such as smoked sausage with masses of lentils, and pastry or cheese, all for

35F50 including service, with red wine at about 4F50. Open 11:30 a.m. to 2:30 p.m. Go before 12:15 or after 1:45 or you won't get in. If you are staying nearby, go as early as 7:30 a.m. for coffee and croissants fresh from the bakery across the street.

Le Trumilou

84 quai de l'Hôtel-de-Ville, 4e
Métro: Hôtel-de-Ville

This used to be the secret restaurant of the knowledgeable painters, writers, craftsmen of the neighbourhood. Now it has appeared in (mostly French) guidebooks, but there seems to be no way it can be spoiled or changed. Biggish, brightly lit room lined with paintings and flowers everywhere; from the street it looks like a bar with pinball machines and so on, but wait until you get in. Mme Rouby, who runs it, looks like the archetype of the motherly French restaurant *patronne*, in her neat black dress and with darting eyes. She is laughing, loving, embracing, and the food is very good indeed. It offers two menus, at 44F50 and 59F20, both including service but not drink. Even the cheaper menu offers such good things as pintadeau (guinea hen) when it's in season – lavish helping of crudités to start with – and very good desserts. Open noon to 2:45 p.m., 7:15 to 10:00 p.m., closed Mondays and September. Good place for Sunday lunch or supper.

5e arrondissement

Au Bouche Trou

24 rue des Boulangers, 5e
Métro: Jussieu

The Trou is truly in the heart of the student district, therefore always crowded, but nevertheless well away from the more touristy parts of the 5e. A genial atmosphere, where a good meal costs only 45F including service and wine – try rillettes to begin, then the star turn, daurade au riz, a beautifully cooked fish, finishing with something like apricot pie or chocolate mousse. It's the kind of place where a debate can flare up at any moment among students, workers, foreign visitors. Yves Bariot, who owns it and cooks the delicious food, is as knowledgeable about history and Paris life as he is about cooking. Discussions can go on long after official end of serving at 10:15. Open noon to 2:00 p.m., 7:15 until the arguments run out of steam. Closed Sundays, and for a month in the summer.

Aux Savoyards

14 rue des Boulangers, 5e
Métro: Jussieu

Again, jammed with students, so don't expect to have a quiet meal. But good food and a cosy ambience. The menu changes every day: don't expect any gastronomic miracles, but you will be given good portions of crudités, well-cooked chicken or boeuf bourguignon, nice selections of cheeses or pastries, and a quarter-litre of ordinary but passable wine, for about 45F. Closed Saturday nights, Sundays and holidays. Open noon to 2:00 p.m., 7:30 to 10:00 p.m., closed in August.

Le Baptiste

11 rue des Boulangers, 5e.
Métro: Jussieu

A beautiful little room with provincial decoration on stone walls, with copper jugs, plants and so forth. Lovely food. Menus are written on wooden paddles, and include a well-peppered pâté, or museau de boeuf for starters; then steak au poivre, entrecôte with shallots, chicken in red wine. Desserts: almost the best pastry ever, which is going some, or cheese. At lunch, a three-course menu is 46F, service included but drink extra, and it may include a plat du jour 'whatever the chef thinks up', and an 'avalanche of desserts' which one day recently was a masterly raspberry tart smothered in whipped cream. At night the menu is 56F, wonderful value.

Le Bouté Grill (Chez Hamadi)

12 rue Boutebrie, 5e
Métro: St-Michel

One of the best 'couscous' places in Paris, and considering its location just off the boulevard St-Germain, no wonder there is always a queue. The menu is 62F50, including wine and service, for a huge meal including more couscous than you can eat. À la carte not too expensive: couscous from 25F, other plats du jour 25 to 33F, a quarter-litre of quite good wine 7F, all plus 15% service. Open noon to 5:00 p.m., good to know if you want a late lunch; then from 6:00 to 11:00 p.m., or even later, seven days a week. No annual closing – open on most holidays.

Le Bouvillon

3 rue des Grands Degrès, 5e
Métro: St Michel or Maubert-Mutualité

This isn't the least expensive restaurant we know, but it offers beautifully cooked food in a most attractive ambience, and it is open every day of the year. Their two-course 'Formule' is 49F50, plus service and drink, so it can work out to about 65F; considering the quality of the cooking, this is not too dear. Poached eggs meurette (in a red wine sauce) as a starter is something you are not offered every day, and the main courses might include turkey escalope with lemon, with two vegetables, among other interesting dishes. Open noon to 2:30 p.m., 7:30 to 10:00 p.m.

La Brouette

rue Descartes, 5e
Métro: Cardinal Lemoine

No wonder it is crowded with the young and hungry. The menu at 42F, including service, gives you six snails or stuffed mussels (or hot mushroom tart), then frogs' legs or boeuf bourguinon, finishing with prunes in wine, or sorbet, or profiterolles. But look out for the drink prices – wine is only available in half bottles at 25F, and mineral water is an incredible 12F! La Brouette is one of many inexpensive restaurants that line rue Descartes, which leads into rue Mouffetard – full of strolling musicians, leisurely crowds, boutiques. Open 12:30 to 2:30 p.m., 7:00 to 10:00 p.m. Closed Sundays. No annual closing.

Crêperie des Poetes

54 bis boulevard St-Marcel, 5e
Métro: St Marcel

The boulevard St-Marcel is a delightful tree-edged street in the quietest part of the 5th arrondissement, not far from the Jardin des Plantes; this crêperie is a delicious discovery. Although it doesn't have a fixed-price menu, the main-course galettes are very big and very interesting: filled with Roquefort and crème fraîche, for 18F, or mushrooms, ham and spinach at 21F, with a most exotic one of salmon, crème fraîche, lemon and vodka at 37F! Two courses – a big galette and a sweet crêpe, from 6F50 up, are very reasonable. Wine, however, is 10F50 for a quarter-litre, so go easy on drink. The room is simple and attractive, with plants and gentle lighting, the service is quick and friendly. Open noon to 2:30 p.m., 7:00 to 10:00 p.m., closed Sundays and holidays, and usually from 15 August to 1 September.

Grenier de Notre Dame

18 rue de la Bûcherie, 5e
Métro: Maubert-Mutualité

We have had varying reports about this vegetarian restaurant – which always has queues outside. The set menu at 38F50, *service compris*, is very limited – only two courses and two choices within each course, but imaginative – potage de miso and vegetable couscous, for instance. A la carte, the bill can run up steeply to as much as 100F. But those who recommend it seem to love it. Open noon to 2:30 p.m., 7:30 to 11:30 p.m., seven days a week in summer, in winter closed on Tuesdays. No annual closing in 1985, but possibly closed in August in 1986.

Le Perraudin

157 rue St Jacques, 5e
Métro: Luxembourg

There's a limited menu here, with not too many choices – at 42F including service, but not wine. The *cadre* (decor and ambience) is pretty and pleasant, and it has a lot of neighbourhood regulars, always a good recommendation. Not exciting, but useful if you have been visiting the nearby Luxembourg Gardens. Crudités, pork chops, andouillettes, steak, chicken – and the usual tempting array of desserts. Noon to 2:30 p.m., 7:30 to 9:30 p.m., closed Saturday nights, Sundays, holidays and all of August.

Taverne Descartes

rue Descartes, 5e
Métro: Place Monge

Here's one of our most expensive restaurants, and one of the best values in Paris (so say friends who live near and dine there frequently). For 72F, including service and a half bottle of wine per person instead of the usual quarter-litre, you can have this sort of food: to start, 12 snails or a whole avocado stuffed with crabmeat, or moules marinière, then very tender steak au poivre or grilled with Roquefort cheese, or coquilles St Jacques, roast lamb, etc.; several kinds of cheese or tartes or well-chosen really ripe fruit. Noon to 2:30 p.m., 7:30 to 10:00 p.m., closed Sundays. No annual closing – and you'll enjoy the ambience of the street, which is full of shops and boutiques, often open late into the evening.

6e arrondissement

Les Byzantins

33 rue Dauphine, 6e
Métro: Odeon/St Michel

Here's a good new one in a neighbourhood where you are apt to find everything very expensive or very 'touristy'. It's Greek, popular, crowded – and the decor of stuffed birds slung from the ceiling, boar's heads and zebra hides, can be off-putting for animal-lovers. However, the menu at 37F, plus service and drink, is really excellent: vine leaves served with cucumbers in a garlicky, lemony yoghurt sauce among other starters, and a choice of calamares, shish kebab, pastitsio (Greek macaroni and meat casserole), with lemon pudding or ice cream or halva or a choice of cheese. So for about 50F, all in, you'll have a flavoursome and filling meal. Open noon to 3:00 p.m., 7:00 to 11:30 p.m., every day of the year.

La Crêperie

38 rue Monsieur-le-Prince, 6e
Métro: Odéon or Luxembourg

Menu: galettes (savoury pancakes) – a choice of ham, spinach, mushrooms, cheese, sausage, or what-have-you, from 10 to 22F. Sweet pancakes: 6 to 24F, with sugar, lemon, chestnuts, liqueurs, honey, fruit, and so on. If you want a quick light meal, a crêperie is always a good idea. This one, about ten yards from the Luxembourg Gardens, is small but has a fairly large menu. For example: galette of egg, ham and cheese for 17F, lemon and sugar crêpe for 7F, cider at 7F a glass. Total: 38F including cider and service. Open noon to midnight, seven days a week, except that in June and July they close Friday lunchtimes, all day Sundays, and are closed for the month of August.

La Grande Muraille

47 rue Monsieur-le-Prince, 6e
Métro: Odéon

Chinese, and hence heavy on the *carte*, although the *prix-fixe* costs only 32F; service included, wine extra. Pâté impérial (quite good), a spicy boeuf aux oignons, rice, wine and coffee came to 30F à la carte. The desserts are (as always in Chinese restaurants) dull – kumquats, pineapple in syrup, sawdusty gâteau chinois. But our Paris student friends strongly recommended the beignets de poisson as a main dish, and say that the 'curry de porc' is tasty and unlike what English Chinese restaurants cook. Don't drink wine, they advise, but do have beer or tea, both about 6–6F50. Open 11:45 a.m. to 2:30 p.m., 6:45 to 11:00 p.m., useful for a late evening snack meal. Closed Mondays. No annual closing.

Jardin des Prunus

37 rue Mazarine, 6e
Métro: Odeon

This simple but elegant Chinese restaurant is truly amazing value – the menu is 37F50, *tout compris*, and the food is exceptionally good. A soup with poached egg and vegetables was delicious – or one could have had bean-sprout salad or egg roll. Chicken with pineapple, or pork or beef with vegetables, were among the main courses, with the usual Chinese desserts: macaroon-like gateau chinois or arbutus fruits in syrup. Open noon to 2:30 p.m., 7:00 to 10:30, closed Sundays, open on holidays and no annual closing.

Orestias

4 rue Grégoire-de-Tours, 6e
Métro: Odéon

The 5e *arrondissement* is famous for its Greek restaurants (all along the rue Mouffetard, for instance), but here's a good one in the 6e near the Odéon. The menu is pretty standard, but the food is above average. First courses, recently, included tomato and cucumber salad, pâté or great vine leaves stuffed with rice, then grilled lamb chops, spit-roasted chicken and tender skewered beef with tomatoes and green peppers. Halva, peaches in syrup, or cheese or crème caramel for dessert. Menu 39F including service but drink extra. Open noon to 3:00 p.m., 6:00 p.m. to midnight, closed Sundays and major holidays, no annual closing. A pleasant, busy, very friendly place with piped music (bearable) and quick service.

Restaurant des Arts

73 rue de Seine, 6e
Métro: Odéon

A 41F menu, service included, but wine extra (and rather expensive, offered only in half-litre carafes, 15F). Really spectacular value, this restaurant run by the second generation of owners, which never changes in its warm welcoming feeling. We, and our French friends, have never had a meal less than good here. For example, not long ago one of us had delicious lentils vinaigrette to start, among choices such as cucumber salad, pâté, potato salad with capers; then cold poached colin, a hake-like fish, with mayonnaise that tasted home-made; another dish the same day was a large and succulent escalope de veau milanaise with sautéed new potatoes. Desserts include fresh fruit salad, cheese, and yoghurt. Rich tartes and gâteaux are offered, but cost 2 to 4F extra. All in all, much more choice, as you will have observed, than most cheap restaurants. Closed Friday night, Saturday and Sunday, and major holidays. Closed in August. Don't go in really hot weather as it is always crowded and you can feel uncomfortably close to a lot of warm bodies.

Restaurant Florin

61 rue M. le Prince, 6e
Métro: Odéon

Worth visiting if only for the decor! Multi-coloured walls and stairs and the room is crammed with junk that seems to be a lifetime collection of the antique couple who run it: pictures, mirrors, old street lamps, wind chimes, candelabras. Huge, rather van Gogh-like bunches of flowers on each table. The food is pleasant but not very distinguished – soup or a big plate of rather unusual crudités, followed by steak or boeuf bourguignon, and yoghurt or pineapple in kirsch or ice cream, 45F *service compris*, with inexpensive and drinkable wine at 6F50 the quarter-litre. They are open on Sundays, when many Paris restaurants close. Open noon to 2:30 p.m., 7:00 to 9:30 p.m., closed Mondays and usually the last two weeks of August.

7e arrondissement

Au Babylone

13 rue de Babylone, 7e
Métro: Sèvres-Babylone

Decidedly eccentric, this is a very family restaurant where the best choices on the menu go very fast, so the waitress reels off what's left when you order. When you pay, you tell the *caissier* what you've had, they glance at your table to verify it, and between you a bill is estimated faster than a calculator could do it! For 37F recently, service included but wine extra, we had a simple lunch – crudités or oeuf mayo, roast lamb or pork chops, and fruit tart or cheese. Wine is about 4F the quarter-litre. Open 11:30 a.m. to 2:30 p.m., closed Sundays, holidays, and August.

Au Ciel de Shanghai

33 avenue de Suffren, 7e
Métro: Bir-Hakeim

A good solution to eating in the neighbourhood of the Eiffel Tower, where most restaurants are either tacky or expensive. Undistracting Chinese music, and a largely Chinese clientele, always a good sign. For openers, Chinese salad with chicken, or Pekin soup; then sautéed crevettes in a crisp batter, with vegetables, or pork with mushrooms or spicy sautéed beef, with moderately interesting desserts – apple fritters, nut sorbet, lychees. The menu is 45F, service compris – wine extra and expensive, half bottles only at 20F. Open noon to 2:30 p.m., 7:00 to 10:30 p.m., seven days a week, open on most holidays and no annual closing.

Chez Germain

30 rue Pierre Leroux, 7e
Métro: Vaneau

You *must* go early, otherwise prepare to queue for ten to twenty minutes – it is that good, and that popular. Great atmosphere, especially for non-smokers as the *patron*, M. Babkine, says *interdit de fumer*. The menu, incredibly, is 32F, including service but not drink, and of course the choices are few (salads or crudités, sausage, liver, cheese or crème caramel) – but for 40F plus 15% service you can eat such delicacies as melon, tender steak, pastries, cheese, or really good fruit in season. Red wine is only 3F90. 11:30 a.m. to 2:30 p.m., 7:00 to 9:00 p.m., closed Saturday nights, Sundays and August.

Le Roupeyrac

62 rue de Bellechasse, 7e
Métro: Solférino

A wonderful menu for 50F, *tout compris*. A very large plate of pâté, or crudités, or oeuf mayo (1½ eggs), then brains in black butter – immense! – or steak, or côte de porc provençale. Then a very big serving of delicious tarte, or cheese. Wine, beer, mineral water. It gets crowded on weekdays with people from nearby ministries – go early. Open noon to 2:30 p.m., 7:00 to 9:30 p.m., Monday to Friday. Saturday, lunch only, and closed Sundays, holidays and 7 August to 9 September.

Le Select

18 rue Jean Nicot near rue St-Dominique, 7e.
Métro: Latour-Maubourg

Its hours are limited – 11:30 a.m. to 8:00 p.m., with last orders about 7:30 p.m., but it's a great place for lunch or an early supper. It looks like an ordinary *tabac* but if you can push through the bar past the pinball machines into the back room it's a find, and just off the great rue St-Dominique. No menu, but the à la carte is cheap: plat du jour could be a cheeseburger at 18F, or a steak with frites at 25F. A first course of pâté is 8F, herring fillets 9F, a huge omelette 13F, a croque madame with salad only 20F, all desserts 10F. Wine is expensive, in half-bottles for 20–55F. Add 15% for service. Closed Sundays, holidays, and August.

La Trattoria

99 rue de Sèvres, 7e.
Métro: Vanneau

In the big, modern, rather featureless Galerie de Séverins, a shopping centre which also has an entrance on the pretty little rue du Cherche-Midi. It's a beautiful, large restaurant with a glass-roofed, enclosed courtyard. The size means that the waiters and waitresses haven't time to be more than routinely courteous, and you may have to wait some time for service, so don't go if in a hurry. The food is fairly routine French–Italian, but good enough. Two menus: 39F10, very limited choices; the 59F menu including service (but not drink) is better, with such main dishes as trout with almonds and some rather super ice-cream desserts. À la carte choices include good inexpensive pizzas (17F50 to 27F). 'Desserts are brilliant, best part of the menu,' reports a Paris friend. Very classy loos. Open noon to 2:30 p.m., 7:00 to 9:00 p.m., seven days a week. No annual closing. Closed on Sundays and public holidays in August.

8e arrondissement

Les Cloyères

9 rue de Laborde, 8e
Métro: St-Lazare

The food is superb, the atmosphere non-existent unless you count the charm of the owners, who also cook and run the bar and chat with customers. It's hidden in a sort of courtyard, and wouldn't have been found if the *patron* of a hotel hadn't led us to it. You serve yourself, and the most expensive things on the menu (leeks vinaigrette, veal escalope milanaise, raspberry tarte, and wine) came to 47F – no service charge of course. Usually there's a short but good menu conseillé, about 39F. Lunch only, 11:45 to 2:00 p.m., closed Sundays, holidays and August. This is serious food, so lunch here should be your main meal of the day.

Étoile d'Asia

24 rue Jean-Mermoz, 8e
Métro: Franklin D. Roosevelt

A pleasant, not-too-expensive, Chinese-Vietnamese restaurant in a ritzy neighbourhood; clientele mostly French. A few nice touches, such as wood-panelled walls. First course: Chinese salad or omelette foo yong, filled with strange and delicious vegetables; then duck in pineapple sauce, chicken curry, beef chop suey; followed by lychees or the usual beignets of apples, pineapple, or banana with icing sugar. Menu 47F50, *service compris*, drink extra and not too exorbitant if you stick to mineral water (6F90) or beer (9F). Open noon to 2:30 p.m., 7:00 to 10:30 p.m., closed Sundays, holidays, and all of August.

La Salade Condorcet

7 rue de Havre, 8e
Métro: St-Lazare

Another good place for a freshly made and lavishly served salad – the 'salade Condorcet' is a big bowl with ham, cheese, hard-boiled egg, olives and tomatoes for 23F. A large cheese omelette is only 15F, and two people could split the 22F salade chef or salade niçoise. Hot plats du jour 30–39F. Add 15% service on all prices. Noon to 3:00 p.m., closed Sundays, no annual closing.

Le Volnay

6 rue de Laborde, 8e
Métro: St-Lazare

One of the deceptively simple little restaurants that could easily be passed without a glance. Go in. It's very much a family place, management and customers, and a tourist seems to be rather a surprise. The desserts are always good, and include crème de marrons and some special pastries. A regular customer who works in the area says it's the best and most consistently good neighbourhood restaurant. A meal could be about 44F, including wine (3F50) and service (15%). Open noon to 3:00 p.m., 6:45 to 8:30 p.m., closed Saturdays, Sundays, holidays and July.

9e arrondissement

L'Auberge du Père Louis

7 rue du Boule Rouge, 9e
Métro: Rue Montmartre

A big place, filled with lots of people getting together to have a good time. If you're alone or a twosome, make for the first or second floor and try for a table near the window, as the ground floor is mostly big groups. Typical meal: terrine, boeuf bourguignon or entrecôte grillé with frites, then chocolate cake or ice-cream. The beef is tender and served with steamed potatoes; the pâté, is fresh and good; the wine like any other. Menu 46F, plus service, wine extra and expensive – 17F50 for half a bottle. Lunch noon to 2:30 p.m., dinner 6:00 to 10:00 p.m., seven days a week. No annual closing, open most holidays but not Christmas or New Year. Diner's Club cards accepted.

Au Pupillin

19 rue Notre-Dame-de-Lorette 9e
Métro: St-Georges or Notre-Dame-de-Lorette

We don't usually recommend places that have a 'formule', which is usually only two courses, plus service and drink; but this glamorous wine bar is a good place to observe the BCBGs (Bon Chic, Bon Genre), France's equivalent of Sloane Rangers. And the food really is delicious, light, unusual, beautifully presented. The 52F 'formule' offered such delights as smoked salmon salad or avocado and apple salad, followed by salmon trout in green sauce or breast of duck in sherry vinegar with apricots. However, desserts (and very exotic they are, such as chocolate and mint mousse cake) are 26F, plus service. A special-occasion place, open 365 days a year, Monday through Friday, from noon on into the afternoon, then from 7:00 p.m. to 2:00 a.m. Booking is essential: telephone 4 285 46 06.

Chartier

7 rue de Faubourg Montmartre, 9e
Métro: Rue Montmartre

A cliché restaurant, listed in all guidebooks, but the value is so good it must be included. It's possible to eat a really superb meal for 56F, everything included – or a less lavish but well-cooked one (shrimp pâté, médaillon of veal à la crème, pastry, wine and service) for as little as 34F50. Service is quick, not too much Gallic charm, but the customers are always an interesting mixture of students, tourists and impecunious Parisians. Look for the menu conseillé, which is always good value, but note that 12% service is added to its basic cost. The 1920 décor makes Chartier worth a visit. Open 11:00 a.m. to 3:00 p.m., 6:00 p.m. to 9:30 p.m., seven days a week. No annual closing.

Chez Maurice

44 rue Notre-Dame-de-Lorette, 9e
Métro: St-Georges

A pretty 1930s room with mirrored pillars, flowers, big linen napkins – and recently, service with a touch of the Fawlty Towers. However, the menu at 42F50, plus service and drink, offers avocado with shredded carrots and tomato, a thin but delicious steak with 'cottage fried' potatoes rather than the usual frites, finishing with a rich mocha cake. A more extensive menu is 67F plus service and drink, with such goodies as moules marinière, steak tartare, and an imposing fresh fruit salad buried in whipped cream – adding up to a little less than £9. Noon to 2:00 p.m., 7:00 to 10:30 p.m., 365 days a year.

Chez Yolande

48 rue de Clichy, 9e
Métro: Liège

This is the epitome of the small, good, Paris restaurant which one friend describes as 'chic à prix choc', meaning very good value and beautifully decorated. The *patronne* comes from Provence, and she serves you herself – so there is no service charge. While Yolande no longer offers a multi-choice menu, she has opted for a well-thought-out fixed menu which changes often. A characteristic meal: salad with pine nuts, an excellent steak with herbes de Provence, and a choice of desserts which included passion-fruit tart. It's 65F, and wine is extra, so this is a place to go the night you feel like spending about £7–£8 for a lovely meal and delightful ambience. Open noon to 2:00 p.m., 7:00 to 10:30 p.m., closed Sundays, and for five weeks from 1 July to end of first week in August.

L'Outa

26 rue de Caumartin, 9e
Métro: St-Lazare or Havre-Caumartin

This is a useful place to know if you're shopping at Au Printemps or Galeries Lafayette, but try to be there by 12:15 for lunch, or wait until about 1:30. Always several well-cooked hot dishes at lunch, such as an entrecôte, or baked pasta with cheese, each 30F, or cold beef vinaigrette with potato salad in a tarragon dressing, 21F. Best of all, their range of salads: a huge bowl of tuna with céleri remoulade, tomato, olives, shredded carrots and lettuce is 25F. Desserts are 6 or 7F, a quarter-litre of red wine is 4F, and they don't blink if you don't order a drink – a carafe of really cold water is on every table. One can lunch quickly, sitting on a high stool at the bar. They do take-away salads and sandwiches too. Open 11:00 a.m. to 6:00 p.m., closed at 2:00 p.m. Saturday and all day Sunday. No annual closing.

Taverne d'Auvergnate

30 rue des Bergères, 9e
Métro: Rue Montmartre

The menu at 46F, service included but wine (4F50 per quarter litre) extra, has some fairly remarkable choices: fish salad with a rich creamy sauce among other starters, then such main dishes as braised rabbit, steak with sautéed potatoes or omelette paysanne with salad. It's one of the few places that offer an omelette at night,

on the menu, which makes it a good place for a not too heavy meal. The service is excellent, the waitress always smiling no matter how busy she is, and it's a very typical Paris restaurant, with plants, dark wood bar, and candlelight. Open noon to 3:00 p.m., 7:00 to 10:00 p.m., closed Saturday evenings, Sundays, and 1 to 15 August.

Taverne des Dauphins

8 rue de Châteaudun, 9e
Métro: Cadet

A cosy, lively little restaurant where you can amuse yourself watching the other customers – entirely French – or find a seat by the window and look out on the busy street. The menu at 36.50 includes service but not drink. Begin with mackerel in white wine, a tuna coquille, melon or oeuf mayo, all remarkably good. Main course could be paella on certain days, or roast pork, or couscous. Try the lemon meringue tart if it is offered for dessert. Paella is offered by more expensive restaurants for up to 80F a serving, and the Dauphin couscous is the equal of that served in more costly, better-known places. Open noon to 2:00 p.m., 7:00 p.m. to midnight, Monday to Friday – weekends, by reservation only. Closed in August.

10e arrondissement

Maison de Confit

9 rue St-Laurent, 10e
Métro: Gare de l'Est

This excellent Basque restaurant in a neighbourhood that hasn't much to offer otherwise, serves good rich spicy food on a menu for 42F including service – drink is expensive, with half-bottles of wine about 20F. Recently a meal included rillettes de canard (a rich duck paté), sirloin steak haché in a highly charged Spanish sauce – or one could have had a huge omelette stuffed to bursting with ham, peppers and tomato. Open 11:45 a.m. to 2:30 p.m., 7:15 to 10:00 p.m. Closed Saturday lunch, Sundays and August.

Paris Liège

36 rue de St-Quentin, 10e
Métro: Gare du Nord

If you've staggered off the train at the station, which is the main arrival point for English travellers from Hovercraft or plane, consider this shabby but useful place. The food is conventional – pâté or oeuf mayo to start, chicken or andouillette or ham with pasta or frites, then cheese or pastry – but at 34F including wine or Vittel and service, you'll have a good filling meal. And they're open on Sundays. Open noon to 2:30 p.m., 7:00 to 10:30 p.m., closed Mondays and holidays, no annual closing.

11e arrondissement

Chez Justine

96 rue Oberkampf, 11e
Métro: St-Maur or Ménilmontant

A surprising find in a very racially mixed, working-class area. For 65F, *tout compris*, you help yourself to an array of hors-d'oeuvres, pour wine – as much as you want – from cask to jug, then choose among entrecôte, onglet (a tender and expensive cut of steak), lamb, or plat du jour, which was poulet basquaise – chicken with ratatouille – when we were there. Unbelievably crowded and like a tremendous party, with many family gatherings and people from all over Paris. Service is not very fast because the tables are jammed together. At lunch, the same menu is 54F *tout compris*. Amex and Visa accepted. Open noon to 2:30 p.m., 7:30 to 10:30 p.m., Closed Sundays and Monday noon. No annual closing, open most holidays including Bastille Day but not Christmas or New Year.

L'Artisan

9 rue de Charonne, 11e
Métro: Ledru-Rollin

An undiscovered delight in the street of furniture-makers. The menu begins with jambon persillé, or four other choices (but the JP is

extraordinary), goes on to roast pork with fresh cauliflower; or a dish of kid cooked like boeuf bourguignon; or poached calves' liver; and ends with chestnut cream smothered with whipped cream. 37F50, including service; wine at 5F. *And* they take Visa cards. Open noon to midnight, but the menu is served only from noon to 2:30 p.m. After that à la carte. Closed Sundays, holidays and August.

Le Fort National

97 avenue Ledru-Rollin, 11e
Métro: Ledru-Rollin

This new discovery is about five minutes' walk from the place d'Aligre (see Flea markets, p.188), and two minutes from the Métro stop. Their couscous is sensational, with large portions of chicken, beef, or merguez sausages in a sauce that is spicy without being raging hot, from about 26F up to a sumptuous Couscous Royale with chicken, mutton and sausages, at 45F. A big salade niçoise 15F, a really 'sensuous' chocolate cake (our researcher's word) 10F. Wine is expensive, half-bottles only, 18F. Very pretty place with tranquil green-and-white décor, cloth napkins, flowers, pleasant, friendly service – open the year around, including Christmas, but not Sundays. There are tables outside, but the street is roaring with traffic, and it's cooler and more relaxing inside, on summer days or evenings.

12e arrondissement

Le Bercy

corner of rue de Bercy and avénue Ledru-Rollin, 12e
Métro: Gare de Lyon

About eight minutes' walk from our favourite small flea market at place d'Aligre, the Bercy is one of those corner cafés that Parisians take for granted. They make the city – real Paris, not tourist Paris – what it is. For 39F, *tout compris*: artichoke hearts, petit salé – smoked ham with lentils – and an orange tart, with very good red wine. Although there are few choices of main dish, they are invariably well cooked. The waitresses literally *run* from opening time at 11:45 a.m. to closing at 2:00 p.m. Closed Saturdays, Sundays, holidays and August.

Café Melrose's

Corner rue de Charenton and avenue Ledru-Rollin, 12e
Métro: Ledru-Rollin

Delightful décor, with tile floors, lace curtain, fringed lampshades, soft taped music, and the food is sensational. The clientele is elegant, discreet, not exactly straight (except for the lunch crowd), but not campy. Menu 56F plus wine and service: various salads and terrines to start. We had a frisée aux lardons, which is curly lettuce with bits of hot smoked ham scattered through it, a big bowl, then paper-thin jambon d'auvergne (cold) with tomatoes and cucumbers, which was like the world's most wonderful lightly smoked prosciutto. You might try the cold salmon trout with mayonnaise, or brochette de boeuf. Desserts: pêche à la canelle, poached in white wine and cinnamon, many tartes and such. Wine is expensive: no quarter-bottles, no beer, and the cheapest house wine 30F a bottle; some half-bottles available at 23F and up. Hours: noon to 2:30 p.m., 8:00 to 11:00 p.m., closed August and Sunday lunch, open Sunday evenings.

Le Vaucluse

2 rue Traversière, 12e
Métro: Gare de Lyon

No tourists have discovered this one – although it is only one street away from the station. Very French, very local, and deserving of praise. The menu is 42F *tout compris*. A 'gorgeous lunch' described by a hard-to-please American friend consisted of a big helping of tuna and potato salad, then thick slices of beautifully cooked roast pork with fresh spinach and 'home-fried' potatoes, not frites, ending with coffee mousse. The cafe is small, serving only about 20 people, so go earlyish for lunch. Open noon to 2:30 p.m., 7:00 to about 9:00 p.m.; closed Sundays and holidays. No annual closing.

13e arrondissement

This neighbourhood is restfully free of tourists for most of the year, and a surprising number of good restaurants turned up in a very short time of searching. Around the Gobelins neighbourhood, there are a number of interesting-looking places if none of our choices suit you.

La Fauvette

58 avenue des Gobelins, near rue Véronèse, 13e
Métro: Gobelins or Place-d'Italie

A simple but very pleasant, conventional French restaurant which offers a limited menu, everything beautifully cooked and served, for 42F, including wine, beer or mineral water, plus 15% service. Lunch on the busy terrace, one sunny day last summer, was well-seasoned rillettes of pork, veal chops with frites, and a piece of brie in all its ripe perfection. Open noon to 2:00 p.m., 6:30 to 11:00 p.m., closed Wednesday, Christmas and New Year's Day but open on other holidays, and no annual closing. Good for an inexpensive Sunday lunch.

14e arrondissement

L'Alésia Brasserie

103 rue d'Alésia, 14e
Métro: Alésia

Menu at 32F, plus service and wine: six choices of main course, including pot-au-feu; eleven hors-d'oeuvres, including an omelette. Inexpensive à la carte, with omelette fines-herbes at 10F50, and pavé – a very tender steak – 26F. The restaurant is open every day of the year, so if you want a very inexpensive agreeable and unpretentious Christmas or New Year's Day dinner, go to L'Alésia. 12:00 to 2:30 p.m., 7:00 to 10:30 p.m.

15e arrondissement

Crêperie Dutot

48 rue Dutot, 15e
Métro: Pasteur

This restaurant opened in May 1983 and has already attracted a large, happy crowd of eaters. White plastered walls, beamed ceilings, and friendly (but not very fast) service. Not the cheapest place in Paris, but the crêpes are wonderful and so are the salads. Salade auvergnate at 23F, with roquefort, nuts, and grilled 'lardons' – bits of hot smoked ham – is very filling. Galette marseillaise, with tomatoes, sardines and mushrooms, at 22F, is sensational. And incredible desserts – from four sugared crêpes at 6F50, to crêpe surprise with orange sauce and Grand Marnier, flambé, at 20F. Service included in all prices, but drink extra and not cheap: Heineken beer 12F, half-litre of wine 18F. Lunch noon to 2:00 p.m., dinner 7:00 to 10:00 p.m., closed Sundays, Mondays, holidays and the first three weeks in August. Not to be missed.

Le Falca

3 rue Castagnary, 15e
Métro: Plaisance

A very homely place, with old-fashioned lamps and pictures on stucco walls, the service friendly and quick. Specialities are paella and couscous. A 37F menu, *tout compris*. First course: delicious artichoke hearts with a sharp vinaigrette, then a fairly conventional choice of main courses: pork chop, grilled steak or spicy merguez sausages, all served with vegetables. Finally, cheese (roquefort, camembert, or brie), or fruit salad or pineapple in kirsch. A good place for the hungry, as portions are large. Lunch noon to 2:00 p.m., dinner 7:00 to 9:00 p.m., closed Sundays, holidays, and August.

16e arrondissement

Le Paris Passy

place de Passy, 16e
Métro: Muette

A Paris friend writes: 'Several people who know the area between the Eiffel Tower and the Trocadéro said that this was the only good restaurant. Everything else is either wildly expensive, or really no good, or catering to tourists who have little choice. It's about 15 minutes' walk from the Métro to the Eiffel Tower, but worth the trip. It's very busy, and I found it somewhat lacking in friendliness. But the food is good, and you eat at tables in the courtyard, directly on the place Passy where you can watch the chic habitués of the neighbourhood go by. The menu is 49F, plus 15% service and drink, so it's not cheap. Nice céleri remoulade, or a good helping of fine pâté; then beautifully grilled entrecôte with frites. The desserts were extra-special, tasted homemade . . . prunes soaked in wine, and the best crème caramel.' Open noon to 3:30 p.m., 7:00 to 10:00 p.m., seven days a week. No annual closing, open on holidays – this all adds up to a very special place.

17e arrondissement

Jacky Loize

17 rue Biot, 17e
Métro: Place de Clichy

Most restaurants in this Montmartre neighbourhood are to be shunned, as the cooking is usually indifferent, the prices nonsensical, the attitude towards travellers almost contemptuous. This one, recommended by a Paris friend, seems to be the exception. The menu is short but very good, with starters such as carottes rapées, sardines in olive oil, or garlic sausage; followed by trout meunière or steak with fresh un-greasy frites, or very good, unusual sausages from Brittany. Linen napkins, a rose on the table, and our information is the trout was large and cooked to perfection, served with steamed potatoes, parsley and butter, and the crème caramel was double the usual serving and very caramelly. All for 50F, with service but not wine. A quarter-litre of red is 4F, white wine as usual more expensive. Open noon to 2:00 p.m., 7:30 to 9:00 p.m., no weekly or annual closing, but between 1 July and 15 August they close on Sundays.

18e arrondissement

Au Caprice No. 4

4 rue de Caulaincourt, 18e
Métro: Place de Clichy

A nice little maman-et-papa café, decorated with flowers and plants, and away from the more raucous parts of this otherwise rip-off neighbourhood. A three-course menu for 39F includes service, but not drink: you are offered crudités, tomato salad or oeuf mayo, then steak in mustard sauce, grilled andouillettes, fish with good lemon mayonnaise or cold ham and potato salad or frites, ending with a peach compôte or ice-cream (no cheese offered). The à la carte menu is inexpensive, but of course you must add 15% service to its prices. Open noon to 2:00 p.m., 7:00 to 10:00 p.m., closed Wednesdays and 1 August to about 5 September. For a light Sunday supper, it's a delight – airy, clean, and friendly beyond words.

Le Fait-Tout

4 rue Dancourt, 18e
Métro: Anvers, Pigalle

The rue Dancourt is a short street leading up to the peaceful and pretty place Charles-Dullin, and it has several small restaurants. Le Fait-Tout is family-run, clean and simple and pretty, with wooden tables and benches, flowers on tables. The food is fairly conventional (such first courses as terrine de lapin or herring fillets, then steak or roast veal or chicken, finishing with fruit tart or fresh fruit salad or the usual ice cream or crème caramel), at 36F plus service and drink. About 52F *tout compris*, which is fairly remarkable so near Pigalle. A menu with more interesting choices is 46F, plus service and drink. As they are open 365 days a year, it could be useful. Lunch from noon to 2:30, dinner 6:00 to 11:00 p.m.

19e arrondissement

Au Petit Laumière

avenue de Laumière, 19e
Métro: Laumière

A friendly, clean, and very French neighbourhood restaurant that is only one Métro stop from Stalingrad, convenient if you have come on a Euroways coach (p.20). Usually, it's packed with people who work nearby and lunch here on the 41F20 menu which includes service and drink. At night, the price is the same, and the diners are usually those who live nearby and find it's easier than cooking at home, and not that much more costly. No wonder: you can pick from seven choices of hors d'oeuvres, eight or ten main dishes such as duck with orange sauce and steamed potatoes, steak cheval (this is *not* horsemeat, but a usually super-expensive dish), then some unusual cheeses or tartes, gâteaux and so forth. The *patronne* is at the bar, and if you make the first conversational move she's most friendly. The lovely avenue de Laumière leads you to the gates of Parc des Buttes Chaumont, see p.133. Lunch, noon to 3:30 p.m., dinner 6:00 to 9:20 p.m. – not a misprint for 9:30! Closed Sundays, open on holidays, no annual closing.

20e arrondissement

Mère Grand'

20 rue Orfila, 20e
Métro: Gambetta

Sadly, this will probably be the last year in *Pauper's Paris* for this lovely little restaurant – which has been written about three times in three years by the very critical Gault-Millau team. Its lunch prices have leapt up to 56F, *tout compris*, and at night a meal costs 86F. Still, it's very good value for hearty eaters on a special night out. Begin with stuffed vine leaves, and continue with large portions of roast beef or chicken, then a selection of really perfect cheeses or unusual pastries. It's not far from Père Lachaise, if you've been indulging your melancholy. Open noon to 2:00 p.m., 6:45 to 8:30, Monday through Saturday. Closed in August.

'Le Self' – yes or no?

As the pace of Paris life becomes faster, self-service groups are proliferating, and they're a very good bet if you want to eat à la carte, inexpensively, and without the usual hour and a half over lunch. The great advantage of *les Selfs* is that if you have a fancy for making a meal of starters instead of a main dish, it's easy and cheap: ideal for vegetarians. The disadvantage is that if you let yourself go among the rather dazzling choices you can spend as much in a *Self* as in a prettier, more comfortable restaurant with some character.

The best-known *Selfs* in such fashionable venues as the rue de Rivoli and around the Louvre are distinctly *not* good value for money. They are over-praised, over-crowded and over-priced, and especially at lunchtime can be more of an ordeal than a pleasure.

However, there are a number of lesser-known *Selfs* which can be an agreeable surprise to anyone whose idea of a self-service place is based on McDonald's. Can you believe a meal that begins with stuffed avocado with shrimp (7F50), goes on to steak au poivre with a heap of crisp frites (18F), and ends (if your liver holds out), with a coupe chantilly – fruit salad with whipped cream, at 7F. Add a quarter-litre of drinkable wine for 4F50, and a piece of bread, 2F, and the whole really luxurious meal comes to only about 40F. These were the most expensive choices in a really nice *Self*. The quality was higher than many neighbourhood restaurants could have provided on prix-fixe menus. In one good *Self*, a complete meal – starter, main course, salad, bread, dessert and wine, beer or mineral water – was only 37F, in a clean, bright, air-conditioned room.

Les Selfs are, on the whole, quite attractive though without much character in the decoration. At lunchtime, they are lively with chatter and laughter; not so gay in the evening when those who eat there tend to be, as in any big city, people who haven't much else to do. Certainly they are worth trying, especially on a day when you are going to be extravagant elsewhere with museum entrance fees, theatre tickets or a spot of shopping. Try these:

Samaritaine

19 rue de la Monnaie, 1er
Métro: Louvre or Pont Neuf

For lunch or snacks, in the big department store – go early and get a table near the window, for the astounding view across the river and over the city. The food is very good and reasonably priced. A steak with frites at 25F was tender and cooked just right, mushrooms in a spicy red sauce for a starter were good and the blueberry pie with whipped cream, 9F50, pleased even an American friend in Paris. Open 11:30 a.m. to 6:30 p.m., but the earlier the better at lunchtime as it gets very crowded and the best choices go quickly.

Le Self Bourse

8 rue St Marc, 2e
Métro: Bourse

Crowded with young stockbrokers and their secretaries, who read company reports while tucking into things like poulet basquaise for 20F, bouchées à la reine (chicken and mushrooms in flaky pastry) 20F, roast veal with potatoes and vegetables, 22F80, and drinking what a poor but aspiring young French lawyer called 'a not bad young Côte du Rhône' for 5F the quarter-litre. A 3-course *menu conseillé* is only 42F50. Open 10:30 a.m. to 3:00 p.m., closed Saturdays, Sundays, holidays. No annual closing.

Le Self Panoramique

12 rue de Rome, 8e
Métro: St-Lazare

For lunch or supper. The food is very good, with especially fine salads, hors-d'oeuvres, and quarter-litres of wine better than you would find in most small restaurants. A good meal, with everything from start to finish, and drink, for about 32F. 11:00 a.m. to 8:45 p.m. seven days a week including public holidays! And a fine view of the street-life below.

La Petite Bouchée

24 rue de la Pepiniere, 8e
Métro: St-Lazare

This must be the classiest small 'self' of Paris, a charming little room up the stairs from the useful snack bar Pomme de Pain. It is wall-to-wall with well-dressed young secretaries and office workers from the quartier, who are both value- and figure-conscious – many good salads for about 18–22F, well-prepared grills and vegetables. A three-course meal would cost about 38F. Open 11:30 a.m. to 3:00 p.m., closed Sundays.

Baltazar

rue René Boulanger
corner rue de Lancry and boulevard St-Martin, 10e
Métro: République

If we had to choose one 'self', this would be it. The walls are papered with enlargements of the 18th-century Plan Turgot of Paris, and there is a small outside terrace in the triangle where three streets meet. A large chef's salad with ham, chicken, tomatoes, cheese and excellent crisp greens was 20F, 'the best couscous', says an enthusiastic couscous eater, 21F. Many starters and desserts to choose from, and coffee brought to your table for 2F60 – better than most 5–6F coffees in bars and tabacs. Open every day of the year, from 11:00 a.m. to 9:30 p.m.

Self-Service de Paris Monte Carlo

9 avenue de Wagram, 17e
Métro: Charles de Gaulle-Étoile

Incredibly, this *Self* in the glossy Champs-Élysées district is open from 11:30 a.m. to 10:00 p.m., 365 days a year – something worth knowing on Christmas or New Year's day when you are truly stuck. The food isn't all that distinguished, but much better than in English or American cafeterias: tender grilled faux filet steak 29F50 is the most expensive, other hot main dishes 15–25F, hors-d'oeuvres from 4F50, and desserts including good fresh fruit salads 8–15F. A complete 3-course meal could cost as little as 38F, including a quarter-litre of wine for 4F50.

Take-away – all of rue Huchette, 5e

Métro: St-Michel

The street of take-away food: delicious charcoal-grilled souvlakia (skewered lamb and vegetables) or shawarma (barbecued, thinly sliced spiced lamb), both in pita bread, at Meteora. Next door, Aux Trois Amis, pick up a container of frites, and sweet Mideast pastries. El Hammamat offers for 8F50 a sandwich tunisien (tuna, olives, tomatoes, peppers, lettuce, and the usual blazing sauce, in a hard roll). Le Minos Snack has Greek and Middle Eastern sandwiches. Au Gargantua, corner of rue de la Harpe, has giant pan bagna (huge roll stuffed with salade niçoise and olive oil) for 9F; big sandwiches of ham or gruyère in French bread, 7F80. You can take all of this to the nearby park in the rue de la Bûcherie. Open every day except major holidays.

M. Benvisti

boulevard de Belleville, near rue Ramponeau, 20e
Métro: Belleville

Food in the extraordinary quarter called Belleville – the Arab and old Jewish Paris – is dealt with at greater length in 'Getting around', (pp.51–2). Tunisian-Jewish take-away called M. Benvisti. You tell the cashier what you want, pay him, and then take a ticket to the counter where they make with great speed huge sandwiches crammed with tuna, olives, capers, cucumber, tomato, and a blazing hot sauce slopped over it all for 12F. Ask for sandwich tunisien or have an assiette tunisienne, same things, on a plate, plus 'brik à l'oeuf' which is the delicious Tunisian pastry with fried egg inside, for 16F, to eat at a sort of stand-up counter. Also available to take away: five kinds of olives, capers, hot peppers, everything to make a great antipasto lunch with a loaf of bread – and beautiful very sweet Arab pastries. Open from about 10:00 a.m. to 9:00 p.m., closed Saturdays.

Les spectacles
(Sights and sounds)

The number one attraction in Paris is Paris. A little footwork can provide all the entertainment you need. Parisians have always relied on their feet for diversion – there's a Parisian art of strolling – the city is inexhaustibly explorable. For a few possibilities, see the chapter on 'Getting around' (p.36).

For incomparable theatre, there are the Parisians themselves. They dress distinctively, and carry themselves with a certain air; they have a highly developed vocabulary of gesture; their voices range from a croak to a twitter; they love to see and be seen. Almost any place will do for Paris- and Parisian-watching: park benches, Métro stations, the *zincs* in local cafés, outdoor markets. It's up to you to be receptive.

Should street-life pall, there are other, more organized entertainments – a surprising number of them free, or very cheap.

Paris parks

There are dozens of parks scattered through the city: tiny, intimate parks in the shadow of churches; parks that are 'wild' and rambling in a curiously artificial and very French way; vast, arid, formal parks consisting of gravel and neoclassical sculpture. All are meticulously kept. Here are a few (you'll find many more yourself):

Jardin des Plantes

bounded by the Seine and the rue Geoffroy-St-Hilaire, 5e
Métro: Jussieu, Gare d'Austerlitz or Place Monge

Part formal garden – minimal grass – part botanical station, with some lush peripheral areas. Contains the Natural History Museum and the Ménagerie. The latter, like every other 'caged' zoo in the world is dismal, smelly, and to be avoided.

Parc de Monceau

boulevard de Courcelles, 8e
Métro: Monceau

Large, full of artificial waterfalls and ponds, glades, romantic statuary. Like most upper-echelon Paris parks, good nanny territory. Two steps away, at 63 rue de Monceau (southern edge of the park), is the Musée Nissim de Camondo: an 18th-century mansion, preserved inside and out.

Square des Batignolles

directly behind Église Ste-Marie-des-Batignolles, 17e
Métro: Brochant, and a fair walk

A charming, unpretentious park in a quiet neighbourhood, with duckponds and a population of elderly park-sitters. The low iron fencing along the paths resembles a lattice of bent twigs – a reminder of the French love for 'natural' artifice.

Parc des Buttes Chaumont

bounded by the rue Manin and the rue Botzaris, 19e
Métro: Buttes-Chaumont

This is a park which most tourists miss because it is so out of the way – a pity, because it is charming. Set on a hillside in the not very fashionable 19e, it was created by Baron Haussmann in response to his monarch's love for anything English. It was once a much more sinister place, where corpses blackened on the gibbet of Montfaucon in the Middle Ages; later a slaughterhouse for horses, finally a general rubbish-heap. The gypsum gave Haussmann the idea of making rock gardens *à l'anglaise*, and there it is, a perfect and peaceful park, only slightly twee.

It's rich in waterfalls, grottoes, rustic chalets, a fake-Greek temple, even fishponds (for which you need a permit from the gendarmerie). It's sixty acres of lovely strolling and picnicking ground, with a fresh breeze always blowing. If you have been in Belleville in the neighbouring 20e, and have collected a sandwich tunisien and a bottle of beer for lunch, get on the No. 26 bus heading towards St-Lazare, step off at the Botzaris-Buttes-Chaumont stop, and find a sheltered grotto for lunch. Even the local dogs, which run to neatly clipped poodles and brushed spaniels, have good manners, and despite the English look of the park, people walk lightly, if at all, on the tidy grass.

Bois de Boulogne

from Porte d'Auteuil to Porte Maillot, 16e
Métro: Porte de Neuilly, Porte Dauphine or Les Sablons

When Parisians say 'Le Bois', they are referring to this park. It's a 19th-century creation, roughly modelled on Hyde Park, at the suggestion of that passionate Anglophile Napoleon III. Its history as a green wooded space dates back centuries, to the days when it stood just inside the fortified boundary of Paris. It was a favourite duelling-ground until, and even after, that sport of the court was outlawed by Louis XIV. Now it is 2000 acres of beautiful, varied, country-like terrain: with one museum, two world-famous race courses, a small zoo, a rose garden, a polo ground, a 'Shakespeare Garden' where grow all the plants mentioned in his plays, two lakes, broad avenues for riding, paths for biking. One can literally live in the Bois – there are camping grounds for tents and caravans.

Of the Métros which serve the Bois, Les Sablons takes you closest to the charming Jardin d'Acclimatation with its little zoo and playground. And one of the most delightful of Paris museums is nearby: the Musée des Arts et Traditions Populaires. This is great for a rainy day; a compendium of everything from country crafts (butter moulds, bee-keeping), to games (*boules*, royal tennis), to bagpipes, Breton headdresses, lace, sixteenth-century toys – the list is endless.

Boats in the Bois can be hired by the hour, at an office near the Lac Inférieur, and the pretty little man-made islands can be visited. Take a picnic: and stay away from the restaurants, which are calculated for the rich.

The exquisite park of Bagatelle, within the Bois, is nearly 60 acres surrounding a fairy-tale palace, and in June it is a paradise of roses. Sir Richard Wallace, said to have been the illegitimate son of the Marquis of Hertford (and a passionate lover of Paris), lived here.

In the daytime the Bois is peopled with strollers, dog-walkers, kite-flyers, riders, cyclists, lovers, and dreamers. But at night it's a different story. Stay away. It's not romantic even in moonlight, and it's very, very dangerous. For years it was the pickup place for certain kinds of Paris prostitutes. The latest group of *les girls* turns out to be South American transvestites. Vandalism and violent crime have taken over the Bois at night.

Bateaux-Mouches

Glass-enclosed excursion boats glide up and down the Seine for about an hour, under various names but generically called Bateaux Mouches.

Bateaux-Mouches: from the Pont de l'Alma, right bank (*Métro*: Alma-Marceau), every half hour. From 10:00 a.m. to noon, then from 2:00 p.m. to 6:00 p.m. 20 F. From 8:30 p.m. to 10:00 p.m, 25F.

Bateaux-Vedettes Pont Neuf: from the Square du Vert-Galant on the Ile de la Cité, (*Métro*: Pont Neuf): every thirty minutes from 10:00 a.m. to noon, then 1:30 to 6:30 p.m. 20F. Evening cruises at 9:00, 10:00 and 10:30, 25F.

Cemeteries

A taste for these is not as macabre as you think (but it does help to go on a rainy day. If you're depressed, they're great places to wallow in despair). There are at least thirteen within the city limits. The best known, and the best for browsing, is **Père Lachaise** (you could win bets as to its real name, which is Cimetière de l'Est). Bounded on two sides by the avenue Gambetta and the boulevard de Ménilmontant; *Métro*: Père Lachaise. It consists of 19th- and 20th-century tombs and sepulchres: some mouldering and decrepit;

some sprucely cared for; some distinctly spooky; others – shiny
granite and plastic photographs – very sentimental. Here lie Colette,
Proust, Wilde, Chopin, Hugo, Balzac, Piaf, Gertrude Stein. And
Jim Morrison. On sunny days the cats come out to bask on the
tombeaux. A map of the cemetery is 1F from the gendarme at the
gate.

If you haven't exhausted your taste for the illustrious dead, your
next stop should be the **Cimetière de Montmartre** in rue Caulaincourt, 18e; *Métro*: Place de Clichy or La Fourche. Contents: Dumas
père (where is *fils?*), Stendhal, Berlioz, Fragonard, Baudelaire.

Open air markets

As you must have gathered by now, food is an object of worship in
Paris. It's appreciated on the plate, and almost as much on the
hoof. Paris abounds with open air markets where everything is
displayed to perfection: fruits and vegetables placed just so; incredible conglomerations of fish and shellfish; poultry and game hung
disconcertingly at eye level. There's nothing antiseptic about the
markets, and nothing haphazard – the stall proprietors are there to
sell (voices that can be heard streets away), and those who come
to buy are determined to get the best. It's hard to know whether
to look at the sellers, the clients, or the merchandise.

Street markets are liveliest on Saturday mornings, often open on
Sundays before lunch, usually closed Mondays. Some of the best,
although not best known:

rue de Lévis, 17e	*Métro*: Villiers
place Monge, 5e	*Métro*: Place Monge
rue de Belleville, 19e	*Métro*: Pyrénées or Belleville
Sundays, 9:00 to noon	
place d'Aligre, 12e	*Métro*: Ledru-Rollin

A big covered market, with outdoor stalls and a flea market
outside. See pp.190–1.

marché Sécretan, avenue   *Métro*: Jean-Jaurès
Sécretan between place de
Stalingrad and rue de
Meaux, 19e
More raucous and infinitely more real and interesting than the
better-known ones; especially Sundays from 9:00 a.m. to noon.

rue de Buci, 6e   *Métro*: St-Germain-des-Prés
   Over-photographed, over-publicized, but still a knock-out. Prices
   tend to be high.

marché de la Madeleine, 8e   *Métro*: Madeleine or St-Lazare
   At the bottom of an office building, this enclosed market is
   entered from rue de Castellane, between rue Tronchet and rue
   de l'Arcade, and is a little world in itself. Tuesday to Saturday
   from about 9:00 a.m. until about 6:30 p.m.; and a little, inexpensive Tonkinese counter restaurant for lunch.

Window-shopping

Food

For museum-quality displays, go to Fauchon, *the* de luxe shop which
faces two sides of the place de la Madeleine, 8e (*Métro*: Madeleine).
Early morning is best, when the terrines and pâtés are arranged in
the window, the crayfish and lobsters set out. Unbelievable gelées,
pâtisserie, arrangements of bread, displays of wine, cheeses you
never dreamed of. On the opposite side of the Madeleine is Hédiard
– smaller, more compact, and just as expensive. Michel Guérard,
known for Nouvelle Cuisine, has a glamorous shop nearby, and,
unbelievably, a cafeteria.

   Exquisite pâtisseries and charcuteries can be found all over Paris,
in the most surprising *quartiers*, some that are nearly slums. No one
hesitates to spend five minutes or more peering in the window,
choosing one pastry or a *tranche* of a wild boar terrine. One wonders
how all this intricately decorated food ever gets eaten, much less
prepared from day to day. A partial answer is the restaurant trade:
the thousands of restaurants large and small rely on the shops of
their *quartier* for the day's terrines and tartes. Somehow, Parisians
have overlooked the idea of mass-marketed, prefabricated victuals,
and they do seem to be happy in their ignorance.

Clothes

As you know, they are of vital importance to the French sense of
self-esteem and to their economy. The couturiers' windows are
accordingly magnificent. Whether sedate or outrageous, they

display their wares beautifully, imaginatively, both inside and in the windows of the great houses. The smaller boutiques, too, have a fresh and lively approach to display. The department stores, however, in comparison to almost any American store and some English ones, are a dead loss – frozen in the display techniques of the 1950s. The only worthwhile window among them is the dome of the Galeries Lafayette, and that's spectacular.

Walk up the rue Royale, along the rue du Faubourg-St-Honoré, along the side streets and avenues of St-Germain-des-Prés, along the avenue Matignon, the avenue du Pierre-Premier-de-Serbie, the rue Boissy d'Anglas, and you come away reeling with the great inventive talent and daring of Hermès, Cardin, Chanel, Dior, St Laurent, Givenchy. It costs you nothing to look in the windows of Cartier, Bulgari, Van Cleef and Arpels, and unconsciously you are absorbing what makes for elegance, quality and flair.

Antique shopping

The pleasure of 'antiqueing' in Paris, too, is for the eye only. Prices are high and rising, as the rich take their panic money out of gold and put it into irreplaceable objects of beauty and luxury. So consider the time you dally in front of windows or in shops as part of your education in what constitutes value in craftsmanship and materials.

If you love antiques and want to see an incredible collection all under one roof, an obvious but good answer is Le Louvre des Antiquaires, in the place Palais Royal, 1er. This three-storey building is a mass of showrooms run by some of the best-known dealers of Paris. Unless you are conspicuously well-dressed, don't expect much attention or friendliness from the dealers: they know their customers, and are fairly sure as soon as they set eyes on you that you're not a prospect. (However, a rich friend with one foot in Oklahoma and the other in Eaton Square – in her jeans and ski-jacket – gave them something of a comeuppance one year when she bought an art deco table for 30,000F in cash, after having been ignored by the dealer for an hour and a half as she wandered around the room. Being wealthy and secure in herself, she bargained him down from 35,000F. It just shows.)

The back streets of the Marais, around the rue des Francs-Bourgeois, are beginning to be lined with elegant small antique shops, but here again you will find few if any bargains. Look, too, at the new Village St-Paul, in the rue St-Paul near the Seine (4e), a beautifully reconstructed cluster of grey stone mansions now housing some lovely shops. Then cross to the Left Bank, and wander around the side streets that make up the St-Germain-des-Prés area: rue Jacob, rue Furstenberg, rue du Bac, rue des Beaux Arts, rue de l'Université.

In the more rarefied reaches of the 7e, you'll find the Village Suisse – a collection of rather expensive dealers – at 78 avenue de Suffren (*Métro*: La Motte-Picquet), open Thursday to Monday, 11:00 a.m. to 7:00 p.m.

What is conspicuously missing in Paris is fine antique silver: much of the best table silver and decorative pieces owned by the aristocracy and the rich bourgeoisie were melted down to pay for the wars of Louis XIV, and most of what remained went into the fires of the Revolution. The few pieces that escaped are now in museums. You will now find that the best silver on offer is elaborate late-nineteenth-century work, a few fine art nouveau pieces – and more available – some of the chic, stark creations of the 1930s, at prices about one-third *more* than a London or New York dealer would charge. You may be lucky in a flea market or a small semi-junk shop, but don't bet on it.

Again, all this comes under the general heading of education. Remember, too, that if you find anything you like and can afford, and it's too big to go in your luggage, you will have to deal with shipping, insurance, customs, and collection at the other end, which can easily double the original price.

The flower markets

If it's not food, clothes, paintings that separate Parisians from the rest of the world, maybe it's their intoxication with flowers. The flower shops and stalls are fantasies of scent, colour, life, and the sort of instinctive flair for arrangement of even quite humble flowers that is absolutely French. The markets are found on the Ile de la Cité, at the back of the Madeleine (8e, *Métro*: Madeleine), and at the place des Ternes. The first two are thick with tourists in high summer, but don't let that deter you. The place des Ternes is well off the tourist beat and has a fine street-market as well as flower stalls. A few blossoms in a water glass or Perrier bottle will cheer up your hotel room.

Plants: walk along the quai de la Mégisserie, 1er (*Métro*: Pont Neuf), if you want to see how the French approach the whole question of gardening, with an emphasis on windowbox plants, kitchen and herb gardens, small-scale city adornment. One of the great seedsmen of Europe, Vilmorin, has a big shop here. A packet of real French basil grown from their seed seems to have a special flavour which may be more in the imagination than in reality (but check to see if your country allows you to import seeds). A Paris-wise pauper bought a little pot of chives and kept it in her very humble hotel room for two weeks, using it to liven up salad lunches and cream cheeses when she was having a more than usually flat-broke period. Weekdays only.

Ducks, deer, swans: also on the Quai de le Mégisserie are the caged animals, birds, tortoises, domestic and wild fowls – which can break your heart. Two swans in a cage; a miniature deer for some rich child's private zoo; even the chickens are pitiable. Week-days only.

Museums

Paris glories in the existence of nearly a hundred museums: from the largest in the world (the Louvre) to one of the most specialized, which displays only the crystal of Baccarat. Many are in the area of central Paris (see museum map, pp.240–1), others within half an hour's travel on the Métro, bus or RER express lines. Some are small and exquisite and so highly specialized that in their best week they get no more than a dozen visitors. Some are great private houses now open to the public, worth seeing even if you didn't look at the contents. One of the most extraordinary, the Musée Nissim de Camondo, is a frozen slice of eighteenth-century France, created by the grieving parents of a First World War hero. Still another has an enticing collection of mechanical toys and clockwork gadgets. There are not one but *two* modern museums in Paris, while poor London struggles on without any.

Most of the major Paris museums are free or half price on Sunday. Some give discounts to students (an International Student Identity Card helps) and to those under or over a certain age. Details under each museum mentioned. If you're under 18 or over 60 (women) or 65 (men), show your passport and ask for *demi-tarif* which cuts museum charges in half. Two elderly friends of ours were admitted free to the Petit Palais on production of passports.

It's true that almost every museum charges an entrance fee, and if you are a conscientious pauper used to the generous free museums of Britain, this comes as a shock. Brace yourself, do without lunch if you must, but either pay the sum asked or wear yourself out on Sundays. You will be rewarded in every sense by the thrill of the beautiful, the odd, the heart-warming or the blood-chilling.

Most museums close on Tuesdays, a few on Mondays, some both days. A few are open on public holidays but most are closed. All are near a Métro stop or within five minutes' walk. All have free cloakrooms (obligatory) for carrier bags, umbrellas, briefcases, but they won't take anything that holds money, jewellery, passport or camera. Some let you take photographs, some forbid flash equipment. Check for rules when you go, as they change from time to time.

Most Paris museums, as one would expect from the general French attitude towards civilized comfort, have benches or chairs on which to fall when your feet, eyes and mind give out. The attendants on the whole give good directions as to what's where, and will do their best to answer questions in English. They have eyes in the backs of their heads and voices that when raised can cut like a laser beam. Don't touch, don't breathe on, don't put a finger near the surface of a painting or a sculpture unless you are prepared for a loud metallic French shout.

Be prepared to queue for admission to the Louvre, and to the Jeu de Paume (Impressionists, Post-Impressionists), and to any major exhibitions which may be open. For these, take along a thermos of coffee and sandwiches to sustain you: for the Manet exhibition at the Grand Palais in 1983 and the Renoir show of 1985, people stood for three hours in cold, rain or heat before they could even get to the ticket window. This can leave you too exhausted to enjoy what you came to see. Sometimes queues are shorter at lunchtime, or when an exhibition has just opened and is not yet highly publicized.

The museums listed and described in this section include our own personal guide to the lesser-known ones as well as the more popular leaders.

1er arrondissement

The Louvre

Métro: Palais Royal or Louvre

Hours: 9:45 to 5:00 for some rooms, to 6:30 p.m. for others, every day but Tuesday and major public holidays. On Mondays and Wednesdays all rooms are open.
Admission: 16F weekdays, 8F for under-25s and over-65s. Sundays free.

To avoid the unbelievable queues at the main entrance of the Louvre – made worse in the past two years by the construction of the controversial glass pyramid in the Cour Carrée – make for the Porte Jaujard in the west wing of the Louvre, or for the riverside Porte Barbet de Jouy. There's a tiny lift in the Pavillion de Flore, (Porte Jaujard), and you walk through the first floor back to the main building to see the most famous paintings. (But don't carry anything that must be left in the cloakroom, as if you do, you'll have to walk all the way back to collect it!)

Because of staff shortages and a lot of reorganization, some rooms and wings are closed on certain days but the major collections are always on view. The big three (Winged Victory of Samothrace, Venus de Milo, Mona Lisa) may be over-exposed, but certainly at least on your first visit to the Louvre, you must see them. For the rest, you'll need one of the many well-produced catalogues, on sale on the ground floor of the museum, and at the bookstall on the first floor. A guided tour, booked in the main entrance hall, isn't a bad way to spend money on your first visit. After that you will home in on your favourites – the Poussins, the Chardins, the Rembrandts, the Italian primitives.

The shop that sells posters, postcards, and reproductions of some Louvre treasures is on the ground floor. The best way to reach it is by the riverside (Barbet de Jouy) entrance. The loos of the Louvre are free, very clean, and located just inside the riverside entrance, so you can avoid the endless lines at the main entrance.

There's a snack and tea bar of sorts on the first floor, but it's expensive and not very good, only to be considered if you're parched with culture and numb in the feet.

If you had but one day in Paris (or one lifetime) the Louvre would be the one indispensable museum. You could move in with camp bed and food for months and probably never get to the end of this great city within a city. Set on the site of royal palaces that date back to the twelfth century, the Louvre stretches over acres along the Seine. Much of the present structure is 'new', as things Parisian go. Both the great Napoleon and the later, lesser Louis-Napoleon had a hand in building or reconstructing. François I was the first royal collector – or looter – in the sixteenth century. He picked up trifles like Giottos, Leonardos, Veroneses on his way through Italy and Spain.

The incredible Egyptian collections owe their existence to the Napoleonic campaigns. Louis XIV housed most of his 'finds' at Versailles, but after his death they were dispersed, some to the Luxembourg Palace but most to the royal palace of the Louvre. After 1798, the Louvre became the Central Museum of the Arts of the infant republic, and was almost at once opened to the public.

This is a sketchy description of what may be the world's greatest museum: to do it justice the rest of this book would have to be dropped. Go early in the morning, go often, leave before you develop visual fatigue. Remember that if you are lucky you will return to it many times in the future.

The Jeu de Paume

place de la Concorde, 1er
Métro: Concorde or Tuileries

Hours: 9:45 a.m. to 5:15 p.m. every day except Tuesdays and major public holidays. Saturdays and Sundays, 11:30 a.m. to 5:15 p.m.

Admission: 16F on weekdays, 8F Sundays. 8F for under 18 and over 65 years, on production of passport.

It's a classic irony of the art world that the young tearaways who provoked Paris with their blurs and splotches in the middle of the nineteenth century are now the Old Masters of the art auctions. The pyrotechnic publicity of the 1970s when the prices of Gauguins, Van Goghs and Monets were on the front pages has brought endless crowds to the Jeu de Paume, partly wondering what all the fuss is about, partly captivated by the radiance that glows from the walls. Not one painting in the museum should be missed. But there are some that draw all eyes: the Cézannes, the Manet 'Déjeuner sur l'Herbe', Van Gogh's sunflowers and his room at Arles, Rousseau's sinister snake charmer. In 1986 all these treasures, and more, will move to the more spacious Musée d'Orsay on the Left Bank, which is now being renovated in an old disused railway station.

The Orangerie

place de la Concorde, 1er
Métro: Concorde

Hours: 9:45 a.m. to 5:15 p.m., every day except Tuesday and major holidays. The Monet 'Nymphéas': 9:45 a.m. to noon, 2:00 to 5:00 p.m.

Admission: 14F, 6F for under 18 and over 65, 6F on Sundays.

A hundred yards closer to the Seine from the Jeu de Paume, this is a museum with (so far) no queues. It houses the Guillaume-Walter collection, mostly early 20th-century paintings, reflecting the highly personal choices of Mme Walter and her two husbands (Paul Guillaume and Jean Walter.) There are 14 ravishing Cézannes, some fine Picassos, many Derains and Soutines, some unusual Douanier Rousseaus – and acres of creamy, satiny, plushy Renoirs. Certainly worth seeing – many critics hated it; those who find out about it seem to love it. The great Monet water-lily paintings (the Salle des Nymphéas) is re-opened, in the Orangerie, and not to be missed.

The Museum of Decorative Art

107 rue de Rivoli, 1er
Métro: Palais Royal

Hours: 12:30 to 6:30 p.m., Tuesdays to Saturday; closed Mondays. Sundays 11:00 a.m. to 5:00 p.m.

Admission: 18F. Reduced price for students, and depending on the mood of the admissions desk, half-price (*demi-tarif*) for over-65s with passport.

A magnificent collection of furniture, tapestries, arts and crafts, books about the decorative arts. It often has fine special exhibitions (early 1981, for example, a show that started with the Middle Ages, took in Art Nouveau and Deco, and ended with modern furniture).

3e arrondissement

Musée Carnavalet

23 rue de Sévigné, 3e
Métro: St-Paul or Chemin-Vert

Hours: 10:00 a.m. to 5:40 p.m., closed Mondays.

Admission: 15F, free on Sundays. Half-price for students. Free for over-65s. These prices may change for special exhibitions here.

Classically elegant 17th-century house in the Marais – almost the oldest continuously-inhabited part of Paris. The Carnavalet is the museum of the City of Paris. History and beauty right back to Roman times, with drawings and scale models of long-vanished streets and squares, and fantastic relics: fans, buckles, tiny satin shoes said to have belonged to Marie Antoinette, jewellery excavated from the Roman settlements of Lutetia (the ancient name of Paris). The garden is lovely too.

4e arrondissement

The Conciergerie

1 quai de l'Horloge, 4e
Métro: Hôtel-de-Ville

Hours: 10:00 a.m. to 6:00 p.m., every day.

Admission: 20F weekdays, 10F Sundays, holidays.

Don't go unless you feel fairly strong. Deep in the huge and pretty formidable Palais de Justice, the Conciergerie puts the Terror of

1789 right at your throat. No matter how you feel about the pre-revolutionary aristos, the sight of Marie Antoinette's cell, and the rooms where philosophers, writers, artists and the nobility waited for death, cannot leave you unaffected.

Musée National d'Art Moderne

Centre National de l'Art et de Culture
Georges Pompidou, 4e (this mouth-filling
title is usually shortened to *Beaubourg*)
Métro: Hôtel-de-Ville or Rambuteau

Hours: Noon to 10:00 p.m. weekdays, 10:00 a.m. to 10:00 p.m. Saturdays and Sundays, closed Tuesdays.

Admission: 13F, 18–25 years, and over 65, 10F. Sundays free. A pass for the entire Beaubourg centre for the day is 25F and lets you enter the museum and all the other shows that otherwise charge separate fees. An annual pass to Beaubourg is 90F, reduced to 65F for those under 18 and over 65 years of age.

A dazzling collection of every important modern painter of the twentieth century. Sit down from time to time to rest and stare, because these paintings aren't meant to soothe the eye or the spirit.
   Beaubourg itself is like a great museum on its own, and much of it is *free*, including the escalator that snakes up the front of the building and gives you an unmatchable view of the city. But the *small* escalator that leads to the big one is narrow, short, and often jammed with queues that even crowd the huge entrance courtyard.

5e arrondissement

Musée de Cluny

6 rue Paul-Painlevé, 5e
Métro: St-Michel

Hours: 9:45 a.m. to 12:30 p.m., 2:00 to 5:15 p.m. Closed Tuesdays.

Admission: 9F weekdays, 4F50 Sundays.

Utterly fascinating medieval monastery buildings which now house one of the world's great collections of arts and crafts of the Middle Ages. Spurs, chastity belts, sculpture, ivories, bronzes – and, except in the high summer months, almost empty of visitors. Often you find yourself in a small dark room staring at some endearing little object that no one has bothered to document or catalogue. And of course, the high point is the haunting tapestry series called, collectively, La Dame Aux Licornes. Bonus: when your feet finally give out, you can hobble a hundred yards to any of twenty inexpensive and good restaurants on and around the boulevard St-Michel.

7e arrondissement

The Invalides

Esplanade des Invalides, 7e
Métro: Invalides, Latour-Maubourg, École Militaire

Hours: 10:00 a.m. to 6:00 p.m.

Admission: 14F; 7F for students and *Carte Vermeil* holders. This ticket entitles you to all three of the museums and to Napoleon's tomb, and can be used on two consecutive days.

The Invalides is a catch-all name for the complex of museums which deal primarily with Napoleon, but also with everything to do with French armies from the shot-torn battle flags of Louis XIV to more modern armour. Napoleon's tomb, under the dome of the Invalides, is majestic, solemn, and always surrounded by a silent, circling group. In summer there's usually a son-et-lumière production. Two performances a night, in English 9:30 and 11:15 p.m., 23F.

Musée d'Orsay

quai Anatole France, 7e
Métro: Chambre des Deputés

This huge new museum is scheduled to open late in 1986, to house art of the nineteenth century, and some of the early twentieth century. Master works in all fields – painting, sculpture, design, architecture, photography, cinema – will be taken from French museums, such as the Jeu de Paume, the Palais de Tokyo and the Petit Palais. But no one museum collection will be totally transferred to the immense new space. In late 1985, work was in progress but the 1986 opening was still debatable. Opening hours not yet set.

Musée Rodin

77 rue de Varenne, 7e
Métro: Varenne

Hours: 10:00 a.m. to 5:45 p.m. Closed Tuesdays.

Admission: 6F, for students, *Carte Vermeil* holders and over-65s on production of passport. Sundays 6F for everyone.

This old and beautiful house in a rather pompous part of Paris holds many of Rodin's most superb works – their power and vigour fairly bursts the walls. More sculpture in the remarkably beautiful garden. And a place to eat in the museum. A nice Paris touch: on the Métro platform at Varenne, lifesize reproductions of the greatest Rodins, and some small ones in a dramatic spotlit glass cage.

8e arrondissement

Musée Nissim de Camondo

63 rue de Monceau, 8e
Métro: Villiers

Hours: 10:00 a.m. to noon and 2:00 to 5:00 p.m., closed Mondays, Tuesdays and holidays.

Admission: 12F; 6F students and with *Carte Vermeil*.

Very quiet: most tourists pass it by, which is their loss. A museum dedicated to the memory of a young aviator shot down in the First World War, which sounds both dull and depressing. Not so. His father, a wealthy art collector, recreated the interior of a house as it would have been done by an eighteenth-century tycoon. French furniture, objets d'art, then were of a luxury and perfection seen nowhere else in the world, and there they are, gleaming with care, love, and polishing, and waiting for the minuet to begin.

Musée du Petit Palais

avenue Winston-Churchill, 8e
Métro: Champs-Élysées-Clemenceau

Hours: 10:00 a.m. to 5:30 p.m., closed Mondays.

Admission: 9F for the museum, usually about 14F for big temporary shows. Students 4F50, Over 65, free on production of passport.

This museum, also often neglected by Paris visitors, has some fine works bequeathed by private collectors – beautiful Manet pastels, Berthe Morisot, Mary Cassatt, Toulouse Lautrec pastels, Bonnard, Vuillard, Cézanne – and historic French furniture, bibelots, clocks and so forth. The peaceful, flowering circular garden is usually deserted; a good place to rest, read, meditate. However, they courteously discourage picnicking so don't try it. Often there are fine temporary exhibitions: check *Pariscope* or street posters.

10e arrondissement

Musée de la Publicité

18 rue de Paradis, 10e
Métro: Château d'Eau

Hours: Noon to 6:00 p.m. Closed Tuesdays.

Admission: 16F, 9F for the unemployed, for students and *Carte Vermeil* holders or over-65s with passport. The ticket admits you to their little *cinémathèque*.

The poster museum has now widened its scope to include all forms of advertising (signs, prints and cinema and TV ads). It sells reproductions of historic French advertising posters, and good postcards. Its own *affiches* are well worth buying for the pure pleasure of the graphic design – something the French have been doing with wit, flair and irony for decades. The admission charge is steep, and the museum is small, so don't go unless you're really interested. The building itself is interesting and you can see *that* free of charge!

12e arrondissement

Musée des Arts Africains et Océaniens

293 avenue Daumesnil, 12e
Métro: Porte Dorée

Hours: 10:00 a.m. to 5:30 p.m., closed Tuesdays.

Admission: 16F weekdays. 8F for students and over-65s. 8F Sundays. It's worth trailing all the way out to this fairly remote part of Paris to find an almost unknown treasure. The arts of black Africa – bold statements in wood, bone, leather, brass – the delicate beauty of carvings and leather from Moslem North Africa – and some gem-like artifacts from the Pacific islands colonized by the French. Poster collectors: don't miss the museum's own magnificent *affiche*.

16e arrondissement

Musée des Enfants

12 avenue de New-York, 16e
Métro: Alma-Marceau

Hours: 10:00 a.m. to 5:30 p.m., closed Mondays.

Admission: 9F; 4F50 for students and *Carte Vermeil* holders. Sundays free. Ticket also admits you to the Modern Museum of the City of Paris, in the same building, which is open the same hours but also on Wednesdays until 8:30 p.m.

An ever-changing delight for children, and for grownups, with dance events, play-groups, paintings, constructions. See *Pariscope* for what's going on when you are there. Whoever runs this museum is rich in imagination and a sense of fun.

Musée Guimet

6 place d'Iéna, 16e
Métro: Iéna

Hours: 9:45 a.m. to noon, 1:30 to 5:15 p.m., closed Tuesdays.

Admission: 12F weekdays, 6F on Sundays, 6F for under-25s and over-65s.

The exact opposite of the Beaubourg Modern Museum: calm, soothing Far Eastern art. The Asiatic Art Collection of the Louvre, and worth return visits if you can afford it – save money with picnic lunches these days. Japanese and Chinese masterworks, irreplaceable sculpture from parts of Cambodia that have vanished for ever in wars, art of India and Pakistan, and an important exhibition on Japanese Buddhism. All rooms open Monday, Wednesday, Friday, but some are closed other days.

Musée Marmottan

2 rue Louis-Boilly, 16e
Métro: La Muette, and about ten minutes' walk through a park

Hours: 10:00 a.m. to 6:00 p.m., closed Mondays and public holidays.

Admission: 18F; 8F for students.

Worth the high price only if you are a Monet fan. Beautifully organized permanent collection, plus many paintings by his artist friends and contemporaries. Often there is an additional exhibition of great interest – check *Pariscope*. Don't miss the touching collection of letters and postcards to friends and patrons, a haunting record of difficulties, illnesses, lack of money.

Musée Moderne de la Ville de Paris

11 avenue du Président-Wilson, 16e
Métro: Iéna

Hours: 10:00 a.m. to 5:30 p.m., closed Mondays. Open until 8:30 p.m. Wednesdays.

Admission: 18F weekdays; 9F for students and over-65s. Free on Sundays. Prices may change for special exhibitions.

This is the modern museum of the city, and always has important shows such as the Modigliani retrospective of spring 1981, as well as good permanent collections. At the sales desk on the ground floor you can find, for as little as 5F, beautiful posters from past years of many Paris galleries (not museums).

18e arrondissement

Musée de Montmartre

12 rue Cortot, 18e
Métro: Lamarck-Caulaincourt; Montmartrobus

Hours: 2:30 to 5:30 p.m. weekdays.

Admission: 10F, students and over-65s, 5F.

An eighteenth-century house crammed with souvenirs of the legendary artists' quarter. The Toulouse-Lautrec posters may have been reproduced on cheap paper a million times, but the originals can still stop you in your tracks. Many drawings, relics, and costumes of the days when Montmartre was a place to be enjoyed, not where one is ripped off as at present.

This list of museums, of course, is the merest scratching of the surface. We have missed out (but you don't have to) such esoteric delights as the Musée Bricard (locks and keys from Roman times to the 1950s, some as fine and intricate as jewellery), the Delacroix and Balzac houses, the Victor Hugo Museum in the place des Vosges, the Grévin (waxworks to make Mme Tussaud melt with envy), and a great crazy one devoted entirely to the art of the counterfeiter. If you can read French and want details of every museum in Paris and the surrounding area, get the brochure *Musées, Expositions, Monuments de Paris et de l'Ile de France*, published every two months by CNMHS, Hôtel de Sully, 62 rue St-Antoine, 4e (*Métro*: St-Paul), and often available from the Tourist Office at 127 Champs-Élysées.

Galleries

Welcoming and forbidding, worthwhile and not to be bothered with. One of the best ways to refresh the eyes without paying entrance fees to museums, or trying to get to all the main museums in the one free day (Sunday).

Most of Paris's galleries are to be found in the avenue de Matignon, the boulevard Haussmann, the rue Miromesnil (establishment art, for the most part, in the 8e), and near Beaubourg and the area around St-Germain (progressive, experimental). Most galleries hibernate in August. Check *Pariscope* or *L'Officiel des Spectacles* for specifics. A few possibilities:

Daniel Templon

30 rue Beaubourg, 3e
Métro: Arts-et-Métiers

Contemporary abstractionists, with emphasis on big American names.

Beaubourg

23 rue du Renard, 4e
Métro: Hôtel-de-Ville

Contemporary European realist painters and sculptors.

Zabriskie

37 rue Quincampoix, 4e
Métro: Rambuteau

Pioneer photography gallery: Arbus, Brassai, Steichen, Strand, Weston, and newer work.

Claude Bernard

5–9 rue des Beaux Arts, 6e
Métro: St-Germain-des-Prés

Contemporary realists, including Bacon, Hockney, Wyeth; and a strong collection of twentieth-century greats.

Dragon

19 rue du Dragon, 6e
Métro: St-Germain-des-Prés

Figurative.

Isy Brachot

35 rue Guénégaud, 6e
Métro: Odéon

Surrealists, current and traditional.

Galerie de Seine

18 rue de Seine, 6e
Métro: Odéon

Contemporary surrealists and abstractionists.

Denise René

196 boulevard St-Germain, 7e
Métro: Bac

Contemporary abstractionists, kinetic art.

Artcurial

9 avenue Matignon, 8e
Métro: Franklin-D.-Roosevelt

Huge complex of galleries: established artists from Max Ernst to David Hockney.

Galerie Maeght

13–14 rue de Téhéran, 8e
Métro: Miromesnil

Large and *very* prestigious.

Cultural centres

You can take advantage of nationalistic self-promotion by attending free, or almost free, events at various cultural centres. Some are dull beyond belief; others – among them the ones listed here – are full of life, even explosive.

Centre Culturel Américain

261 boulevard Raspail, 14e
Tel: 4 321 42 20
Métro: Raspail

Concerts, courses and spectacles, exciting and well organized, with emphasis on the contemporary.

Centre Culturel Britannique

9–11 rue de Constantine, 7e
Tel: 4 555 54 99
Métro: Invalides

Lectures, films and concerts, and a good library. Closed Saturdays and Sundays.

Centre Culturel Canadien

5 rue de Constantine, 7e
Tel: 4 551 35 73
Métro: Invalides

Art galleries, a sculpture garden, a library, and an auditorium
for concerts. Monthly children's concerts. Admission free. Closed
Sundays.

Centre Culturel de la Communauté Française de Belgique

7 rue de Vénise, 4e
Tel: 4 271 26 16
Métro: Les Halles or Rambuteau

Theatre, films, concerts, art shows and dance – burgeoning activity,
from 5F to 30F.

Centre Culturel Latino-Américain

6 rue des Fossés-Saint-Marcel, 5e
Tel: 4 336 56 04
Métro: St-Marcel

Exhibitions, concerts and conferences.

Institut Néerlandais

121 rue de Lille, 7e
Tel: 4 705 85 99
Métro: Bac

Classical music concerts, and Dutch jazz and contemporary music.
Free. Closed Mondays.

Centre Culturel Portugais

51 avenue d'Iéna, 16e
Tel: 4 720 86 84 and 4 720 85 94
Métro: Étoile

Classical music concerts.

Centre Culturel Suédois

11 rue Payenne, 3e
Tel: 4 271 82 20
Métro: St-Paul

Exhibitions, concerts, theatre, film – usually free.

Goethe-Institut

17 avenue d'Iéna, 16e
Tel: 4 723 61 21
Métro: Iéna

German music, film, and art.

Check also (if your interests run in these directions) the cultural centres of Yugoslavia, Egypt, Mexico, Spain, Italy, and Brazil. They're all in the phone book.

Concerts

The French are not the most musical nation on earth, and the dearth of classical music in Paris seems to be worrying quite a lot of people. Compared to London, New York, Manchester, Chicago, Cleveland, it's a bit of a desert. The 'major' composers rank as minor compared to Germans, Austrians, Italians. French popular music is unoriginal, not even a good copy of American or English. But there is music to be found, and more of it every year. Much of it is vastly overpriced, but we've tracked down a number of concerts that are either free, or very nearly so.

In churches

You can hear some of the finest organ music in the world, played in the incomparable settings of Paris churches, often on Sunday afternoons, and it's free. For current listings, check the magazine *Pariscope*, published every Wednesday (3F50).

Maison de la Radio

An orchestra organized by the French National Radio Service (ORTF) often gives free, or very inexpensive, concerts. For details, send a self-addressed stamped envelope to Radio France, 116 avenue du Président-Kennedy, 16e. Or drop in and see what you can find out. *Métro*: Ranelagh or Passy.

Métro music

Classical music students at the Conservatoire National are encouraged by their teachers to learn to perform, not just to practise, and a very good way for them to do so is to pick a spot in a Métro corridor and play for the passers-by. It's a neat way to pick up some change, too. The quality is often exceptionally good, although the acoustics may leave something to be desired. Some fairly good Irish bands, accordionists, provincial flute-and-drum ensembles, and even expatriate American blues and jazz singers also make use of the Métro, and are not to be sneezed at (they're impossible to ignore, anyway).

Beaubourg

The cobblestoned vastness in front of the Georges Pompidou Centre, 3e (*Métro*: Hôtel-de-Ville or Rambuteau) often plays host to musicians of very good standard, mixed in with the mimes and fire-eaters.

Rue de Provence, 9e

Of all unlikely places, a pedestrian square between Au Printemps, the department store, and Prisunic frequently has chamber groups, soloists, or blues or pop singers performing to people sitting on the steps of the nearby church. *Métro*: Havre-Caumartin.

Student discounts: reduction in ticket prices for classical music in the big concert halls is usually available. Check listings in *Pariscope*, or apply with student card to COPAR, 39 avenue Georges-Bernanos, 5e (*Métro*: Port-Royal).

Senior citizens: with the *Carte Vermeil*, which the French generously provide for women over 60 and men over 65 *of any nationality*, discounts for musical events are given. See p.199 for details of this marvellous card. Look for the initials 'CV' in the price listing of any event. Or show your passport at the box office.

Free music – a typical week's offerings*

Carillon concert in the belfry of the Mairie (town hall) of the 1er *arrondissement*.

Pascal Bouret, guitarist, playing at the Carrefour de la Différence 'Les Vendredis Musicaux d'Auber', part of the Festival Estival of Paris, in the Salle des Echanges at the RER station Auber. Pierre-Michel Bedard, organist, at the Chapelle-St Louis de la Salpetrière.

Bach Cantatas, in the Festival Estival, a consort of mediaeval instruments, church of St-Séverin

Flute, violin and clavichord concert at the Carrefour de la Différence. University of California Choir at the American Cathedral, 23 avenue George-V.

American chamber music at the American Church, 65 quai d'Orsay

* See *Pariscope* and *L'Officiel des Spectacles de Paris*, both published Wednesday mornings, for very complete listings of all musical events, and look for the words *Entrée Libre* or *Gratuit*, which means you.

Spectator sports

Racing

There are eight tracks to go to, some literally within the city limits, others within easy reach by a combination of Métro and suburban bus lines or trains. If you can resist betting, a day at a French track with the sun shining, the crowds shrieking and stamping on losing tickets, is an experience not to be missed. You'll also see some very classy animals, hot competition, and a mix of people from working-class to the truly elegant racehorse owners and followers.

The two racecourses at the southern end of the Bois de Boulogne are enchanting. **Longchamp** is by all odds the smartest and most modern. The stands have escalators, tickets are distributed by machine, and if standing in the fresh air bores you, you can even watch the racing by closed circuit television. It's the world's longest track, and said by horsey people to be one of the most difficult. The Prix de l'Arc de Triomphe and the Grand Prix are the great social events – go very early if you hope to get in, and expect to feel like a pariah unless you are perfectly dressed. However, on other days, go for the fun, and the beauty, and try to refrain from betting as, unless you really understand the monumentally complicated French system, you may find that in the end you didn't have your money on the horse you chose at all.

To get to Longchamp, take the Métro to Porte d'Auteuil, then the special bus which costs 7F50 (*Billet de Tourisme* and RATP tickets not valid). Inside the Bois, on the bus route, you will see several gates marked *Pelouse*: entrance here is to the infield, standing among the crowd, and costs 3F. If you stay on to the gate marked *Pesage*, you enter the elegant grandstand which costs 15F weekdays, 30F Sundays and holidays, for unreserved seats on wide bare stone steps. Take a newspaper to sit on, they're dirty.

Here, we recommend splurging on a 15F entrance fee, as the surroundings are beautiful and comfortable, and you can follow the knowledgeable to watch the horses from above the saddling enclosure behind the stands. Take the lift to one of the towers marked 'Restaurant Panoramique' for a most lovely view over the course and the park, and some extremely posh lavatories, free.

Racing at Longchamp goes on from early April to October.

Auteuil, the other racecourse in the Bois, is for steeplechasing, and gets a very mixed crowd (i.e. pickpockets). If you can get there for the Prix des Draggs in early summer, it's one of the best almost-free sights of the world. Admission to the *pelouse* is 2F. Grandstand admission is 12F on weekdays, 20F on Sundays, special prices for big races.

Vincennes, in the Bois de Vincennes at the other end of Paris, is another city track, this time for trotters, which look like something out of Dégas. There's daytime racing all year around; night racing from the end of March to the first week in December – a great way to spend a spring or summer evening. Don't believe anyone who tells you it is a ten-minute walk from the Château; it's fifty minutes dusty or muddy foot-slogging. Get there by RER to Joinville-le-Pont (free with your *Billet de Tourisme*, or a 4F ticket), then about fifteen minutes' walk.

The **Hippodrome** at St-Cloud is reachable in either of two ways: quickly by RER to Rueil station, then by bus 431 to the stop 'Laboratoire Débat' for the *pesage*, or 'Champ des Courses' for the *pelouse*; more slowly, the Métro to Pont de Sèvres, then bus 431 to the stops as above. St-Cloud is the place for flat-racing, a lovely track which attracts lots of fashionable people and famous horses at certain classic races. Last week in February to end of July, then from late September to the end of November.

For information about hours and events, the daily newspapers are a washout. French races are listed not by the time of running as in England, but by the name of the individual race. You must consult *Paris-Turf*, the horsey paper. Do this free by standing at a newspaper kiosk, as banner headlines always give the hour and place of the main events of the day. If you're a serious racegoer, however, buy the paper and get the small leaflet *Calendrier des Courses*, which lists every race meeting and the name (not the hour) of its main events for the entire year. Or pick this up, free, from the offices of *Paris-Turf*, 100 rue Réaumur, 2e (*Métro*: Sentier).

Tennis

Tennis is generating immense interest in Paris: quite a lot of tournaments with some of the world's great players competing. The scene changes so fast that it is impossible to make an accurate listing here, so check the newspapers if you are really that interested (or bored with what Paris itself is offering). The Stade Roland-Garros (*Métro*: Porte d'Auteuil then – during major tournaments – special buses to the stadium) is world famous, but the prices are high, especially for big events, so don't say you weren't warned.

Theatre

The theatre is all but impossible unless you can understand swiftly-spoken French. And it's expensive. Although the Comédie Française has some seats available for as little as 20F, they must be booked a week in advance. The *Carte Vermeil* (p.199) often gets reductions (e.g., 20F at the Théâtre du Chaillot instead of the normal 45F). At the Petit Odéon, students get in for 12F. If you can book two weeks in advance, a seat at the Odéon itself can cost as little as 20F. Or if you're willing to take a chance at 6:30 p.m., seats unsold at the Théâtre de la Ville are available at 25F instead of 28 to 48F. At the Théâtre Aire-Libre de Montparnasse, students and *Carte Vermeil* holders get in for 25F instead of 40F. And *occasionally*, theatres will allow standing-room customers in free, at the last moment. Don't count on it.

The Bouffes du Nord, Peter Brook's triumphant venture into French theatre, is not wildly expensive: 35F to see, for example, his remarkable re-staging (in French) of *The Cherry Orchard*. Starve for a day or two but try to see whatever he is doing. Closed July and August.

At the Cité Universitaire, students and *Carte Vermeil* tickets are 18F. And at the Conservatoire National d'Art Dramatique, productions are *free*.

Look at *Pariscope* every week to see what's on and how much it costs, as this varies, of course, all the time. Many theatres close in summer – they are listed under 'Relâche' in *Le Figaro*.

Circus

The circus is having something of a renaissance in Paris, after several years of quiescence. When last checked, there were about six, of varying standards of cost and interest. This listing is necessarily fallible, as circuses come and circuses go. Have a look at *Le Figaro* or *Pariscope* while you're there. Fortunately, no French is needed to enjoy these spectacles.

Cirque Aréna, square de l'Amiral-Bruix, 16e. *Métro*: Porte Maillot. Tickets from 13 to 40F. Wednesday, Saturday, Sunday and holidays, at 3:00 p.m. Lots of clowns, jugglers, ladies in spangles, on horseback.

Cirque Diana Moreno, cours de Maréchaux, Vincennes. *Métro*: Château de Vincennes. Tickets 30F for adults, 20F for children. Wednesday, Saturday, Sunday, 3:00 p.m.

Cirque de Paris, Porte de Champerret, 17e. *Métro*: Porte de Champerret. Tickets from 15 to 30F. Wednesday, Saturday, Sunday, 3:00 p.m. and every day during French school holidays.

Cirque d'Hiver, 110 rue Amelot, 11e. *Métro*: Filles de Calvaire. Check *Pariscope* to see whether it's running, and if so, when, and how much. Now (1980s) housing musical comedies instead of circuses.

Puppets

Marionetterie, if there is such a word, is a very old French art, and not to be missed. Although the puppet theatres are nominally for *les jeunes*, parents and hangers-on love them too. These are only a few theatres: check *Le Figaro* and *Pariscope* for more.

Marionettes des Champs-Élysées, Jardin du Carré Marigny, 8e. *Métro*: Franklin-D.-Roosevelt. This is the guignol horror show that has entranced kids since the dawn of history. Wednesday, Saturday, Sunday, 3:00 p.m.

Marionettes du Champ de Mars, Esplanade du Champ de Mars, 7e. *Métro*: École Militaire. Every day in summer at 4:30 p.m. – winter performances may be less frequent, check *Pariscope*.

Théâtre du Carreau du Temple, 4 rue Eugène-Spuller, 3e. *Métro*: Temple. Wednesdays, Saturdays, Mondays at 3:00 p.m. – a marionette show put on by the Théâtre de la Lune.

Théâtre Guignol Anatole, Parc des Buttes Chaumont, 19e (entrance in the place Armand-Carrel). *Métro*: Laumière. 3:30 and 4:30 p.m. every day.

Marionettes du Luxembourg, in the Luxembourg Gardens, 6e. *Métro*: Vavin or Notre-Dame-des-Champs.

Théâtre de la Petite Ourse, Tuileries Gardens, 1er. *Métro*: Concorde. Thursday to Sunday at 4:00 p.m.

Note: many children's theatres in Paris do magic shows, plays and pageants. Often there are extra performances during Christmas and Easter holidays, and in the weeks just following the end of the school year. However, many theatres close for 5 to 8 weeks from mid-July to mid-September, so it's best to refer to the current *Pariscope* or *Figaro* for specific information.

Television

French TV is *very* French. If your hotel has a set in the office, breakfast room or lobby, linger and look. When a big soccer match, race or (best of all) the Tour de France, is on, make for the nearest TV dealer and join the crowd which will stand there forever with boos, whistles, groans and some racy French language. The TV news . . . 'speakerines' are chosen for intelligence and wit – they sparkle – eyes, teeth, lipstick and intellect – in the hard brilliant studio lights.

Paris, plus

Versailles

Some of the most alluring places to visit are within an hour or two of Paris by public transport or by fast train. It would be almost illegal to be in Paris and not to see Versailles. This vast complex of parks, palace, and the pavilions known as Les Trianons, is almost impossible to comprehend when you are on the spot. It's wise to collect and study a good small guidebook before you go. The *Blue*

Guide (p.201) has a very good, succinct and easily followed section on the château, the park and gardens, and if you have already invested in it you really won't need another book. Versailles is easy to reach, and if you have the time to do it, go for a few hours three or four times, rather than wearing yourself out mentally and physically by one long visit.

You can reach Versailles free with your Billet de Tourisme, Métro to Pont de Sèvres, then bus 171, but it takes about an hour. SNCF trains from the Invalides station go every 15 minutes and take about half an hour, but be prepared for long queues at the ticket windows, and make sure you go to Versailles Rive Gauche (RG), nowhere else. *Aller-retour* (return) tickets cost 17F50; make sure you get both tickets when you buy.

Half-day all-inclusive tours, by coach, including transport, entrance to major attractions, and guide, are 142F from many ticket agencies, but in our view are to be avoided. You are shoved through at a brisk trot, told where to look, never allowed to lag or sit down, and returned to Paris more dead than alive. You can do the whole thing at your own pace for half the price.

The main treasures of Versailles – the Chapel, the State Apartments of the King and Queen, and the Hall of Mirrors – must be seen by every visitor. The fee for them is 16F, reducing to 8F if you are between 18 and 25 or over 60. Under 18, it's free. On Sundays, everyone gets in for 8F – but NEVER go then, as queues for tickets can stretch half a mile.

The King's Private Bedroom and the Royal Opera can be seen only by guided tour, for 25F, lasting an hour and a half. . . . the guides are wonderful. After the tour, you can see the State Apartments, the Chapel and the Hall of Mirrors by yourself without paying more.

The Queen's Private Rooms and Madame de Maintenon's Apartment are guided tours too, one hour for 20F, after which you can see the rest, as above.

The Grand Trianon costs 12F, but combined with the Petit Trianon it's 15F.

The Lenôtre gardens carved out of the swamp, and the Mansart fountains, a marvel of hydraulic engineering, are 'musts'. If you can visit more than once, don't miss two of the smaller delights: the Musée des Voitures, with its perfectly preserved state coaches, wedding carriages and hunting calèches; and the extraordinary Hameau, the rustic village where Marie Antoinette went on playing at being a country wife up to 1789.

Guided tours of the Versailles Park and Groves are available; information from the Versailles Tourist Office, telephone 4 950 36 22.

The Château and the Grand Trianon are open Tuesday through Saturday from 9:45 a.m. to 5:00 p.m., the Petit Trianon 2:00 to 5:00 only. Everything is closed on Mondays and public holidays.

Chartres

Again, it can be done by taking a fairly pricey tour bus, which gives you cosy shepherding; or, cheaper, more fun, and infinitely more flexible – take the train from Gare de Montparnasse as early as you can and wander round on your own. They run about every 45 minutes from 6:26 in the morning, with the last train back at 10:53 at night. Return fare is 90F (or free with the Eurailpass).

Wander around the town, which is a delight in itself, and absorb the miracle of the cathedral by yourself, through your own eyes, and not blurred by tour-guide patter. Then find a small neighbourhood restaurant, which will be half the price and twice the pleasure of any suggested by an organized group, and eat what you want at a price you want to pay. Or take a picnic. Get a small, good guidebook to Chartres before you leave Paris, and read it on the train. Henry Adams, the nineteenth-century American writer, did rather a good job on both Chartres and Mont-St-Michel.

A coach tour to Chartres costs about 155F, takes 5½ hours (and since it's 88 miles from Paris, travelling time eats into Chartres time); it gives you a view of Rambouillet and Maintenon châteaux on the way, and a guided tour of the cathedral. Various companies do tours on different days, so check with a travel agent for details.

The Monet Gardens – Giverny

A coach tour to the famous water-lily gardens of Monet costs about 125F for half a day from Paris – don't do it, as the bus trip out is intensely boring and the commentary more so, with piped music all the way back. Instead, take the train from St Lazare to Vernon, for 70F and bus to Giverny, pay about 15–20F for admission to the house and gardens, wander freely, picnic, and come back when you choose. The ponds and bridges and flowers are *exactly* as they were painted.

Mont-St-Michel

Once a month, the RATP (Paris Transport) runs a day trip to this dreamlike mountain village rising from the sea. It's not very expensive, it's all in French, and it's an experience you'll never forget. Coaches leave at 7 a.m. and it's a long day. Get brochures about this and other day trips from RATP, 52 quai des Grands Augustins, 6e (*Métro*: St Michel).

Malmaison

A curiously neglected side trip from Paris, except among those who are passionate about Napoleon. This is the château bought and furnished by him, for Josephine, set in most lovely grounds. Nearby is a museum crammed with Bonaparte memorabilia. Take the RER (the high-speed, extra-fare Métro) from Charles-de-Gaulle-Étoile to La Défense, five minutes away, then the 158A bus to the Malmaison-Château stop. Buses run about every fifteen minutes and take about 25 minutes to the bus stop nearest the château, then it's about an eight-minute walk.

The RER station at the Charles-de-Gaulle-Étoile Métro stop is huge, eerie, depopulated, and if you get lost you'll find yourself asking directions from a weary flower-seller. If you have a *Billet de Tourisme*, travel on the RER and the suburban bus line is free. Otherwise, take a ticket from the automatic dispenser (one way). Follow signs marked 'St-Germain-en-Laye' for trains to La Défense. On the 158A bus, if you're travelling without a *Billet de Tourisme*, the fare is one ticket.

Entrance to the château is 9F (4F50 for *Carte Vermeil* and under 18, free on Wednesdays), and you can't wander around: when a little group has collected, a guide appears. The tour takes about an hour and a quarter, it's all in French, so if you are a true Napoleon fan, read the very good entry in the *Blue Guide*. At the end of the tour (which tells you more than you want to know about the history of the porcelain plates and the very banal paintings), give the guide one or two francs. The château is unexpectedly small for such a great man (and the beds are tiny); but for those who expect Napoleon to rise from the dead and take over France, it's very touching. Open 10:00 a.m. to 12:30 p.m., 1:30 to 5:30 p.m. (last visits noon and 5:00 p.m.), closed Tuesdays, public holidays.

À bon marché
(The shops)

Shopping is distinct from window-shopping, though you can combine the two. What you crave in Lanvin or Kenzo can be duplicated or approximated elsewhere at a discount; or found 'once-worn'. You can use Paris to stock up on often outlandish items of food: pickles and conserves that would cost a mint in Soho, available for next to nothing at the Prisunic. Second-hand books, cheap but thrilling gifts, museum prints, and every kind of flea-market hand-me-down. Remember, you've got to fit it all into your luggage and get it home.

Manners: as everywhere, you can go farther and faster on a few elements of *la politesse* and a smile. In some situations, however, no amount of manners will do you the least bit of good. Salespeople in large establishments tend to be more abrupt than in small ones, less willing to help. Solution: know what you're looking for; find out the correct terms (the name of the article, the colour, the size, the brand); do not be browbeaten into buying something you don't want; if one person won't tell you where to find it, try another.

Avoid paying with anything but cash. A bank will always give you a better exchange rate than a shop (or for that matter a hotel or restaurant) for travellers' cheques or foreign currency. Credit cards are billed at the going rate on the date of billing, not the day you used the card, so you'll have only a rough idea of what you spend.

Bargains

Here we include cheap shops – not resale. Paris is a mine of good clothes at less than Paris prices – if you know where to look. The rue St-Placide in the 6e is lined with shops plastered with signs: 'Dégriffés', 'Soldes Permanents', 'Les Prix Dingues'. The rue St-Dominique, in the 7e, is a magnet for bargain hunters. However, be warned that shops in both these streets have a mushroom growth and disappear just as fast. A big vacant shop can be stocked up with clothes for men, women and children, from various sources, do a roaring trade and vanish in six months or less. La Clef des Soldes was a biggish place in the rue St-Dominique a few years ago, specializing in deluxe ready-to-wear for men and women (Cardin, Hechter, etc.). Then it went completely over to sports and ski-wear; the next year it was gone.

This listing is the current crop of good cheapies, all over Paris. Don't write us a letter of reprimand if they've disappeared. We would rather have a letter from you telling us of *your* discoveries, so that we can look them over ourselves and possibly include them in a future edition.

These shops can be fun to fish around in. They often have bins of oddments, or racks of clothes that can be just what you are looking for (equally good chance of nothing but monster coats and dwarf dresses). With patience you can turn up something.

6e arrondissment

Safran

31, rue St-Placide, 6e
Métro: St-Placide, Sèvres-Babylone

Cheap, nice trendy young clothes of current styling. Perpetual sale prices: French Connection tops, 50 to 100F, rails of fashionable Bermuda-length and short shorts 50F. Open Tuesday through Friday, 11:00 a.m. to 7:00 p.m. Saturdays 10:00 to 7:00 p.m. Closed Mondays.

Philomène

34 rue St-Placide, 6e
Métro: St-Placide, Sèvres-Babylone

Look here for leather skirts and trousers, 600–800F, and thick, bright trendy coats for 730F. But avoid copies of the world's most famous raincoat, which are of poor material and cheaply made.

Week End

40 rue St-Placide, 6e
Métro: St-Placide, Sèvres-Babylone

Jam-packed, floor to ceiling, with men's clothes – some smart shirts, some hideous, at 139F and 169F. Suits can be bought for as little as 250F. Open 10:00 a.m. to 6:00 p.m., Monday to Saturday.

Sido

51 rue St-Placide 6e

Fun to browse around in and perhaps pick up some 1930s and 1940s chunky costume jewellery and scarves. Outrageous and theatrical, their stock has been described – hideous or magical according to your point of view.

7e arrondissement

Declic

80 rue St-Dominique, 7e
Métro: Latour-Maubourg

A crazy mixture of clothes and gifts where *Mil Soldes* shop used to be. Pretty sundresses for as little as 99F, as well as things like tureens, vases, and figurines that might appeal for their sheer kitsch value.

Martinelli

116 rue St-Dominique, 7e
Métro: Latour-Maubourg

This shop has pretty cheap shoes for women, and some for men. Its sister shop across the street, *Do Mil Soldes*, is full of bright, young clothes for girls such as a flounced T-shirt dress in three really loud colours at 119F. Closed Monday mornings, otherwise open from about 10:00 a.m. to 7:00 p.m.

Paris pas Cher

11 rue Jean-Nicot, 7e
Métro: Latour-Maubourg

This is the bargain shop of Paris, with tinned food, umbrellas, linoleum, plastic bins, sweaters, enamel cooking pots; the most attractive thing in the window on the last visit was a huge copper preserving pan, tin-lined, for only 130F. Open 10:00 a.m. to 2:00 p.m., 3:00 to 7:15 p.m. Tuesday to Friday. Mondays, 3:00 to 7:15 p.m. only. Saturdays 10:00 a.m. to 1:00 p.m., 2:00 to 7:00 p.m. Don't miss it for seeing how the other half of Paris shops.

8e arrondissement

Au Printemps

64 boulevard Haussmann at rue du Havre, 8e
Métro: Havre-Caumartin or St-Lazare

Go on a Saturday and enjoy the fun of the stalls outside this elegant department store. Everything from books to wigs, raincoats, pots and pans, plastic rubbish bin liners, right up to very convincing adaptations of expensive designer handbags – all at bargain-basement prices. At the corner of rue de Provence there is often a sleepy little grey donkey laden with paniers of lavender from Provence, which is ladled into plastic bags by his attendant. Often there are spectacular buys for men and women; smartly styled men's trench coats for 225F. Open 9:45 a.m. to 5:30 p.m., Monday to Saturday.

9e arrondissement

Acta

place Georges-Berry, 9e
Métro: Havre-Caumartin

Go out the door of Prisunic into a pedestrianized square facing the Église St-Louis, and rummage Acta's stalls for bargain clothes especially skirts and trousers for women, from 99 to 119F, many jeans and denim jackets.

Parallèle

rue Joubert, corner of rue de Caumartin, 9e
Métro: Havre-Caumartin

Just past Acta, and a bit smarter: Naf-Naf ensembles 145F, printed jumpsuits 179F (half normal price), a classic 3-piece suit for women in blue-and-white stripe with a crisp white blouse a bargain at 299F. Open 10:00 a.m. to 7:00 p.m., Monday to Saturday.

Prisunic

rue de Provence, 9e
Métro: Havre-Caumartin

The enterprising Prisunic chain is the French, very French, equivalent of Woolworth – but there the resemblance ends. You can buy a lightbulb, saucepans in high-fashion colours such as vermilion and cobalt blue, food processors and waffle makers at very low prices; and smartly dressed Parisian girls and young men have been known to find 'the' scarf, or some extraordinary striped sailor-type jerseys, for rock-bottom Prisunic prices. Heavy foulard men's scarves, recently, were 33F and looked triple the price. Elegant sandals for women 49F.

Check out the food department for herbs, mustards, wines, olive oil flavoured with basil – eighty-five kinds of cheese – and pâtisserie. In the cafeteria: quiches, hot pâté sandwiches, pizza, and the inevi-

table hot dog, plus croissants, Danish pastries, and coffee or wine
– all half the price a brasserie would charge. Open 9:00 a.m. to
7:30 p.m., closed Sunday.

Sphinx

31 boulevard Rochechouart, 9e
Métro: Barbès-Rochechouart

Good-looking men's clothes, not as cheap as in some of the tatty
shops around here, but excellent quality, cut, fabric and prices. The
husband of the fashion editor who told us about Club Rochechouart
(see below) buys his expensive-looking suits and sports jackets here
but doesn't mention it to his fellow bankers. Open 10:00 a.m. to
5:30 p.m., Tuesday to Saturday.

Tissus Bouchara

boulevard Haussmann, corner of rue Charras, next door to
Printemps
Métro: Havre-Caumartin or St-Lazare

Great buys in fine fabrics at low prices, considering their quality –
from Provençal-print cottons at 12F a metre, to Liberty prints, lots
of them from 30F a metre up, and magnificent cut-velvet upholstery
fabrics from 110F – anyone who can sew could make an evening
skirt from one metre of that. Open 9:30 a.m. to 6:00 p.m., Monday
to Saturday.

12e arrondissement

Square

26 rue Charles Baudelaire, 12e
Métro: Ledru-Rollin

Not far from the market in the place d'Aligre. A funny little shop
with a window sign 'T' as la Fripe Chic! T'as le Look Choc!' which
translates, roughly, as 'Get cheap rags for the look of chic-shock'.

If you are a 'Retro' fan, clothes from the 1950s and 60s, this is the place to find a stiffly-boned ball dress for 150–500F, or a man's dinner jacket from 250F, real sailor tops for women, 80F, a lot of new or very slightly used cheapies. A good place for leisurely shopping, then take a picnic from the nearby market to the charming park across the street. Open Tuesday through Saturday from 10:30 to 1:00 p.m., 3:00 to 7:00, and Sundays 10:00 a.m. to 1:00 p.m. Closed Mondays. August hours are very much the same, except that in the afternoons they open at 4:00 p.m. and stay open until 8:00 p.m.

18e arrondissement

Childebert

14 rue Custine, 18e
Métro: Château-Rouge

This is an astounding place. Its walls are lined with *closed* shoeboxes, set up according to size in narrow aisles. Each box is labelled by type of shoe and colour, and you'd be surprised at how quickly you pick up the code. *Moc-marron* means 'Low heeled moccasin-type in chestnut brown', and so on. Very good selection of men's shoes and boots, and some for children. It's jammed, uncomfortable, and fun. To give you an idea of the prices: superb black patent leather Gucci copy was 200F. They have some handbags as well – the stock varies in type and quality with the season. Open 10:00 a.m. to 6:00 p.m. Tuesday to Saturday.

Club Rochechouart

50 boulevard Rochechouart, 18e
Métro: Anvers

Unexpected, in this very raffish street which is lined with cheaper-than-cheap shops. Some very smart clothes for women, many in striking and unusual colours – few of a kind, and you may have to go back several times to find what you want. A scarlet-and-white striped jacket and skirt, which was sold in the best boutique in the Marais for 520F, appeared here for 205F. A fashion editor told us about the Club several years ago. Open 10:30 a.m. to 5:30 p.m., Monday to Saturday. Visa cards accepted.

Permanent Soldes

62 boulevard Rochechouart, 18e
Métro: Anvers

If you must have a rabbit-fur coat for 990F, on a Sunday afternoon, here's your place. Other furs ranging up to a bleached fox coat, or musquash – copies of couture models. Women's coats, dresses too. Open seven days a week from 9:00 a.m. until the traffic stops.

Rue Séveste street market

just off boulevard Rochechouart, 18e
Métro: Anvers

A range of stalls offering cheap but interesting men's shirts, jeans, jackets, ties – and women's dresses, blouses and sometimes suits. The quality isn't up to much, but you shouldn't complain when you can buy a striking cotton sundress, very St Trop, for 35F, or a man's wool jacket, reasonably well cut and lined, for 125F. Open Tuesday to Saturday, a few shops open on Sundays and/or Mondays.

Tati

4–28 boulevard Rochechouart, 18e
Métro: Barbès-Rochechouart

This complex of big, untidy, very cheap shops deserves a small book of its own. One of a chain, this Tati is heaven for those who have the time and the knack of picking through racks, shelves, and bins of clothes at prices so low you think they've misplaced a decimal point. Divided into several shops: **Tati Hommes**, for men, has at various times great cheap cord trousers for 49F50, cheap jeans, copies of Levis and Lees, faded blue Levi-style jackets, sweaters in heavy acrylic knit for as little as 40F. Inexpensive shoes from canvas espadrilles for 15F to reasonable facsimiles of very expensive leather shoes at 100F. All these items change from week to week and season to season, so go without any fixed idea and rummage around.

Tati Femmes is equally astounding: quilted nylon dressing gowns for 50F, roll-neck cotton jerseys 8F, tights 1F50, and for 15F, pastel knee-length cotton v-neck t-shirts.

Children's clothes at Tati are particularly good buys: tough jeans and sweaters for 20 to 25F. Open 10:00 a.m. to 7:00 p.m., Monday to Saturday.

Tordy

30 boulevard Rochechouart, 18e
Métro: Barbès-Rochechouart, or Anvers

Inexpensive, fashionable shirts, pullovers, and some very convincing fake-leather jackets, 149F. Open 9:30 a.m. to 6:00 p.m., Monday to Saturday.

Second hand

If you think all the pretty girls of Paris who carry Vuitton bags and wear Charles Jourdan shoes buy them on their salaries, you've missed one of the great features of Paris: the many shops that sell slightly used couture clothes, expensive bags, and such telling accessories as silk scarves and art deco jewellery. The rich women who buy at the couturiers often wear their clothes only five or six times before turning them over to a resale shop – and this is Paris, not in the least like Madame's Dress Agency in the high street: no timid little coats with tired rabbit collars.

If you're lucky, you can find a classic black wool Chanel suit (last year's model, but who's to know) for 1000F. Lined in pure silk, weighted with chains, and trimmed with Chanel braid and gilt buttons. Or a caramel-coloured crocodile handbag, lovingly cared for (the leather lining smelling of Patou Joy) for 390F.

More rarely, you can find superb men's clothes and beautiful, expensive children's clothes.

Some of these shops have been going on for years, and have well-established connections not only with the elegant women of the *quartier*, but with the couturiers themselves: often you will find evening dresses that have been worn only in the seasonal collections, or shoes that have only walked on carpeted runways. These are almost always model sizes (for which read tall and thin), and the shoes are apt to be narrow. If your taste runs to the extreme of fashion, these shops can be a joy. But it takes time and the patience to return several times if you don't find your little Yves St Laurent treasure at first visit. Most of the shops are closed on Mondays, have a clearly posted sign (in French) about their policy on returns or exchanges, and some of them have salespeople who speak English of a sort. Many close in August.

Almost all clothes are legibly labelled with price (and sometimes with the original price). In the few that we found where each garment did not have a price tag, we had the feeling that the owner of the shop matched the price to the customer: in which case, feel free to raise your eyebrows, say something like 'Un peu trop cher' (a bit too expensive), and put the garment back on the rack. This tip was passed on by a friend who brought the price of a Christian Aujard dress down from the (oral) asking price of 420F to a bargain level of 330F. Keep a steady nerve and be prepared to leave the shop without buying anything. Check seams, hem, buttons, linings in men's suits and coats, insides of shoes and handbags, and point out any weak spots which might bring the price down. In every resale shop we checked, the merchandise was in superb condition – having been cleaned, brushed or polished before being put on view.

These vendors of de luxe merchandise sometimes have a few rails of women's and men's clothes that come from the better French ready-to-wear manufacturers at the end of a season – special purchases in small quantities. They're often worth going through carefully, as the colours, fabrics, and general air of Parisian smartness – masculine as well as feminine – will delight you when your Paris visit is only a memory.

Some 'resale' shops spring up hopefully in fashionable parts of Paris, buying fairly ephemeral clothes from the young and capricious. By their nature, these rather tentative shops may not be very long lived, as their survival hangs on their supply of customers to bring in clothes as well as to buy them. It is hoped that all the addresses below will still be in business for a while: they are the best-established and most trusted by the more fashion minded of our Paris friends. But don't lose your cool if you find they have moved or gone out of business. Most of the neighbourhoods in which they are located are worth a visit for local colour; and if one shop is gone, another one a hundred yards away may catch your eye.

8e arrondissement

Anna Lowe

55 avenue Matignon, 8e
Métro: St-Philippe-du-Roule

Investment clothes, according to our Paris shop spy, sell for a fraction of the price they might command round the corner in the rue du Faubourg St-Honoré. Anna Lowe was a model and has connections with important couture houses from which she gets end-of-season clothes, and with the best ready-to-wear lines from which she gets fashions only two months after they go on sale. Not long ago, you could have found a yellow Ungaro suit (originally 8000F) for 2500F, or a Jean Louis Scherrer suit, not 4940F but 1200F. Ms Lowe also has handsome clothes made especially for the shop, and to *her* taste which is perfect. Simple alterations are free! Open Monday to Friday, 10:30 a.m. to 7:00 p.m., Saturday 3:00 to 6:30 p.m. Closed in August.

15e arrondissement

Capriverseau

46 rue des Entrepreneurs, 15e
Métro: Félix-Faure

For men, women and children, a resale shop in the non-touristy and very bourgeoise 15e. Very good clothes at real bargain prices. 'A rose linen jacket,' says our informant, 'only 140F, a knockout which I instantly bought.' Open Tuesday to Saturday, 11:00 a.m. to 2:00 p.m., and 3:00 to 7:00 p.m.

16e arrondissement

Catherine Baril

25 rue de la Tour, 16e
Métro: Pompe

A small elegant resale shop, which buys from the rich and well-dressed women of the quartier. Some of the designer clothes have labels left in – an Ungaro wool skirt was 590F, Nina Ricci scarlet skirt and long sleeved silky top was 1300F, YSL shirts for 400F, and a bargain rail of last year's models at 100F. Open Mondays 2:00 to 7:00 p.m., Tuesday through Saturday 10:00 a.m. to 7:00 p.m. Usually closed from about 15 July to 15 August. Visa cards accepted.

Maxipuces

18 rue Cortambert, 16e
Métro: Pompe

In the elegant Passy district you'll find several of the best high fashion resale shops. This one sells slightly-worn couturier clothes, and some end-of-season closeouts from the factories who actually manufacture for the ready-to-wear lines with couturier labels. Also hats, a few furs or fur accessories, sometimes jewellery, scarves (you could find an immaculate Hermès silk, one metre square), and beautifully polished shoes. Open Tuesday to Saturday, 10:00 a.m. to 7:00 p.m.; Monday, 2:30 to 7:00 p.m. Next door is Mme Vecchi, who will alter your Guy Laroche to fit you – she is said to be a skilled dressmaker who can copy a photo or sketch, if you can afford it. Maxipuce is closed in August.

Réciproque

95 rue de la Pompe, 16e
Métro: Pompe

This big well-established shop now has an annexe, next door, for children's wear, and for scarves, handbags, etc. for men and women.

The main shop has good couture clothes worn a few times by private clients, or in fashion shows – and a lot of well-made ready-to-wear things. A good buy recently was a suede-finish wool coat from Kenzo, second hand but looking new, for 620F. Open 10:00 a.m. to 6:45 p.m., Tuesdays to Saturdays. Closed 29 July to 2 September.

Other fascinating, slightly second-hand shops you might like to visit are:

8e: **Lady Change**, 37 bis rue du Colisée, *Métro*: St-Philippe-du-Roule.

11e: **Rétro Manoli**, 74 rue Léon Frot. *Métro* Charonne.

15e: **Saint-Frusquin**, 1 villa Juge, *Métro* Dupleix.

16e: **Maguy**, 30 rue de la Pompe and **Patricia Archange**, 106 rue de la Tour, both *Métro* Pompe; **Le Truc et Troc**, 70 avenue St-Didier, *Métro* Victor Hugo.

Gift shopping

The shops of Paris are crammed with perfect gifts – at a price. Wander along the rue du Faubourg St-Honoré, or the rue de Rivoli, or rue Royale, or among the boutiques of the Left Bank, and you will begin to feel like a poor relation outside a rich man's door. But once you get your eye in, you can with some perseverance find an enticing selection of small portable presents at a fraction of the big-name shop prices.

Note: many shops close during August for the annual holiday; and hours can change, from time to time. If a shop has closed, or even disappeared entirely, it's not a disaster, you'll wander the neighbourhood and find places of your own.

Monoprix, Prisunic, Uniprix

These have turned up frequently in these pages as perfect hunting grounds for food, clothes, household gadgets. Consider them for gifts, too: make for the larger shops, in the more fashionable areas of the Right Bank, which quickly seize upon the year's fashionable ideas and copy them down to a price. Monoprix at 21 avenue de l'Opéra, 1er, *Métro*: Opéra, usually has silk-look scarves in subtle colours, with a very 'designer' look, for as little as 25F. Their scarves and mufflers for men, in wool or wool and acrylic, are elegantly designed in stripes, patterns or muted plaids, and look much better than their price of about 42–45F.

Look in Prisunic for traditional French earthenware plates and cups; a big café-au-lait bowl for breakfast, in a shape that dates back to the eighteenth century, is 11F50.

1er arrondissement

FNAC

forum des Halles, 1er
Métro: Les Halles

Two of the biggest and best of Paris's bookshops are under this name. The other can be found at 136 rue de Rennes, 6e. Both are open from 10:00 a.m. to 7:30 p.m., closed Sundays and Mondays.

Au Grenier de Cunégonde

208 rue de Rivoli, 1er
Métro: Tuileries

The shop for collectors of puppets, pierrots and their clothes. Open 10:30 a.m. to 7:00 p.m., Monday to Saturday.

Il Etait Une Fois

10 rue Jean-Jacques Rousseau, 1er
Métro: Palais Royal, Louvre

A crowded treasure-house of clothes for men and women, from the 1900s onwards; wonderful for browsing – and if you are looking for investment clothes for the next 30 years. Exquisitely made camisoles, old lace, velvet and embroidered bodices and short jackets, lace collars, gloves, buttons, boas, beaded headbands, handbags, costume jewellery crowd its walls. For what they are, the prices are not exorbitant: a velvet and lace jacket could cost from 350F, but it's one of a kind and of a workmanship that will never be seen again. Look for original Dior, Lanvin, Balmain, and for men, the much-prized Burberrys and Harrods jackets! Open 11:00 a.m. to 7:30 p.m., Monday through Saturday, but it's wise to telephone first (4 233 81 17.)

Madame Bijoux

13 rue Jean-Jacques Rousseau, 1er
Métro: Palais Royal, Louvre

If you don't find what you want at Il Etait, cross the street and see what Bijoux has on hand – more of the theatrical fantasies including masks, hair slides, beads, shoes from the 1920s, more feather boas, some junk, some gems. Open 11:00 a.m. to 7:30 p.m., Monday through Saturday, but check by phone (4 236 98 68) before making a special trip.

Centre Franco-Americain

1st floor, 71 rue d'Aboukir, 2e
Métro: Sentier

As it has now been found that the duty-free shops at Paris airports are the second most expensive in Europe, you might do better to check out this small place where perfumes etc. are tax free, and 25% off the marked prices: Givenchy eau de toilette, 200 ml, was 360F, less 25%. They also stock Dior, Hermès, Armani, YSL scents, as well as makeup and skin treatment products. Open Monday through Friday, 9:00 a.m. to 6:30 p.m., closed most of August. Its prices are keener than the more well-known and crowded shops under the arches of the rue de Rivoli, around the Louvre.

4e arrondissement

52 rue des Archives, 4e
Métro: St-Paul

This shop without a name, at the corner of the rue des Francs-Bourgeois in the Marais, is bursting with gift ideas, from frightful provincial kitsch, to some really charming small things in brass, pewter, glass and porcelain. For example, a beautiful little enamel, gilt and coloured glass box for earrings was 20F not long ago. Others, looking like the antiques they are copied from, range from 22 to 65F. Open 9:30 a.m. to 5:30 p.m., Monday to Saturday.

Librairie du Vieux Paris

62 rue François-Miron, 4e
Métro: St-Paul

Old books and prints. Open 3:00 p.m. to 7:00 p.m. only, Tuesday to Saturday.

La Licorne

38 rue de Sévigné, near rue des Francs-Bourgeois, 4e
Métro: St-Paul

The shops in the Marais change almost overnight, and if this is still here, it's a delightful place to find not very expensive costume jewellery. Open 8:30 a.m. to 6:30 p.m., Monday to Saturday.

À L'Olivier

77 rue St-Louis-en-L'Ile, 4e
Métro: Sully-Morland, Pont Marie

The street is delightful, the shop is irresistible. A litre of the best extra-virgin cold-pressed French olive oil is 50F70 and worth it. Also walnut oil, avocado oil, spices, rare peppers, every kind of olive you could imagine, dried fruits, nuts. Open 10:00 a.m. to 7:00 p.m., Monday to Friday. August hours are 11:00 a.m. to 1:00 p.m., 3:00 to 7:00 p.m. Visa, Diners' Club and American Express cards accepted.

La Vide Gousset

rue des Blancs-Manteaux, corner of rue Vielle-du-Temple, 4e
Métro: St-Paul

Prices here range from ridiculously low to somewhat staggering, for early 1900s treasures such as chemises, camisoles with lace, tea-glasses set in silver filigree holders, elaborate coffee cups and so on. Open 10:00 a.m. to 5:30 p.m., Monday to Saturday.

5e arrondissement

La Tuile à Loup

35 rue Daubenton, 5e
Métro: Censier-Daubenton

A shop scented with herbs, filled with beautifully designed, rather rustic gifts: wicker, wood, earthenware casseroles, baskets and cook-books (in French). Old-fashioned wicker heart-shaped *coeur à la crème* baskets, classic glazed earthenware wine pitchers, bread-boards. Best buy: the Imagerie d'Épinal prints, made to be cut out and turned into paper dolls but nicest left as they come – 8 to 15F. Open 10:30 a.m. to 12:30 p.m., 3:00 to 7:30 p.m., Monday to Saturday.

6e arrondissement

Au Chat Dormant

15 rue du Cherche-Midi, 6e
Métro: Rennes

A minuscule paradise for cat lovers, with gifts ranging from post-cards to antique silver boxes, everything saluting cats. Figures of cats in marble, metal, porcelain, plastic. Umbrellas whose handles are heads of cats. Paintings, prints, posters. Open Mondays 2:00 to 7:00 p.m., Tuesday to Saturday 11:00 a.m. to 7:00 p.m.

8e arrondissement

Casoar

15 rue Boissy-d'Anglas, 8e
Métro: Concorde, Madeleine

Mainly fine antique jewels, but you will find some beautiful vermeil (silver-gilt) jewellery not too expensive. For a friend who likes to cut a dash, a great pair of dangling earrings, bogus onyx set in 'diamonds', 199F. Less flashy, rings, necklaces and bracelets with a costly look, at lowish prices. Open 11:00 a.m. to 6:00 p.m., Tuesday to Saturday. Closed August.

9e arrondissement

32 rue de Provence, 9e

Métro: Chaussée-d'Antin

This shop seems to have no name but it's paradise for finding French paperbacks from 2F (thrillers are good for increasing your knowledge of Paris argot), or for superb leather-bound sets of the classics, for prices up to 200F the set. Visa accepted. Open 9:00 a.m. to 6:30 p.m., Monday to Saturday.

10e arrondissement

rue de Paradis, 10e

Métro: Poissonnière

Walk down this street between the rue d'Hauteville and rue de
Fidélité, and you will find a nexus of attractive shops with an infinite
variety of porcelain and crystal, not all that extraordinarily cheap
but of great beauty. At that, prices seem slightly lower than in the
Galeries Lafayette or the pricier gift shops of the Left Bank. Such
names as Daum Cristal and Havilland are everywhere; almost
everything available is small, portable and desirable, although
breakable. At Au Paradis, 55 rue de Paradis, look for exquisite
porcelain handmade vases and jugs in subtle colours. Most shops
seem to open around 10:00 a.m. and almost everything is closed on
Saturdays.

11e arrondissement

Carabosse

58 rue de Roquette, 11e
Métro: Bastille

A feminist bookshop in an otherwise unattractive neighbourhood
(but if you walk along to No. 43 and 45 you will find two great
shops with old advertising prints, stamps, beer mats, from the
1920s). Carabosse sells books, posters, and has a noticeboard with
advertisements for holidays, flats, lifts. Also a little coffee shop.
Tuesday to Saturday, from about 12:00 to 7:30 p.m. Closed from
23 July to 6 September.

14e arrondissement

La Salle des Ventes

117 rue d'Alésia, 14e
Métro: Alésia

In this lively, very untouristed area, a real discovery: a salesroom
which, although specializing in huge pieces of furniture, has glass

cases full of small treasures (different every week, of course). It's a wonderful place to browse – and you might find some delightful very French *objet* to take home. A pretty little carriage clock for 600F (about £50), an ivory necklace for 80F, an amethyst choker 310F, a silver art nouveau hand mirror 140F, were among recent temptations. Open 10:00 a.m. to 7:30 p.m., Monday to Saturday.

15e arrondissement

L'Art Populaire

157 rue Lecourbe, 15e
Métro: Sèvres-Lecourbe

This entrancing small shop is crammed with beautiful little gifts, all in natural material – wicker, wood, willow, stone, earthenware, glass. Look for the shiny black abacus, 35F. Classic French café-au-lait bowls, 8F, bamboo frames from 12F and sometimes exquisite old oil lamps, unconverted, fragile but irresistible at 50–60F. The stock changes constantly but is never less than beautiful. Open 9:30 to 1:30 p.m., 2:30 to 7:30 p.m., except Mondays, when the shop closes at 2:30 p.m.; closed Sundays.

Flea markets

Les Marchés aux Puces – one of those romantic conceptions of Paris, whose faded glamour lingers somewhat past its prime. As there are now 'flea markets' of sorts all over the world, your chance of finding a nice little precious object for almost nothing is probably as good in a Sunday morning sale in Salford, as in the most famous flea market in Paris. However, if you think you want the fun of scrabbling through bins and tables, or just watching Parisians striking bargains in rapid-fire slangy French – and you still hope to find something everyone else has missed – so be it. Here is the latest, most realistic information, from French sources.

The flea market at St-Ouen

Métro: Porte de Clignancourt and a fair walk

Acres of sprawling market-stalls, crammed with people on the hunt for bargains or for 'the picturesque', which these days means German tourists photographing American tourists. It is the best known, and the most expensive. Much of the stuff you see is pure and simple junk, brought in to unload on the unwary. For the rest – the dealers know where the good buys are, and by the time you have reached here by public transport they have come and gone. Most of the best-looking stalls are owned by merchants who also do business from flossier premises, in the 1er, 8e and 16e *arrondissements*. The prices you see in the flea market will be no lower than in the rue du Bac. However, it's an experience, and if you are willing to make the longish journey, rummage and enjoy the bargaining, it could be fun. Saturday, Sunday and Monday from dawn to about 1:00 p.m.

Despite the apparent haphazardness of the market, it is actually laid out in a fairly comprehensible and sensible fashion. Outside, on the fringe, are the inevitable buses, station wagons and hand carts spilling over with second-hand jeans, Indian blouses, 'Afghan' rugs, damaged transistors, and such-like. Inside, you will find a number of individual markets, well sign-posted. Most interesting:

Marché Vernaison, 136 avenue Michelet. Everything from gilt buttons off Napoleonic tunics, to small walnut prayer-stools, toys, jewellery, lamps, glassware. Forget about any art nouveau *trouvailles*, the Paris, London and New York dealers got there three years ago. Go for the small pieces of the thirties, forties, fifties, even the sixties now, and hope that fashion catches up with you.

Marché Malik, rue Jules-Vallès. Mostly old clothes, umbrellas, walking-sticks, tatty fake-sheepskin coats, scratched records. Bins of lace, twentyish dresses, earthenware, glass, tin, perfume bottles – sometimes these are fun, smelling in a ghostly way of scents no longer made. The clothes may need washing or dry cleaning.

Marché Biron, rue des Rosiers. Expensive, elegant furniture and *bibelots*, on stands run by professionals who know precisely the worth of everything they stock. You might beat them down ten to twenty per cent, but as the original price is usually astronomical to begin with, you'll still end by spending a lot, if you buy at all. However, everything is good value, and backed by reputable names in the business.

Marché Paul Bert, rue Paul Bert. Some really exquisite crystal, modern gilt, bronze, polished wood furniture, ornaments, mirrors. They could easily fetch double the asking price if put up at Christie's – that is, if you could afford to pay what the vendors are asking in the first place.

Marché Jules-Vallès, rue Jules-Vallès. The most fun, and the most promising for finding something unusual and not too expensive, if you feel your stay in Paris isn't complete without something from the flea market. Look for small bisque-headed dolls, theatrical costumes, 1930s shoes, decorative glassware, candlesticks, ashtrays, doll trunks. Bargain if you can, most of the dealers speak some kind of English, but don't be disappointed if the final price is not really rock-bottom.

The other flea markets

These are where the knowledgeable Parisians find their bargains. As they become better known, the quality of merchandise brought to them goes up, and prices are rising fast. A few years ago, these were true junk stalls, set up along the edge of an established street market. Some still qualify, just, for this status, but foreign dealers are moving in to buy, smart young stallholders are setting up their stands, and the time to go is *now*.

Place d'Aligre, 11e

Métro: Ledru-Rollin

Look for signs to 'Marché Beauvau'. The surrounding market of fruit, vegetables, meat and seafood is one of the lesser-known and most delightful in Paris, and worth a visit for itself. In the square, about twenty tables of odds and ends are set up. Boxes of the most astounding old clothes – cracked leather shoes, a furry bowler hat, a pair of striped trousers, a stack of fourth-hand handbags. But look for old postcards, small pieces of silver or silverplate, glassware, cooking utensils of every age and condition, books, odd boxes of jewellery – mostly Woolworth stuff, but occasionally a piece of once-expensive jewellery turns up. There's a table of buttons old and new that will send button-collectors wild. Everything quite cheap, the atmosphere quiet, the dealers pleasant.

Early in 1985, it shrank by about 20 stalls, as the Mayor of Paris apparently decreed that it was bringing too much traffic to the surrounding streets, but by the end of the summer many of the long-established vendors had crept back. The street market around it is a wonderful place to shop for fruit, flowers, North African olives and hot peppers, good breads, and the corkscrew you forgot to bring. Plenty of picnicking material, for a snack in the square bounded by rue Vollon and rue Trousseau. Every day but Monday, from about 9:30 a.m. to about 1:00 p.m.

Porte de Vanves, 14e

A very good small flea market is in the avenue Marc Sangnier (*Métro*: Porte de Vanves), 14e, Saturday and Sunday mornings. It's mostly junk, but if you have a quick eye you can spot some real bargains. Look for oldish Dinky toys; copper jelly moulds; old glass lamps; costume jewellery of the 40s and 50s, comics, postcards, pots, bottles. A few small (rather pricey) antiques. The grander end of this market in avenue Georges-Lefenestre, around the corner, is described below.

Marché aux Puces de la Porte Didot

You will find this mentioned in *Pariscope* as to be found at 54 boulevard Brune, *Métro* Porte d'Orleans – don't believe it, it's a long walk. Instead, take the Métro to Porte de Vanves, much closer, walk through the tatty part, and in the avenue Georges-Lefenestre you find 'the real market of grandpapa'. This means delectable junk and little treasures, not rock-bottom cheap. You have to be able to bargain in French if you want to get prices down. Good for pretty china, glass, silver, ornate little picture frames, small antique furniture. Not many (foreign) tourists yet, but a lot of beady-eyed young French couples decorating their houses cheaply. Photographers come here for props. On a summer weekend, it is an agreeable stroll under the trees and through the good-natured, ambling crowd. You can even find places to sit and have a picnic while your feet recover; or find a café in the nearby rue Raymond Losserand. Saturday and Sunday, from 8:00 a.m. to about 6:00 p.m., but best before lunchtime as by mid-afternoon most of the best stallholders have begun to pack it in. The Porte de Vanves/Porte Didot market has been under threat of closure for the last few years, as local shopkeepers complain that it takes away trade from them and sometimes brings undesirable characters into the *quartier*. Police show up regularly to chase away the unlicensed who spread their odds and ends on newspapers on the pavement. But the market still goes on, at this writing at least.

Paris pratique
(Staying afloat)

The quality of your stay in Paris – reverie or nightmare – is going to depend on some very basic circumstances: the state of your digestion, your feet, your French. The amount of time you spend looking for a post office is stolen from the time you spend looking at paintings. The confusion you encounter when dealing with telephones, tipping and traffic detracts from your pleasure in everything else Parisian. The information that follows, alphabetically arranged, is simple and practical – it can make the difference between two weeks of fretting about mechanical details and ten minutes of dealing intelligently with them.

Animals (see also 'Au secours', p.227)

Parisians are unsentimental about animals, but they like to have them around. Small dogs of peculiar breed on leads trail every other person – on the Métro, in restaurants, everywhere. The sidewalks are consequently treacherous. You can get entangled, or step in something, but you'll rarely be snapped or barked at.

Cats run wild in certain areas, notably the cemeteries, and are not to be petted. This goes for all animals in France, except those personally known to you. See Animal bites, p.235.

Live animals for food are closely caged and brusquely treated. If this puts you off your feed, avert your eyes.

Babysitters

Association Générale des Étudiants en Médecine

103 boulevard de l'Hôpital, 13e
Tel: 4 586 19 42
22F per hour.

Especially recommended for children 18 months or younger.
Medical students are called *carabins*. After midnight, provide taxi
fare home.

American College in Paris

31 avenue Bosquet, 7e
Tel: 4 555 91 73,
extension 19 or 24
22F per hour.

Give the sitter something to eat if the evening begins before 6:00;
provide two Métro tickets, or, after midnight, either take the student
home or offer taxi fare.

Baby Sitting Actif

34 rue Delambre, 14e
Tel: 4 327 82 38
22F per hour.

Price decreases to 15F from 8:00 p.m. to midnight, with an agency
fee of 35F.

Baths, public

If your hotel doesn't provide a shower – or if it's too expensive –
try the Bains-Douches Municipaux. Bring a towel, soap, and slip-
pers (the flip-flop variety). More about this on p.61. Cost: 4F60.

Open Thursday, noon to 7:00 p.m., Friday and Saturday, 7:00 a.m. to 7:00 p.m.; Sunday, 8:00 a.m. to noon.

8 rue des Deux Ponts, 4e	18 rue de Meaux, 19e
50 rue Lacépède, 5e	place des Fêtes, 19e
38 rue du Rocher, 8e	27 rue de la Bidassoa, 20e
40 rue Oberkampf, 11e	66 rue de Buzenval, 20e
188 rue de Charenton, 12e	148 avenue Gambetta, 20e
34 rue Castagnary, 15e	296 rue des Pyrénées, 20e

There are also 64 fountains donated to Paris by Richard Wallace (he also tried to give Paris his furniture collection; it was turned down and wound up in London). The fountains are scattered throughout the city, contain clean water, and are good for a *toilette de chat* ('a lick and a promise').

Bicycle hire

Paris-Vélo (Rent-a-bike): 2 rue du Fer-à-Moulin, 5e. *Métro*: Censier-Daubenton or Gobelins.
Rental: daily, 40–60F, depending on type of bike. Weekend, 65–95F. Four days to one week, 120–190F. *Deposit*: 400F or your passport.

Roue-Libre Velo: You can rent bikes cheaply in and around Paris, from mid-March to late November. For the Bois de Boulogne, take the Métro to Porte Maillot or Bus 244 to the 'Bagatelle' stop, bikes are available near the Relais du Bois. For the Bois de Vincennes: *Métro* Château de Vincennes, bikes rented on the esplanade of the Château. For the beautiful Valley of the Chevreuse just outside Paris, take the RER to St-Germain-en-Laye, bikes are rented in the parking place.

Books (in English)

When French newspapers begin to give you indigestion, revert to English. Remember, though, that imported books are expensive – about double their home price.

Brentano's

37 avenue de l'Opéra, 1er
Tel: 4 261 52 50
Métro: Pyramides

Galignani

224 rue de Rivoli, 1er
Tel: 4 260 76 07
Métro: Tuileries

Shakespeare and Company

37 rue de la Bûcherie, 5e
No listed telephone
Métro: St-Michel

W. H. Smith & Son

248 rue de Rivoli, 1er
Tel: 4 260 37 97
Métro: Concorde

Clothing sizes

Women:
Dresses/Suits

British American	10	12	14	16	18	20
French	38	40	42	44	46	48

Stockings

British American	8	8½	9	9½	10	10½
French	0	1	2	3	4	5

Shoes

British	4½	5½	6½	7½
American	6	7	8	9
French	37	38	40	41

Men:

Suits/Overcoats

British American	36	38	40	42	44	46
French	46	48	50	52	54	56

Shirts

British American	15	16	17	18
French	38	41	43	45

Shoes

British American	7	8	8½	9	9½	10	11
French	41	42	43	43	44	44	45

Discounts – *for students*

Carte Jeune

A nifty little item for those between 18 and 25. Entitles you to a 50 per cent reduction on all French railways, and free couchette. It's good only between 1 June and 30 September. Get it from main railway stations or travel agents. Cost: 125F.

Council for International Educational Exchange (CIEE)

49 rue Pierre-Charron, 8e
Tel: 4 359 23 69
Métro: Alma-Marceau

Provides International Student Identity Cards, useful for discounts on museum and film entrances, Eurail-passes, and much more. You must have proof of full-time student status, a passport-sized photo, and 30F.

Using the card: Look for prices under 'Tarif spécial pour étudiants'.

Ligue Française des Auberges de Jeunesse (LFAJ)

38 boulevard Raspail, 7e
Tel: 4 548 69 84
Métro: Bac

For Youth Hostel cards. Hostels are cheap (15–25F per night) but offer little privacy. Not for long stays. See 'Au lit', p.88, for more information.

Student restaurants *(les restos U.)*

About 6–7F per meal.

Albert Châtelet
10 rue Jean-Calvin, 5e
Métro: Censier-Daubenton

Assas
92 rue d'Assas, 6e
Métro: Notre-Dame-des-Champs

Bullier
39 avenue Georges-Bernanos, 5e
Métro: Port-Royal

Censier
3 rue Censier, 5e
Métro: Censier-Daubenton

Cuvier
8 bis, rue Cuvier, 5e
Métro: Jussieu

Mabillon
3 rue Mabillon, 6e
Métro: Mabillon

Mazet
5 rue Mazet, 6e
Métro: Odéon

Discounts — *for those over 60*

Carte Vermeil

With great generosity, the French provide this discount card for those of 'the third age' – a much nicer phrase than the unctuous Anglo/American 'senior citizens' – available to anyone, of any nationality, who is over 60 years of age (women) or 65 (men). Take proof of your age – your passport – to the Abonnement office in any major railway station, or to the SNCF (French Railways) office in the lower ground floor of the Office de Tourisme at 127 Champs-Élysées, 8e (*Métro*: George-V). Pay them 65F, and get in return the *Carte Vermeil*, which is valid from 1 June to the next 31 May; during that time it entitles you to manifold discounts on entertainment, travel, and many museums.

The office at the Gare St-Lazare is an easy one to deal with, as the station is served by several Métro and many bus lines, and is not so crowded as the one at the big Gare du Nord or at the SNCF-Champs-Élysées. Don't expect anyone to speak English, but you won't need much French to communicate your wishes, as they are used to dealing with foreigners who have cottoned on to this very useful offer.

As you look through *Pariscope* for theatres, music, cinema, etc., note the price reductions available to holders of the *CV*; it can be 40 per cent or more. Most museums and special exhibitions (such as those at the Grand Palais and Petit Palais) give half-price admission to holders of the *CV*. Notable exception: at the Jeu de Paume, women as well as men must be 65 or over to get the reduced charge. However, we've been told that here, even without the *CV*, presentation of your passport as proof of age will get you in at half price; it's worth a try.

Holders of the British Senior Citizens Railcard should note that they will need the £6 Rail-Europ supplement card for discounts on: rail/boat/hovercraft: check British Rail, in England, or at 55 rue St. Roch, 1er (*Métro*: Pyramides), for details of specific offers. Dates and hours may be restricted; read the small print to make sure you can get back from your holiday when you want to.

Dry cleaning

It's called *Nettoyage à sec* or *Le Pressing*. Sample prices:

Trousers – 20F
Jacket – 25F
Dress – 30F

Le Pressing is also available everywhere for a touch-up.

Electricity

Although the current, in most modernized hotels, is 220 volts, as in the UK (in older hotels it may still be 110 volts, so inquire before using any appliance), you must fit a *European* two-round-pin plug to the flex of electrical gadgets. Many ironmongers sell these (or get one in Paris). If you have an appliance with a three-cord flex, make sure the earth wire (green and yellow) is securely bound and covered with electricians' tape, so that it cannot touch the other wires nor the wall socket. Or buy one of the pricey but safe adaptors sold in ironmongers. Also do be considerate: you might check with the concierge about using a hairdryer, which draws a lot of current.

Embassies

See 'Au secours', pp.227–37.

Emergencies

See 'Au secours', p.227.

Entrances and exits

French doors open inward. This takes a while to get used to.

Entrée = Entrance
Sortie = Exit
Tirez = Pull
Poussez = Push
Passage Interdit = No Admittance

Guide books

The only ones worth having, to our knowledge, are:

Blue Guide to Paris

(In English, detailed information on museums and areas of historical interest.)

Michelin Green Guide

(In English, good overview, and excellent maps.)

Gault-Millau: 'Le Nouveau Guide'

(In French, published monthly – 20F. About £2 in the UK, $4.50 in the US.) An invaluable source of inside information on restaurants, hotels, travel, holidays. However, most of its restaurant recommendations are well above our price limits. Gault-Millau are utterly frank about the places they write about, and they write wittily and often colloquially. In one of their issues they actually had a feature called 'Restaurants to Flee From'.

Le Nouveau Guide is almost too much of a country-wide or world-wide magazine to be of use to those staying in Paris, but you might have a look at the cover of the magazine of the month, and buy it only if it is featuring something inexpensive and Parisian.

Survive in French

Combined, cassette/ phrasebook/mini-dictionary from Longmans. Fairly basic, and therefore useful, 'how-to' phrases, with a question and answer format in the cassette to help accustom you to listening to, and understanding, what people tell you in reply to your stumbling inquiries. Get it well before you go, and *practise*. This kit is especially useful for motorists, as it includes a long illustrated section on everything (always more than you think) that can go wrong with a car in France; from booksellers, £7.95.

Berlitz cassette/phrasebook

Very much the same idea, but with less emphasis on cars, more on everyday situations (hotels, trains, emergencies) so perhaps pointed more towards paupers. From bookshops.

Pan Travellers' French

Small, thin, truly pocket-size, and packed with useful words, phrases and pronunciations to cover almost anything that can happen to you. Particularly strong on medical emergencies, chemists, camping. A good buy. From booksellers, £1.25p.

French for your Travels

An even smaller phrasebook/pocket dictionary, well organized and succinct. Very good for shopping, postage, asking directions. Regrettably, they have dropped some gem-like phrases from an earlier edition long treasured in our family, including 'You dance

very well' and 'I think your sister is beautiful'. From Berlitz, or
booksellers, £1.95.

Paris Pas Cher

In French, good for bargains and 'consumer' information, but don't
rely on it for realistic prices, as they rise every year. M. A. Éditions,
Paris, 69F.

Hairdressers

Le training – a first-class example of *Franglais* – offers you a chance
to get a free or reduced rate haircut or styling in some very good
salons. These sessions are popular with the young and broke of
Paris, so you may have to wait or return another day. For women
only, as far as is known now: although the trendier unisex salons
may by now have 'training' sessions, too. You are sure of getting
something smart and professional, as the cutter who works on your
hair is actually employed in the salon at normal times, not just a
learner-driver, so to speak; and there is always one of the top stylists
of the establishment hovering near to criticize or comment or direct.
Don't mind if you are treated rather as an object than a client to
be flattered and soothed. And you probably will find that your own
wishes are not paramount. Don't go in with long straight hair and
expect to come out with just a trim. Get an idea beforehand of the
general attitude of the salon before you put your head in their
hands.

Bruno

15 rue des Saints-Pères, 6e
Tel: 4 261 45 15
Métro: St-Germain-des-Prés

Tuesdays, 6:00 p.m. Shampoo, cut, blow-dry 30F. No appointment
necessary. Not July and August.

Jean-Jacques Maniatis

35 rue de Sèvres, 6e
Tel: 4 544 17 37
Métro: Vaneau

Tuesdays and Thursdays, 5:00 to 10:00 p.m. Free – but you must stay for the whole session.

Marianne Gray

52 rue Saint-André-des-Arts, 6e
Tel: 4 326 58 21
Métro: St-Michel

Training sessions are once a week, telephone for current information. Not July or August. If a first-year student does your hair under the eye of a senior stylist, it's free. Work by an advanced student is at half the normal salon cost, or about 40F for a complete restyle. Tip the *coiffeuse* about 4F, even if the treatment is free.

For a non-training (paid) coiffure, expect to pay about 40F for a cut, 20F for a shampoo, and blow-drying or setting about 28–30F, all plus 15 per cent.

Note that although prices were accurate at the time of going to press, they may have risen by the time you read this book.

Health

See 'Au secours', pp.227–37.

Holidays

1 January; Easter Sunday and Monday (Pâques); 1 May (French Labour Day); Ascension Day; Whit Monday; 14 July (Bastille Day); 15 August (Feast of the Assumption); 1 November (All Saints Day – Toussaint); 11 November (Remembrance Day) and Christmas.

The entire month of August is high season for tourists, low season for Parisians. The city trades its population in for a flock of provincials and foreigners. Stay out of town unless you don't mind being asked directions by passers by.

Information sources

For basic information, consult the Offices de Tourisme. The Hôtesses speak English, and will provide information on hotels, transportation, sight-seeing, travel in France, and such.

Office de Tourisme: Main office

127 avenue des Champs-Élysées, 8e
Métro: George-V
Tel: 4 723 61 72
Hours: Monday to Saturday, 9:00 a.m. to 8:00 p.m.; Sundays and holidays, 9:00 a.m. to 6:00 p.m.

Branch offices:

Gare de Lyon

Hours 8:00 a.m. to 1:00 p.m. and 5:00 to 10:00 p.m., Easter to 1 November. Other months to 8:00 p.m., Monday to Saturday.

Gare de l'Est

Hours: 8:00 a.m. to 1:00 p.m. and 5:00 to 10:00 p.m. Easter to 1 November. Other months to 8:00 p.m., Monday to Saturday.

Gare du Nord

Hours: 8:00 a.m. to 10:00 p.m., Easter to 1 November. Other months to 8:00 p.m., Monday to Saturday.

Gare d'Austerlitz

Hours: 8:00 a.m. to 10:00 p.m., Easter to 1 November. Other months to 3:00 p.m., Monday to Saturday.

The Yellow Pages are known as *Le Professionel* in Paris.

Language courses

Berlitz

29 rue de la Michodière, 1er
Métro: Opéra

Alliance Française

101 boulevard Raspail, 6e
Tel: 4 544 38 28
Métro: Notre-Dame-des-Champs

Office National des Universités et Écoles Françaises

96 boulevard Raspail, 6e
Tel: 4 222 50 20
Métro: Notre-Dame-des-Champs

Offers information on French language courses from French universities.

Launderettes

The idea of self-service laundries is catching on very quickly in Paris, and a good thing for all us paupers. You may well find one very close to your inexpensive hotel, or choose one from this short list.

24 place Marché-St-Honoré, 1er

4 rue Léopold Bellan, 2e

98 rue St-Antoine, 4e

1 rue de la Montagne Ste-Genevieve, 5e

91 rue de Seine, 6e

108 rue du Bac, 7e

6 rue de la Tour d'Auvergne, 9e

96 rue de la Roquette, 11e

13 rue de Crussol, 11e

9 rue Jean-Pierre-Timbaud, 11e

4 rue de Wattignies, 12e

7 boulevard Arago, 13e

3 avenue Georges-Lefenestre, 14e

There are many *Laveries Automatiques Libre-Service* in the 5e and 6e *arrondissements*, as you would expect from student quarters – but as they seem to come and go with some frequency, we don't feel sure enough of their locations to put them down here. All the ones above are secure enough to be listed in the Paris telephone book.

A launderette charges 18F per load to wash, 7F for 20 minutes in the dryer (*séchoir*), and 2F for soap (*savon*). *Blanchisseries* are expensive, but they'll starch, fold and wrap your shirts.

Lavatories, public

There are still a few *vespasiennes* in Paris, but don't count on stumbling across one. Métro stations frequently (but not always) have lavatories (marked WC-Dames, WC-Hommes); for once, correct vocabulary is *essential*. The attendant expects ½-franc in the saucer. Superb new automatic lavatories are being sited at many street corners: a 1F piece gets you up to 10 minutes in an immaculate white cubicle.

Café and brasserie toilets offer various states of hygiene and civilization – about half the time, you'll find the 'à la turque' kind, which can be very clean or very dirty, especially in the smaller out-of-the-way places which as a pauper you will frequent. *Never* leave home without a pack of humane loo-paper, as advised on page 19.

If your need for a lavatory doesn't quite coincide with your desire for a cup of coffee, you might try the *Jeton* Trick. Find a café or brasserie and ask to use the phone. Buy a *jeton* (phone token – 1F) if you must, at the bar. The phone and lavatory, if you're lucky, will be found next to each other. Don't use the phone. On your return to the *caisse*, sell the *jeton* back to the management. Your party didn't answer.

Libraries

If you expect to be able to use one of the great French libraries (the Bibliothèque Nationale or the Bibliothèque Ste-Geneviève) you will need some authoritative support: a letter from your university describing your research, or from your corporation. The more official the better. Count on bureaucratic resistance.

Lost and found

We have found the Lost and Found charming and helpful, and they have at least one person who speaks good English.

Bureau des Objets Trouvés
36 rue des Morillons, 15e
Métro: Convention
Hours: Monday, Tuesday, Wednesday and Friday, 8:30 a.m. to 5:00 p.m. Thursday, 8:30 a.m. to 8:00 p.m.

Lost or stolen passport: see 'Au secours', p.233.

Maps

The best we know is the *Plan de Paris*, edition A. Leconte, red cover, 55F, and worth it. For details, see 'Aux alentours', p.36.

Mental health

SOS Amitié (in English)

Tel: 4 723 80 80
7:00 a.m. to 11:00 p.m.

For pouring out your troubles by phone. No advice given, no sides taken, but they lend a sympathetic ear and can recommend other sources of specific help or refuge.

Metric system

To convert centimetres into inches, multiply by .39
To convert inches into centimetres, multiply by 2.54

1 cm = 0.39 in
1 m = 39.4 in = 3.28 ft = 1.09 yd

1 in = 2.54 cm
1 ft = 30.48 cm = 0.304 m
1 yd = 91.44 cm = 0.914 m

1 kilogram (kg) =	2.205 lb
2	4.409
5	11.023
10	22.046

1 pound =	0.45 kg
2	.90
5	2.25
10	4.50

To convert degrees Centigrade into degrees Fahrenheit, multiply Centigrade by 1.8 and add 32.

To convert degrees Fahrenheit into degrees Centigrade, subtract 32 and divide by 1.8.

Money

See also 'Preliminaries', pp.10–20, for an idea of how much to bring with you.

The denominations	Will get you
5 centimes	nothing
10 centimes	nothing
20 centimes	nothing
½F (50 centimes)	nothing
1F	a phone call
2F	admission to the *pelouse* at race-tracks; *or* a paperback thriller in a flea market
5F	Cognac *ordinaire*
10F (paper or coin)	a *filet* string bag for groceries
50F	a very good lunch
100F	a day in Chartres *or* a very good lunch for two *or* a real splurge meal for one

French paper currency (les billets) is whimsical. The portraits on the bills are not of politicians but of artists: Berlioz (10F), Racine (50F), Corneille (100F), Pascal (500F). This is conclusive proof that the French value philosophy above literature, and literature above music.

Bureaux de change

Despite our wise words about sleeping cheap and eating well, within certain sets of limits, money does seem to drip through the fingers in Paris. And when you need it most – on weekends, or just before dinner – where do you go to get it? Even during banking hours on weekdays you can find yourself walking miles, past bank after bank full of busy money-changing citizens, but barred to *you* by the inflexible sign *no change, no wechsel*. Every guidebook lists the exchange facilities in the railway stations: but we can only say that they are a foretaste of hell. Fearsomely crowded, jostling with impatient travellers barging themselves and their rucksacks past you to get to ticket offices and trains. But fear nothing, here are the life-saving addresses:

CCF (Crédit Commercial de France)

115 Champs-Élysées, 8e
Métro: George-V
Hours: Monday to Saturday, 8:30 a.m. to 8:00 p.m.

UBP

154 Champs-Élysées, 8e
Métro: Charles de Gaulle-Étoile
Hours: Monday to Friday 9:00 a.m. to 5:00 p.m., Saturdays, Sundays, holidays, 10:30 to 6:00 p.m.

But watch out – this is the Mug's Bank, charging almost 10F to cash an English bank cheque which others cash for 7F50, and 10F plus for travellers' cheques. It also has a time-wasting double-queueing system. They often refuse cheques drawn on English provincial banks. Use ONLY on Sundays or holidays when desperate.

Bank Tejerat

44 Champs-Élysées, 8e
Métro: Franklin D Roosevelt

Open Sundays during June, July and August; they charge a slightly higher exchange fee than most banks, but are a useful refuge on a Sunday.
Hours: Monday through Saturday, 9:00 a.m. to 6:00 p.m., Sundays 11:00 a.m. to 6:00 p.m. Closed 12–1 p.m. every day.

Barclays Bank

rue Intérieure, 9e (entrance in rue St-Lazare)
Métro: St-Lazare
Just across from the rail and Métro station, a lovely peaceful
English-speaking bank – and cashing Eurocheques there costs less
than at the other commercial places. Open 9:15 a.m. to 5:30 p.m.,
Monday to Friday, closed at noon on days before major holidays.

Banco Borges

30 rue du 4 Septembre, 2e
Métro: Opéra or 4 Septembre
Hours: Monday to Friday, 9:30 a.m. to 6:30 p.m. Saturday 9:00 a.m.
to 5:00 p.m.

Bureau de Change

9 rue Scribe, 9e
Métro: Opéra
Hours: Monday to Friday: 9:00 a.m. to 5:15 p.m. No exchange fee
charged.

Melia Travel Agency

31 avenue de l'Opéra, 1er
Métro: Opéra
Hours: Monday to Friday, 9:30 a.m. to 6:30 p.m., Saturday 9:30 a.m.
to 6:00 p.m.
Days before holidays (e.g., 24 and 31 Dec.): 9:00 a.m. to 4:00 p.m.

Banque Portugaise

5 rue Auber, 9e
Métro: Opera
Hours: Monday to Friday, 9:30 a.m. to 6:15 p.m., Saturday 9:00 a.m.
to 6:00 p.m.

Banks and *bureaux de change* have varying charges for cashing personal and travellers' cheques, so shop around. At Barclays, you can cash a personal cheque for up to £100 per day, backed with a bank card and your passport, for a single fee of 7F50. Other banks insist on two cheques, £50 each, with two fees. American Express travellers' cheques are best cashed (no fee) at their offices, otherwise you pay at least 1%. Barclays' travellers' cheques cost you nothing to cash at their branches.

Eurocheques

Between 1983 and the end of 1985, the major banks opted for the Uniform Eurocheque scheme, to supersede the use of your personal chequebook backed with a Eurocheque card – which, although fairly widely accepted in banks abroad – did not allow you to pay for meals, hotels or purchases with a cheque. You will pay £3.50 a year to your bank, plus 1.25% of the value of each cheque, plus about 30p per cheque to your own bank. In return, you get the privilege of writing cheques in local currency, which can save you a lot of time and the petty annoyance of queueing to cash cheques in a bank and paying a fee each time. In France, you can write cheques for up to 1000F; and can cash cheques at a bank for up to £100. You may be asked to produce your passport as well as the cheque-guarantee card, but there's no point in getting wrought up about this – just do it and don't argue.

It's possible that by the time you read this, you may be able to use this new card to get cash from machines; ask your bank about this, and for a PIN number for such use.

Travellers' Cheques, of course, are the safest way to carry money, as if lost or stolen they will be replaced with varying degrees of speed – but they cost you 1% of their value to buy, and usually about 1% to sell, unless you make for the Paris branch of the issuing company (American Express, Barclays, etc.). Never cash travellers' cheques, or personal cheques, at any branch of the CIC bank! They have a fixed charge of 12F, plus taxes of 18.25% on that for every transaction no matter how small. In London, Thomas Cook and the various *bureaux de change* found in such central areas as Piccadilly Circus and Kensington charge a fee of 1 per cent for selling you francs for pounds, with a minimum charge of 75p (Cook's) or 60p (most *bureaux de change*). Branches of major banks charge ½ of 1 per cent, with a minimum charge, usually, of about 50p. You can change pounds into francs easily at Heathrow and Gatwick, where the big banks have branches, but this can take time because very often arriving air travellers are writing out long strings of travellers' cheques in yen, kroner, rands and suchlike. At the Paris end, at Charles de Gaulle and Orly, there are *bureaux de change* which will change travellers' cheques and pound notes.

National Giro will furnish its account holders with Post Cheques, which can be cashed at any post office in francs – and this can be a tremendous convenience for out-of-banking-hours emergencies. These cheques must be ordered in advance, take about a week to ten days to get, and come in books of ten each worth up to £50. *And* – a real plus – unlike travellers' cheques which must be paid for on the spot, plus the usual 1 per cent charge, the money for a Post Cheque isn't taken out of your Giro account until the cheque is cashed. A charge of about 5F60 – about 50p at the moment – is made for each encashment.

Credit cards can be used to draw cash against your account from French banks displaying the appropriate symbol; the amount varies from year to year and so do the terms. Find out before you leave England whether this cash advance is interest free if you settle up on the normal due date, or if it begins to attract interest – up to 23% a year – the day it hits their computer. American Express cardholders can cash personal cheques, backed by the Amex card, for up to £500 every 21 days. Diners' Club will advance up to 8250F to its cardholders every two weeks, but of course a swingeing interest charge will be added if the account is not promptly settled when the bill comes in. Their office: 18 rue François Premier, 8e.

When it comes to using credit cards to pay for meals, hotels, or purchases abroad, opinions differ. More and more restaurants – even small brasseries and cafés, including one we know in the very working-class area of the rue de Charonne – are offering charge-card services. It lets you have up to six weeks' free credit before you have to pay up. But – and this can hurt, as we found out in June 1981 when the pound was behaving like a kangaroo – you will be billed at the rate on the date when the credit-card company enters the charge on your account, *not* on the date when you incurred the expense, so you have no way of knowing exactly how much you are spending.

If you are from a country outside the EEC, you get a certain break when using travellers' cheques: if you are spending more than a certain amount in shops like Samaritaine and Galeries Lafayette, you will get a discount because your purchase is exempted from the French version of VAT. Ask at the customer service bureau in the store for details.

Newspapers

In French: *Le Monde* is left of centre, *Le Figaro* right of centre (but at the moment, with the Socialists in office, *Le Figaro* veers wildly to the right). Either will give you a morning's occupation if your French is slow. *France-Soir* leans towards the sensational, a good source of crime and scandal stories; *Le Canard Enchaîné*, is a sort of French *Private Eye*; *Paris-Match* is the *Life* of France. A couple of hundred others, of all sorts and persuasions.

In English: the *International Herald Tribune* (daily) for comprehensive stock quotations, news, and American 'Op-Ed' features. Columnists recruited from the *New York Times*, the *Washington Post* and elsewhere. *Guardian, Times, Telegraph* available daily near the Hotel Crillon, place de la Concorde, at Palais Royale, Opéra and other central news kiosks. And discover *Passion*, the monthly English-language magazine for intellectual news, views and reviews, personal ads, fashion, beautiful photographic essays.

Nuisances

Noise: hotel regulations specify quiet before 10 a.m. and after 10 p.m. Bang on the wall or call the manager if you have noisy neighbours. Try *il y a du bruit* (it's noisy), or *c'est trop bruyant*.

Other complaints

Mosquitoes: *Moustiques*
Fleas: *Puces*

Lice: *Poux* (don't complain, leave the hotel)
Inedible: (mild) Cela ne me plaît pas
         (strong) *C'est dégoûtant, ça*
Odour (extreme): *Ça pue!*
Unwelcome advances: *Laissez-moi tranquille. Fiche-moi le camp!*

Beggars: if you're unwilling or unable to give handouts, the best defence is not to understand what they want. *Parle pas* will do.

Thieves see p.232

Smoking: if the smell of Gauloises and Gitanes bothers you, leave the country. It's true that smoking is forbidden in post offices, Métros, buses, and certain other public places, but you can't spend all your time in these. The rule (*défense de fumer*) is generally adhered to, although Parisians will often light up just as the Métro doors open.

Numbers

It's absolutely necessary to understand the difference between, say, *quatorze* and *quarante*; between *cinq* and *cent*. When you can tell in an instant what *quatre-vingt dix-neuf* means, you've arrived. Memorize the following:

1	un	vingt-et-un . . .	21
2	deux	trente-et-un . . .	31
3	trois	quarante-et-un . . .	41
4	quatre	cinquante-et-un . . .	51
5	cinq	soixante-et-un . . .	61
6	six	soixante-et-onze . . .	71
7	sept	quatre-vingt-un . . .	81
8	huit	quatre-vingt- onze . . .	91
9	neuf	cent	100
10	dix	deux cent	200
11	onze	mille	1000
12	douze		
13	treize		
14	quatorze		

15	quinze
16	seize
17	dix-sept
18	dix-huit
19	dix-neuf
20	vingt

premier (ière)	first
seconde	second
troisième	third
quatrième	fourth
cinquième	fifth

Without understanding the numbers, you won't be able to ask information about bus routes; pay for a meal or a minor purchase without getting it in writing; figure out what the gendarme means when he says the Métro is *deux-cent cinquante* metres away.

Open and closed: abbreviations

TLJ – every day (*tous les jours*)
Sauf lundi – except Monday
S, D & F – Saturdays, Sundays and holidays (*samedis, dimanches et fêtes*)

Periodicals

Pariscope and *Officiel des Spectacles*, for weekly listings of cinemas, theatre, concerts, dance, music, cabaret, races and other sports, and art galleries. 3F50, every Wednesday.

Police (see also 'Au secours', pp.227–37)

Paris police come in different guises. The everyday cop, the gendarme (*le flic*), travels on foot, usually in pairs. He is to be addressed thus:
   '*Pardon, Monsieur l'agent . . .*'

Any other means of getting his attention, short of falling in front of a bus, will get a chilly reception.

The CSP are a special anti-terrorist force who guard embassies, certain banks, agencies such as Aeroflot (the Russian airline) and the like. They wear blue windcheaters, carry guns, and look like thugs. Do not ask them what time it is.

If you are a foreigner, and are asked, for whatever reason, to show your *papiers* – your passport – to a gendarme, do so. If you don't have it on you it's a fast trip downtown for you.

In general it would be unwise to break any laws while in Paris.

La politesse

Without which you might as well stay at home. Parisians – if you'll permit the generalization – are formal creatures. What they lack in rigid class distinctions they make up for in the personal carapace of manners that each carries around. It's unlikely that any Parisian will adopt you into the bosom of his family, or spill his inmost secrets to you, but with the right approach you can at least penetrate the first line of defence.

The trick is to use the standard forms of *politesse: Excusez-moi, monsieur; s'il vous plaît, madame; pardon, mademoiselle* . . . and use the honorific (never the *tu* form unless a) you're a member of the family; b) you're a bitter enemy; or c) you're among the more casual student generation, who seem to have given up the second person plural). And say the words as if you mean them. As a rule, Parisians prefer to be spoken to directly; they are all for eye-contact; they enjoy shaking hands (brief – up-and-down only – but firm) on all occasions, once a relationship has been established.

And as a means of establishing relationships – even purely commercial ones – we suggest that you cultivate certain people and places throughout your stay. Even if you spend most of your days in the hinterland of the city, there should be a few characters – the concierge of your hotel, the owner of your neighbourhood café, the woman who sells you the newspaper, the staff of a restaurant or two where you return several times – who will get to recognize you, know you however slightly, welcome your appearance, bid you good appetite or good day. If you make the effort to communicate – in however stumbling French – it will be appreciated. If you enjoy their food, their accommodation, their city, don't feel shy about showing it.

Post

Another exercise in bureaucracy: receiving parcels through the post office is said to be Kafkaesque.

Stamps (*timbres*) are available at post offices (*bureaux de poste*) and at *tabacs* (tobacco shops) for French destinations only. Postboxes are oblong, about two feet by three feet, a pale, Dijon-mustard colour, generally attached to walls, and virtually invisible. In post offices you have a choice of three slots: Paris only, *Avion* (airmail), and *départements étrangers* (anywhere outside Paris).

The French produce some of the prettiest (and biggest) commemorative stamps in the world. They're called *timbres de collection*, and are available at a special window in the post office.

A 24-hour post office is open at 52 rue du Louvre, 1er, but never go on Saturday afternoon or Sunday unless you can face an hour's queuing. At 71 avenue des Champs Élysées, 8e, a post office is open Sundays and holidays, for stamps, telephones and telegrams only – also very crowded.

Letters Paris/United Kingdom cost 2F40 for 20 grams (airmail envelope and two thin sheets of paper); postcards are 1F70. Airmail letters to the US and Canada are 3F40 for 10 grams.

Post codes: the postal code for Paris is 75, and to this is added a zero and the number of the *arrondissement*. Most of the Marais is thus 75004. It's always written 75004 Paris, postal code first and town name second. (These codes are changing and may be made more specific, in the British style, in 1986.)

Telegrams: via the telegram counter at any post office, or call 4 233 21 11. Seven word minimum; the address counts as part of the message.

Telex: public telex offices at 7 rue Feydeau, 2e Tel: 4 233 20 12, or 4 233 20 13. *Métro*: Bourse. Open daily, 8:00 a.m. to 8:00 p.m.

Railway information

The great source of all knowledge about how to get from anywhere to anywhere in France is in the Information Bureau at Gare St-Lazare, near the entrance closest to the rue de Rome. It takes a few minutes to crack the code of how to work the timetables, which are mounted on rollers behind glass, but once you've done that you're in clover. Also available: a certain number of printed time-tables from a central stand in this office, each section labelled by the name of the station from which the train leaves. No one here speaks English, so equip yourself with your pocket dictionary to make sure you understand all the footnotes. And don't leave this planning until the last minute before a journey.

Shoe repair

cordonnerie – cobblers
soulier – shoe
lacet de soulier – shoe lace
cuir – leather
semelle – sole
talon – heel

Slang

The current argot runs to Franglais, which you should have no trouble with (although it does change: jogging, a few years ago, was known as *le footing*, now it's *le jogging*). And abbreviation: you can go to *un resto très sympa* and possibly finish your meal with a liqueur or *un cogna*.

Anyone in deep trouble is said to be *dans le chocolat* which is a delicate way to avoid saying *dans la merde*.

For a complete and very funny read, get Miles Kington's *Let's Parler Franglais!* published by Penguin – he may have invented some of the words, but they sound authentic.

Taxis

Current prices in the City of Paris, as far as the Boulevards Périphériques: from 6:30 a.m. to 10:00 p.m. 'Tarif A':

Pick-up charge   8F
Price per kilometre   1F85
Waiting time: 1 hour   36F
(Same price if the taxi is held up in traffic and can go at only 24 km per hour or less)

From 10:00 p.m. to 6:30 a.m., 'Tarif B':

Pick-up charge   8F
Price per kilometre   2F75
Waiting time per hour   36F

Telephones

A subsidiary of the Post Office. In public places, such as airports, phones are frequently found with post offices and telegraph offices under the sign PTT (Poste, Téléphone, Télégraphe). Otherwise, there are many kiosks on the streets, cubicles in hotels, restaurants, bars, brasseries.

Pay phones: as of October 1985, all Paris telephone numbers must now be prefaced with the number 4, so you have eight digits to dial. Calls cost 1F, and you can use two ½F pieces or a single coin, if you are lucky enough to find an unvandalized phone kiosk. Also, make sure you have your number written down before you begin telephoning, because it's hard to understand a telephone number delivered with machine-gun speed by Directory Assistance, and you will almost never find an intact telephone directory in any kiosk.

Since so many public phones are literally unusable, if you have any serious telephoning to do make for some peaceful place with a handful of coins. At the Galérie Rond Point, 12 avenue des Champs Élysées (*Métro*: Franklin D Roosevelt) there are three good working phones, in the *sous-sol*, all with numbers where you can be called back. The Galérie Claridges nearby has two telephones and, wonder of wonders, complete telephone directories. The Galérie des Champs, 84 Champs-Élysées, has three phones (and free loos, unlike most other public places, although they of course get very crowded by mid-day). Luxury hotels almost always have public telephones, and a place to sit down.

After you have put in the coin or coins, and dialled the number, you will hear a jumble of noise and then a 'ring' tone which sounds like the British 'number engaged' sound. Don't hang up.

You can often phone from cafés, *tabacs* and bars, although some have a notice over the bar telling you that telephones and toilets are reserved for the clientele. You may be asked to buy a *jeton* from the cashier, which will probably cost about 1F20; or the time of the call will be registered on a meter at the bar and you pay later. *Jetons* are not transferable from café to café, so if your party doesn't answer, get your money back. *Jeton* phones require you to press a rectangular button to the right of the phone when your party answers.

Outside the eight-digit area, time and distance come into play. In phone kiosks, there is a table listing the correct amount to pay for a call lasting a specified number of minutes, to a specified three-number 'area code'. Consult the table, dial, wait for an answer, insert the money. When your time is almost up you'll be warned by a tone. Put in more change only then.

Long-distance: in PTT locations, where there is an operator to help you, you can write the phone number, city, and country you want to call on a piece of paper. The operator will place the call for you and tell you the charges when you're through. A pay phone works as well, but requires quantities of small change. Direct-dial instructions are posted in every call-box.

An easy way to call long-distance is to place a collect call (a 'PCV') and have the party ring you back. This is especially useful in hotels, which normally add a surcharge to all phone calls, local and long-distance. Drawback: it may take an hour and a half for a collect call to go through.

Collect calls to the United States and Canada cannot be made on Sundays.

Time

The French use the twelve-hour clock, but run on 24-hour time. Hence, 5 p.m. is 17:00 (*dix-sept heures*); midnight is 24:00 (*minuit*); and so forth. It takes practice.

The days of the week are *lundi, mardi, mercredi, jeudi, vendredi, samedi* and *dimanche*. The months of the year are easier to deal with: *janvier, février, mars, avril, mai, juin, juillet, août, septembre, octobre, novembre* and *décembre*. We narrowly escaped Napoleon's idea of *Germinal, Thermidor, Brumaire*, which, from 1793 to 1806, replaced the more familiar Gregorian Calendar.

And France is one hour ahead of the UK; six hours later than the US (East Coast time). You should be aware of this before you call your friends at 3:00 a.m., *their* time.

Tipping

The rules are clear-cut. Try not to deviate if you want to stay on good terms with your hosts.

Taxis: 10 to 15 per cent.

Lavatory attendants: ½F.

Waiters: 15 per cent is almost always included (you'll note the words *servis compris* on the menu). When service is *non-compris*, your expenses will be itemized, with 15 per cent (rounded off either way) tacked on at the bottom of your bill, and the whole thing totalled.

Cafés: 15 per cent is included (as for waiters) for table service. At the counter, leave some change.

Cloakroom attendants: 1F per person. A *consigne* at a railway station will post its rates: currently 7F50 per piece of luggage. No other tip necessary.

Hotels: Service is added into the bill – but if the concierge or any other personnel have done you special favours (calling theatres, getting taxis), they should be rewarded.

Porters: Set price: 7F50 piece of luggage.

Hairdressers: 10 to 20 per cent.

Theatre and cinema ushers: 1F for the cinema and theatre, per person.

Traffic

Since we assume you're not suicidal, we won't deal with traffic regulations from a driver's viewpoint here. As a *piéton* – a pedestrian – you should know a few rules of the game.

If you're English, Scottish, Welsh, Irish or Japanese, you should know that traffic in France travels on the *right*. Therefore, when you step off the kerb, do not look to your right. *Look left*. Then look right, left again, and in all directions as quickly as possible before you head out, or you'll be mowed down. Most Paris streets, though not all, are one-way.

For pedestrians, a green light is a little green man in the traffic signal; sometimes a pinpoint of green or white light; sometimes nothing at all. A red light is a little red man. Your best bet is to wait for all traffic to stop, and ride on someone else's coat-tails across the street. All traffic lights, red or green, are called *feux rouges*.

Zebra crossings exist, but may be ignored by all concerned. Traffic tends to edge into them even when stopped.

Paris streets are either incredibly wide (the *grands boulevards*) and hence impossible to cross without feeling totally naked; or incredibly narrow, with cars parked halfway up the kerb, pedestrians walking with one foot in the gutter, single file, or face to the wall. Either way it's risky, so watch your step.

Wheelchair access

Paris for the less mobile. To be perfectly plain about it, Paris isn't the ideal city for anyone in a wheelchair or with serious walking difficulties. The Métro and the buses are only for those with a certain degree of mobility on their own two feet. The major museums are out of reach because they are reached by flights of steps (except the Jeu de Paume, whose entrance door is almost on the flat, and many of whose major treasures are on the main floor). The Louvre is said to have a special entrance for those in wheelchairs, but *Which?* magazine, June 1981, reported absolute frustration when attempted by one of their researchers.

That said, one must in all fairness add that Paris itself – its streets, its squares, its buildings, its illumination at night – is infinitely accessible and always rewarding.

In the government-produced *Guide des Hôtels*, there is a 'wheelchair' symbol which seems to promise much in the way of facilities for the disabled. Sadly, it has been impossible to establish any norm of exactly what the facilities are: many hoteliers who offer such conveniences as lifts or bedrooms on the ground floor forget that access to the hotel is up several steps, or through a narrow door. And far too many lifts, because of space restrictions in lobbies, are actually approached by two or three steps which make manoeuvring impossible. Other hotels listed with the 'wheelchair' symbol have split-level lobbies impossible for wheelchairs, and tricky even for those who use crutches or canes.

A useful series of guides for France is published under the title of *Access*, from 68B Castlebar Road, Ealing, London W5. Two or three of the hotels their group has vetted still come within our price and comfort range:

Véronèse, 5 rue Véronèse, 13e Tel: 4 331 20 90 *Métro*: Place d'Italie
Good sized lift; some bedrooms on ground floor.

Aviator, 20 rue Louis-Blanc, 10e Tel: 4 607 79 24 *Métro*: Louis-Blanc
Easy access from street; moderate-sized lift.

Grand Hôtel du Septième, 13 rue Chevert, 7e Tel: 4 551 10 48
Métro: École-Militaire
Easy access from street; moderate-sized lift.

More specific information is available from an excellent publication called *Voyager Quand Même* (Travel Anyway), in French and in English, published by Le Comité National Français de Liaison pour la Réadaptation des Handicapés (CNFLRH), 38 boulevard Raspail, 75007 Paris.

Association des Paralysés de France (APF), 17 boulevard Auguste-Blanqui, 75013 Paris, will furnish information about services and help available, and has representatives in various areas to help, as well as a magazine called *Faire Face* (in French) which often contains useful information.

Women on their own

Word has it that women alone do just fine in Paris (the reverse has also been mentioned). Our sources say that women can eat alone in almost any restaurant (except in an obviously raffish neighbourhood), drink alone in most bars, walk alone in most parks and *quartiers* without being disturbed or made to feel uncomfortable; stay alone in hotels. But use your head; don't walk in parks or lonely dark streets at night – either alone or in company.

Au secours (Emergencies)

Dealing with real trouble at home is bad enough. In a foreign country, and in a foreign language, it can be devastating. But there are resources.

Medical emergencies

If it's more than a minor ailment, you need an English-speaking doctor or nurse, or a supply of medicine dispensed by someone who can understand you and your problem without the aid of faltering French or a translator. Here are the numbers to note. Write them down in your pocket notebook for the times (we hope rare) when you don't have this book in your hand.

Hospitals:

British Hospital

3 rue Barbès, Levallois-Perret
(In a suburb of Paris, but easily reached)
Tel: 4 758 13 12
Métro: Anatole-France
24 hours, 365 days a year

Telephone first for an appointment. Medical only; no dental facilities.

American Hospital

63 boulevard Victor-Hugo, Neuilly
Tel: 4 747 53 00
Métro: Porte-Maillot, then bus 82 to last stop

Appointments: telephone first. Hours: 9:00 a.m. to noon, 2:00 to 6:00 p.m. Sundays: emergency treatment only, no fixed appointments. Dental as well as medical.

Pharmacists

Pharmacie Anglaise des Champs-Élysées
62 avenue des Champs-Élysées, 8e
Tel: 4 359 22 52 and 4 225 25 13
Métro: George V

Well stocked with familiar English and American brands of medicines, or their French equivalents, and attended by professional people who speak English. They will fill a prescription from a doctor, or can give you advice about a proprietary product for minor ills (headache, diarrhoea, streaming cold, strains and sprains, rheumatic pain).

Hours: 8:30 a.m. to 10:30 p.m., Monday to Saturday. Closed Sundays.

British-American Pharmacy

1 rue Auber, 9e
Métro: Opéra

Very much like the one mentioned above, staffed with bright, English-speaking people.

Hours: 8:30 a.m. to 8:00 p.m., Monday to Saturday; closed Sundays.

Pharmacie des Arts

106 boulevard Montparnasse, 14e
Tel: 4 325 44 88
Métro: Vavin

Another late-night refuge. They have been dealing with English and American tourists for years, and can produce an over-the-counter remedy for almost anything, as well as quickly filling medical prescriptions. Prices tend to be high but the extraordinary opening hours make it worth it if you are in real need.

Hours: 8:00 a.m. to midnight, Monday to Saturday; 9:00 a.m. to 1:00 p.m. Sundays and public holidays.

Pharmacie des Champs-Élysées

84 avenue des Champs-Élysées, 8e
Tel: 4 562 02 41
Métro: Franklin-D.-Roosevelt, George V

Open 24 hours a day – very small, but useful in extreme emergency, and they speak about 18 languages.

Pharmacie Le Drugstore

boulevard St-Germain (corner of rue de Rennes)
Tel: 4 548 04 55
Métro: St-Germain

Open 10:00 a.m. to 2:00 a.m. seven days a week. English spoken, and English and American remedies stocked.

Poison Centre

Hôpital de l'Assistance Publique Fernand Widal, 200 rue du Faubourg St-Denis, 10e
Tel: 4 205 63 29
Métro: La Chapelle

Burn Centre

Hôpital de l'Assistance Publique Trousseau, 26 avenue Dr Arnold
Netter, 12e
Tel: 4 346 13 90
Métro: Porte de Vincennes

Drug Crisis Centre

Hôpital Marmottan, 19 rue d'Armaillé, 17e
Tel: 4 574 00 04
Métro: Argentine

Alcoholics Anonymous in English

Tel: 4 806 43 68

SOS Pacemakers

Tel: 4 250 33 08
24 hours a day

If you have a pace-tracer, your pacemaker can be checked through
the telephone. Call 4 532 84 34, 24 hours a day.

VD Clinic

43 rue de Valois, 1er
Métro: Palais Royal

Dispensaire de la Croix Rouge Française de Vénérologie

Service free, English minimal, sympathy non-existent.

Medical bills

English travellers in France get a pretty good deal. Free, or partially free, medical care is available through the reciprocal scheme of the EEC. Good news: this now applies to the self-employed (barristers and such) and the unemployed, as well as to 'full time employees'; and if you're going abroad as a family, a single form covers all of you.

At least thirty days before departure, get Form CM-1 from your local Department of Health and Social Security office, or by mail from the DHSS Leaflets Unit, Stanmore, Middlesex HA7 1AY. Fill it in at once and you are rewarded with Form E-111. If you need a doctor or hospital treatment in France, pay the bill, get a receipt, and present it for repayment (70–80 per cent of the charges) to the French Sickness Insurance Office. Full details accompany Form E-111. Guard your E-111 with your life, as it cannot be replaced by post if lost, and the British Embassy can do nothing about reissuing it for you.

House calls by a doctor will cost from 100F, depending on the neighbourhood. Office calls are about 75F.

First Aid

At night, Sundays, or holidays, your concierge can telephone the nearest Commissariat of Police to get you the name of an emergency doctor. In case of a street accident or emergency, look for the automatic callbox marked *Services Médicaux*, at the nearest intersection of major streets.

Europ-Assistance

A round-the-clock service for the nervous: offering what seems to be the most complete *au secours* operation currently available. It provides the usual range of coverage for lost luggage, personal accident, delays, cancellations and so forth. But in addition, in cases of extreme need it will provide either an air ambulance to fly home an ill or injured person, or will get them back to base on a scheduled air service, along with a doctor or nurse if necessary.

In France, there are 2000 Europ-Assistance agents, most of them multilingual, and you will see their symbols in banks, garages and shops. If you have ignored our one-word advice about driving in Paris (*don't*) have a look at their motoring policies. But perhaps of more interest to paupers in Paris is the non-motoring coverage: for a journey of up to five days, £7.20 covers you against loss of luggage up to £750, money up to £200, delay or cancellation costs up to £800, and medical expenses up to £100,000. For six to twelve days, it costs £9.15, for 13 to 23 days the cost is only £10.80, and if for any reason beyond your control your stay has to be prolonged, you get coverage free for an extra week.

In every insurance policy, it's wise to read the fine print, and Europ-Assistance is no exception. For instance, if you know before you go that there may be a transport strike – and that includes such wildcat numbers as the British Rail strike that tied us all up in the summer of 1982 – your policy won't cover expenses for delay or alternative travel. Riots, civil commotions and such are also excluded, so don't get in the way of a paving block or a Special Forces baton.

Otherwise, there don't seem to be any catches, and many people we know who have used this service swear by it. When you buy a policy, you are given a seven days a week day and night number to phone wherever you are, and this gives one a great sense of having a security blanket at hand.

You must get your coverage before you leave the UK (although on Townsend Thoresen ships, you can buy a last-minute policy from the purser under the name of Gold Cover). For details: Europ-Assistance, 252 High Street, Croydon, Surrey, CR0 1NF. Telephone: 01 680 1234. In the United States, it's available through INA (Insurance Company of North America).

Robbery, attack, rape

Or any other crime of which you are a victim – use the automatic callbox as above, marked *Police Secours*. Ask for someone who speaks English. We are advised by feminist friends in Paris that the police are notably unsympathetic to anyone claiming rape, as they seem to take the attitude that women who wear anything more provocative than an anorak are asking for trouble.

Lost passport

Make sure you have the number of your document noted in your notebook. The minute you lose it, through carelessness or by theft, report to the nearest police station (ask a policeman or a *pervenche* – the blue-clad meter maid), then go at once to your embassy (addresses below). They can issue you a travel document that will get you in and out of most countries, although in some parts of the Continent this can mean at best a sour look and some questioning from the immigration men; at worst a few hours of cooling your heels in airport or train station while they check up on you.

Lost money

Report it to the police, as for passports, then forget it. See Travel insurance, below.

Travellers' cheques

You *do* keep a record of those numbers in that notebook, don't you? Cross off each as you cash the cheques. If you lose the remaining ones, get in touch with the issuing company right away (their European addresses and telephone numbers are in the fine print that comes with the cheques). With varying degrees of speed, they will provide duplicate ones. Report this loss, too, to the Paris police.

Credit cards

Note down the numbers, expiration date, and Paris address of the company. Call them right away and tell them exactly when you discovered the loss, so they can issue a stop-order which protects you against someone booking a round-the-world flight on your Visa card. Each company has a slightly different policy on covering losses on credit cards, so be sure you know your rights when you make your call. If you get an automatic answering service, at night,

Sundays, or holidays, say your piece slowly, and include the phrase, 'As of this moment, X a.m. or Y p.m., of reporting the loss, I am no longer responsible for any charges incurred on this card number: 0000000000000.'

You can now insure your credit cards against loss and fraudulent use – check with the issuing company. Such coverage costs about £6–£7 a year and could save you ££££.

Lost or stolen jewellery, camera, clothing, luggage

Report to the nearest police station (ask someone who speaks French, if you can, to write out a brief description of the lost item in French). Last resort: the Lost and Found office (Bureau des Objets Trouvés), 36 rue des Morillons, 15e (*Métro*: Convention). File a report of what you lost and where you think you lost it. The chances of recovering anything are almost nil, but in dealing with such an emergency you'll be surprised at how your French improves, and you'll get to see the inside of offices and police stations that are right out of Maigret. French functionaries are not noted for their ability to speak English – that's not what they're paid for – so if you can chase up a French-speaking friend to go with you, it will help.

Thefts at airports

This is the 'in' thing in French crime these days. Charles de Gaulle/ Roissy is the mecca for the brighter minds in the criminal world. Most recent ploy is for two or three top-rank snatch men to fly in, mingle with the queue at the check-in desk of a major airline, wait until madame in the mink coat puts down her Vuitton satchel while she deals with tickets and reservations. A quick jostle, many apologies, and *voilà*, the precious case is gone with a colleague, headed for Milan or Amsterdam on the next flight. It may sound like a film plot, but the Paris papers were full of it recently. Brief-cases (for calculators, radio, expensive pens), and garment bags (suede jackets, suits and dresses) are the favourites. When you put down your carry-on luggage at the check-in, put your foot on it or through the handle. If you are robbed at the airport despite this advice, ask the nearest airline desk to call the airport security police. They will do their best, but don't get your hopes up.

Travel insurance

Everything you travel with – clothes, radio, watch, money, luggage, specs – can be covered by comprehensive travel insurance. This should, ideally, include cancellation insurance for plane, train, or boat tickets that may not be usable because of illness or accident. Make sure you have the kind of policy that provides you with instant money to get replacement clothes, luggage, camera, etc., without waiting months for reimbursement. Contact lens wearers should make sure that their insurance policy covers travel. Read the fine print. One friend who thought her fur coat was covered by her household policy had it pinched in a restaurant, and too late found that said coat was only covered in the house – not while being worn. Ask your travel agent for the best deals going, don't buy the first policy offered; check one against the other.

Animal bites

Cat scratches, dog bites, a nip from a horse or a squirrel – don't shrug them off. The best we can advise is *not* to fool around with any animal, tame or wild, on the continent. Rabies is at large in Europe, no joke. The French call it *la rage*, and you will see warning posters in many places. If you are scratched or bitten, get a doctor at once, and report the incident to the police quickly. They will pick up the animal and hold it until it is proved to be either safe or rabid. And they will keep you under observation until your condition has been thoroughly checked. You may need a series of painful, costly, and time-consuming injections which can wreck your holiday: so don't feed squirrels or stray cats, and unless you know an animal and its owner personally, keep your hands to yourself.

Stranded

If you are without money, travellers' cheques, or transport because of loss, theft, or other damage, call on your embassy. If they are convinced that you are a genuine victim without resources, they can arrange for your transportation home (the slowest and cheapest way). You must agree to pay them back as soon as you reach a source of funds. Each embassy has a different policy, so check with yours.

British Embassy

35 rue du Faubourg St-Honoré, 8e
Tel: 4 266 91 42
Métro: Concorde

It's a beautiful, historic house and worth taking a look at if you have legitimate reason to call. Nicer manners than at the American Embassy, and not so many guns in evidence, but the same basic approach.

British Consulate (for other problems)
2 Cité du Rétiro, 8e
Tel: 4 266 91 42
Métro: Concorde

American Embassy

2 avenue Gabriel, 8e
Tel: 4 296 12 02
Métro: Concorde

Brusque but helpful. Don't expect much sympathy or offers of extra money, as they have had to deal with too many feckless tourists in the sixties and seventies who thought they were a soft touch for Uncle Sam's largesse. Lost passports replaced here, but you must produce some evidence of residence and citizenship.

American Consulate
2 rue St-Florentin, 1er
Tel: 4 296 14 88

Canadian Embassy

35 avenue Montaigne, 8e
Tel: 4 723 52 50
Métro: Alma Marceau

Canadian Consulate
4 rue Ventadour, 1er
Tel: 4 296 87 19
Métro: Pyramides

Australian Embassy and Consulate

4 rue Jean-Rey, 15e
Tel: 4 575 62 00
Métro: Bir-Hakeim

New Zealand Embassy and Consulate

7 rue Leonardo-da-Vinci, 16e
Tel: 4 500 24 11
Métro: Victor Hugo

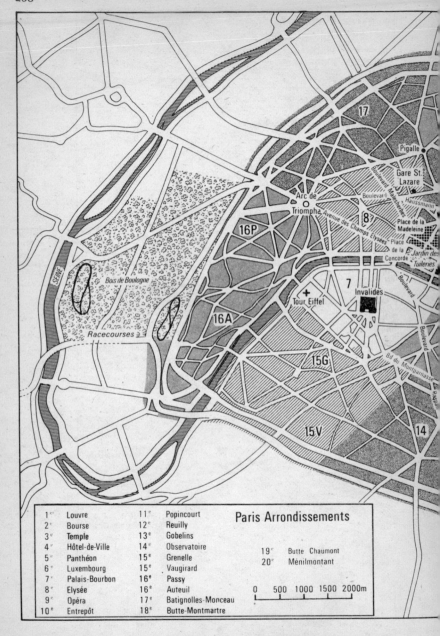

17

Pigalle

Gare St.
Lazare

Boulevard
Haussmann

Arc de
Triomphe

16P

8

Place de la
Madeleine

Avenue des Champs Elysées

Place
de la
Concorde

Jardin des
Tuileries

Boulevard

SEINE

Bois de Boulogne

Tour Eiffel

7
Invalides

16A

Bd. du Montparnasse

Racecourses

15G

15V

14

1ᵉʳ	Louvre	11ᵉ	Popincourt	**Paris Arrondissements**		
2ᵉ	Bourse	12ᵉ	Reuilly			
3ᵉ	Temple	13ᵉ	Gobelins			
4ᵉ	Hôtel-de-Ville	14ᵉ	Observatoire	19ᵉ	Butte Chaumont	
5ᵉ	Panthéon	15ᵉ	Grenelle	20ᵉ	Ménilmontant	
6ᵉ	Luxembourg	15ᵉ	Vaugirard			
7ᵉ	Palais-Bourbon	16ᵉ	Passy	0 500 1000 1500 2000m		
8ᵉ	Elysée	16ᵉ	Auteuil			
9ᵉ	Opéra	17ᵉ	Batignolles-Monceau			
10ᵉ	Entrepôt	18ᵉ	Butte-Montmartre			

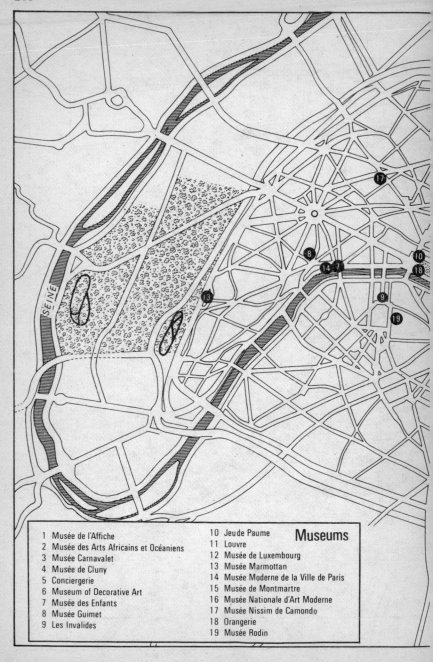

1 Musée de l'Affiche	10 Jeu de Paume **Museums**
2 Musée des Arts Africains et Océaniens	11 Louvre
3 Musée Carnavalet	12 Musée de Luxembourg
4 Musée de Cluny	13 Musée Marmottan
5 Conciergerie	14 Musée Moderne de la Ville de Paris
6 Museum of Decorative Art	15 Musée de Montmartre
7 Musée des Enfants	16 Musée Nationale d'Art Moderne
8 Musée Guimet	17 Musée Nissim de Camondo
9 Les Invalides	18 Orangerie
	19 Musée Rodin

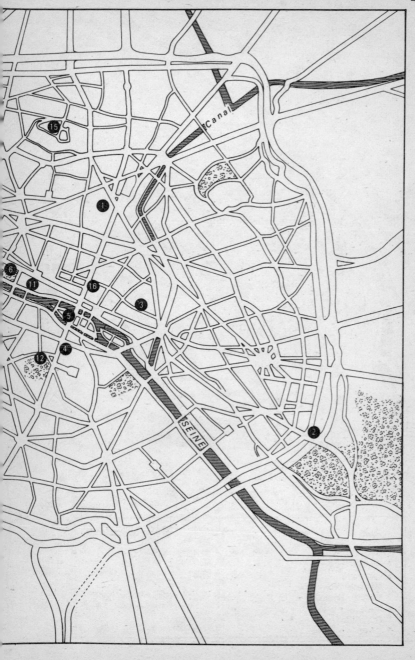

Index

Arthur Eperon
Travellers' France £3.50

Six major routes across France, taking in the best restaurants and hotels, visiting the most interesting out-of-the-way places. This detailed and up-to-the-minute handbook is for the traveller who wants more out of France than a mad dash down the motorway. Each of the six routes across the country is illustrated with a specially commissioned two-colour map, and includes a host of information on where to eat and drink, where to take children, where to stay and how to get the most out of the town and countryside.

The French Selection £4.95

If you've enjoyed Arthur Eperon's recommendations before, you'll welcome this hand-picked selection of good French hotels – and if you're taking advantage of his experience for the first time, you can be sure of an excellent holiday. The author is a professional *bon viveur*, and that means high standards in every hotel chosen. And they all offer good value for money, too. It's packed with all the information you need, so treat yourself to this indispensable guide to the true gourmet's France.

Le Weekend £2.95

Northern France and Belgium are not far away. It's knowing how to get there and where to go when you arrive. *Le Weekend* is Arthur Eperon's guide to getting the best out of your weekend on the Continent. Just a short journey from the terminal to a hotel or inn where you can meet the local people, drink good wine, eat very good food – where 'Monsieur le Patron mange ici' – and find gems within a few miles of the ports. The author of *Travellers' France* is one of the cognoscenti. Let him show you around.

Fiction

☐	**The Chains of Fate**	Pamela Belle	£2.95p
☐	**Options**	Freda Bright	£1.50p
☐	**The Thirty-nine Steps**	John Buchan	£1.50p
☐	**Secret of Blackoaks**	Ashley Carter	£1.50p
☐	**Lovers and Gamblers**	Jackie Collins	£2.50p
☐	**My Cousin Rachel**	Daphne du Maurier	£2.50p
☐	**Flashman and the Redskins**	George Macdonald Fraser	£1.95p
☐	**The Moneychangers**	Arthur Hailey	£2.95p
☐	**Secrets**	Unity Hall	£2.50p
☐	**The Eagle Has Landed**	Jack Higgins	£1.95p
☐	**Sins of the Fathers**	Susan Howatch	£3.50p
☐	**Smiley's People**	John le Carré	£2.50p
☐	**To Kill a Mockingbird**	Harper Lee	£1.95p
☐	**Ghosts**	Ed McBain	£1.75p
☐	**The Silent People**	Walter Macken	£2.50p
☐	**Gone with the Wind**	Margaret Mitchell	£3.95p
☐	**Wilt**	Tom Sharpe	£1.95p
☐	**Rage of Angels**	Sidney Sheldon	£2.50p
☐	**The Unborn**	David Shobin	£1.50p
☐	**A Town Like Alice**	Nevile Shute	£2.50p
☐	**Gorky Park**	Martin Cruz Smith	£2.50p
☐	**A Falcon Flies**	Wilbur Smith	£2.50p
☐	**The Grapes of Wrath**	John Steinbeck	£2.50p
☐	**The Deep Well at Noon**	Jessica Stirling	£2.95p
☐	**The Ironmaster**	Jean Stubbs	£1.75p
☐	**The Music Makers**	E. V. Thompson	£2.50p

Non-fiction

☐	**The First Christian**	Karen Armstrong	£2.50p
☐	**Pregnancy**	Gordon Bourne	£3.95p
☐	**The Law is an Ass**	Gyles Brandreth	£1.75p
☐	**The 35mm Photographer's Handbook**	Julian Calder and John Garrett	£6.50p
☐	**London at its Best**	Hunter Davies	£2.90p
☐	**Back from the Brink**	Michael Edwardes	£2.95p

☐	**Travellers' Britain**	} Arthur Eperon	£2.95p
☐	**Travellers' Italy**		£2.95p
☐	**The Complete Calorie**		
	Counter	Eileen Fowler	90p
☐	**The Diary of Anne Frank**	Anne Frank	£1.75p
☐	**And the Walls Came**		
	Tumbling Down	Jack Fishman	£1.95p
☐	**Linda Goodman's Sun Signs**	Linda Goodman	£2.95p
☐	**The Last Place on Earth**	Roland Huntford	£3.95p
☐	**Victoria RI**	Elizabeth Longford	£4.95p
☐	**Book of Worries**	Robert Morley	£1.50p
☐	**Airport International**	Brian Moynahan	£1.95p
☐	**Pan Book of Card Games**	Hubert Phillips	£1.95p
☐	**Keep Taking the Tabloids**	Fritz Spiegl	£1.75p
☐	**An Unfinished History**		
	of the World	Hugh Thomas	£3.95p
☐	**The Baby and Child Book**	Penny and Andrew	
		Stanway	£4.95p
☐	**The Third Wave**	Alvin Toffler	£2.95p
☐	**Pauper's Paris**	Miles Turner	£2.50p
☐	**The Psychic Detectives**	Colin Wilson	£2.50p

All these books are available at your local bookshop or newsagent, or
can be ordered direct from the publisher. Indicate the number of copies
required and fill in the form below

12

....

Name_____
(Block letters please)

Address_____

_____

Send to CS Department, Pan Books Ltd, PO Box 40, Basingstoke, Hants
Please enclose remittance to the value of the cover price plus:
35p for the first book plus 15p per copy for each additional book ordered
to a maximum charge of £1.25 to cover postage and packing
Applicable only in the UK

While every effort is made to keep prices low, it is sometimes
necessary to increase prices at short notice. Pan Books reserve
the right to show on covers and charge new retail prices which
may differ from those advertised in the text or elsewhere